THE DEATH OF CHRIST

JAMES DENNEY, D.D.

THE
DEATH OF CHRIST

Edited by

R. V. G. TASKER, M.A., D.D.

*Professor Emeritus of New Testament Exegesis
in the University of London*

THE TYNDALE PRESS

39 Bedford Square London WC1B 3EY

First published in this Edition – June, 1951
Reprinted   –   –   – June, 1952
Reprinted   –   –   April, 1956
Reprinted   –   –   February, 1960
Reprinted   –   –   October, 1961
Reprinted   –   –   May, 1964
Reprinted   –   –   November, 1970

STANDARD BOOK NUMBER: 0 85111 561 6

Made and printed in England by
STAPLES PRINTERS LIMITED
at their Rochester, Kent, establishment

CONTENTS

EDITOR'S PREFACE

HALF a century has passed since James Denney, then a professor in the United Free Church College at Glasgow, published *The Death of Christ*. It is not only a tribute to the abiding value of his work, but also a sign of the changed theological atmosphere of our time, that it should be thought fitting to republish this book today. At the beginning of this century British theological scholarship was coming more and more under the influence of the Liberal Protestantism of Germany. As increasing emphasis came to be placed on the fatherhood of God and the brotherhood of man as the essential elements in Christianity, so there was a growing neglect of the doctrinal emphasis of the New Testament upon the atoning nature of the death of Christ. To have studied in Germany under the leading exponents of this school of thought, or at least to be familiar with the last work of biblical criticism from Germany, was regarded in many quarters fifty years ago as the *sine qua non* of eminence in theological scholarship.

Many of the advocates of Liberal Protestantism were men of great erudition; but for the most part they were men of the study and not of the pulpit. They made little attempt to 'preach the gospel'; indeed they had no real gospel to preach! It is not therefore surprising that the steady decline during the last fifty years of vital evangelical preaching based on the exegesis of Scripture (where it has not been due to a false sacramentalism which tends to divorce the sacraments from the gospel) can largely be traced to lack of *first-hand* study of the text of Scripture (coupled often with a *second-hand* knowledge of critical theories) and to the failure to see the centrality of the New Testament teaching about Christ's atoning death. It has only too often been forgotten that the documents of the New Testament were the products of a missionary church, and that the dominant interest of their writers was the preaching of a gospel of salvation won by Christ on Calvary.

Today in the light of two world wars, and confronted by the

7

possibility of a third, a large and, I believe, a steadily increasing number are coming to see that, if the Christian religion is not what the New Testament presents it as being, a religion of redemption, then it is of little consequence: for nothing less than this has power to remove the guilt of the sin-laden conscience.

It was the greatness of James Denney that he refused to separate Christian theology from Christian evangelism. Well acquainted with the biblical criticism of his day, and ready always to evaluate such criticism with the care and patience of the true scholar, he nevertheless remained very sure that the nerve of Christianity is that it is a gospel to be preached; and that the power of that gospel lies in the truth contained in the words 'Christ died for the ungodly'. 'I haven't the faintest interest', he once said, 'in theology which does not help us to evangelize.' And the 'theology which helps us to evangelize' is the theology which recognizes 'the centrality, the gravity, the inevitableness and the glory of the death of Christ', wherein the unity not only of the New Testament but also of the entire Bible is to be found. To put the emphasis anywhere else; or to use the language of the New Testament about Christ's death in a sense other than that given to it by the New Testament writers, is to debase the Christian religion and paralyse the life of the Church. On the other hand, to recognize the death of Christ for what the New Testament asserts it to be is, in Denney's view, to possess the essential clue to a proper understanding of His person, of the purpose of His incarnation, of the working out of His vocation during His earthly ministry, and of the influence He has had upon all who have accepted Him as Saviour.

Denney had already shown his powers as an expositor of the New Testament in commentaries on the Epistle to the Romans and the Second Epistle to the Corinthians before he published *The Death of Christ* in 1902. This first edition was soon supplemented by additional chapters dealing with 'The Atonement and the Modern Mind'. The present volume contains a revised and abridged edition of this larger work. In order to make the book simpler and more suitable for the general reader as well as for the theological student, I have omitted some passages where the exegesis of a particular text is unusually technical and detailed, and others where Denney pauses to deal critically, and sometimes at considerable length, with the arguments of individual contemporary scholars, many of whose works have long since been out of print. The general nature of the various types of criticism with which Denney was confronted remains, however, clearly evident in these pages. I have also rewritten sentences which seemed unduly difficult; and have attempted generally to simplify the narrative without being unfaithful to the thought. My sole desire throughout has been to enable the reader of today to experience as fully as possible the cumulative and compelling power of the evidence which Denney here presents with such sustained reasoning, such quiet fervour, and such profundity of spiritual insight. Scriptural quotations are taken for the most part from the Revised Version. Occasionally, however, the author has introduced his own translation of the original text in order to express more clearly the particular point he is seeking to make.

It is my own conviction that to read this book carefully and thoughtfully is to have one's eyes opened afresh to the real meaning of the New Testament, to enjoy a spiritual experience of a high order, and to be rekindled with desire to spread the gospel. For these reasons I hope that in its new format it may find a large number of new readers particularly amongst the younger generation. Few things, I feel sure, would do more to raise the level of preaching and to restore the cardinal doctrine of the New Testament to its proper position as the foundation rock of true Christianity than the constant study of this book by all who are called to bear witness to Christ in our own day and generation.

R. V. G. TASKER.

THE DEATH OF CHRIST

INTRODUCTION

TWO assumptions must be made by anyone who writes on the death of Christ in the New Testament. The first is, that there is such a thing as a New Testament; and the second, that the death of Christ is a subject which has a real place and importance in it. The first may be said to be the more important of the two, for the denial of it carries with it the denial of the other.

There has been a strong tendency in much Liberal Protestant and modernist theology to depreciate the idea of a New Testament in the sense in which it has rightly or wrongly been established in the Church. It has been asserted that the books which compose our New Testament are in no real sense a unity. They were not written with a view to forming the volume in which we now find them, nor with any view of being related to each other at all. They are merely the chief fragments that have survived from a primitive Christian literature which must have been indefinitely larger, not to say richer. The unity which they now possess, and in virtue of which they constitute the New Testament, does not belong to them inherently; it is the artificial and to a considerable extent the illusive result of the action of the Church in bestowing upon them canonical authority. The age to which they historically belong is an age at which the Church had no 'New Testament,' and hence what is called New Testament theology is an exhibition of the manner in which Christians thought before a New Testament existed. As a self-contradictory thing, therefore, it ought to be abolished. The 'dogma' of the New Testament, we are told, and the artificial unity which it has created, ought to be superseded, and instead of New Testament theology we should aim at a history of primitive Christian thought and life. It would not be necessary for the purposes of such a history to make any assumptions as to the unity of the 'New Testament' books; but though they would not form a holy island in the sea of history, they would gain in life and reality in proportion as the dogmatic tie which binds them to each other was broken, and their living relations to the general phenomena of history revealed.

There is not only some plausibility in this but some truth: all I am concerned to point out here is that it is not the whole truth, and possibly not the main truth. The unity which belongs to the books of the New Testament, whatever be its value, is certainly not fortuitous. The books did not come together by chance. They are not held together simply by the art of the bookbinder. It would be truer to say that they gravitated toward each other in the course of the first century of the Church's life, and imposed their unity on the Christian mind, than that the Church imposed on them a unity to which they were inwardly strange by statute —for when 'dogma' is used in the abstract sense which contrasts it with fact or history, this is what it means. That they are at one in some essential respects is obvious. They have at least unity of subject: they are all concerned with Jesus Christ, and with the manifestation of God's redeeming love to men in Him. There is even a sense in which we may say there is unity of authorship; for all the books of the New Testament are works of faith. Whether the unity goes further, and if so how far, are questions not to be settled beforehand. It may extend to modes of thought, to fundamental beliefs or convictions, in regard to Christ and the meaning of His presence and work in the world. It is not assumed here that it does, but neither is it assumed that it does not. It is not assumed, with regard to the particular subject before us, that in the different New Testament writings we shall find independent, divergent, or inconsistent interpretations of Christ's death. The result of an unprejudiced investigation may be to show that on this subject the various writings which go to make up our New Testament are profoundly at one, and even that their oneness on this subject, a oneness not imposed nor artificial, but essential and inherent, justifies against the criticism referred to above the common Christian estimate of the New Testament as a whole.

Without entering on abstract or general grounds into a discussion in which no abstract or general conclusion can be reached, we would point out that, in the region with which the New

Testament deals, we should be on our guard against pressing too strongly some current distinctions which, within their limits, are real enough, but which, if carried beyond their limits, make everything in the New Testament unintelligible. The most important of these is the distinction of historical and dogmatic, or of historico-religious and dogmatico-religious. If the distinction between historical and dogmatic is pressed, it runs back into the distinction between thing and meaning, or between fact and theory; and this, as we shall have occasion to see, is a distinction which it is impossible to press. There is a point at which the two sides in such contrast pass into each other. He who does not see the meaning does not see the thing; or to use the more imposing words, he who refuses to take a 'dogmatic' view proves by doing so that he falls short of a completely 'historical' one.

The same kind of consideration has sometimes to be applied to the distinction of 'Biblical' or 'New Testament' and 'Systematic' theology. Biblical or New Testament theology deals with the thoughts, or the mode of thinking, of the various New Testament writers; Systematic theology is the independent construction of Christianity as a whole in the mind of a later thinker. Here again there is a broad and valid distinction, but not an absolute one. It is the Christian thinking of the first century in the one case, and of the twentieth, let us say, in the other; but in both cases there is Christianity and there is thinking, and if there is truth in either there is bound to be a place at which the distinction disappears. It does not follow from the distinction, with the inevitable limitations, that nothing in the New Testament can be accepted by a modern mind simply as it stands. It does not follow that nothing in Paul or John—nothing in their interpretation of the death of Jesus, for example—has attained the character of finality. There may be something which has. The thing to be dealt with is one, and the mind, through the centuries, is one, and even in the first century it may have stuck to a final truth which the twentieth will not transcend. Certainly we cannot deny this beforehand on the ground that Biblical theology is one thing and Systematic or Philosophical theology another. They may be taught in separate rooms in a theological college, but, except to the pedant or the dilettante, the distinction between them is a vanishing one.

The same may be said, finally, about the distinction of matter and form. There is such a distinction: it is possible to put the same matter in different forms. But it does not follow that the form in which a truth or an experience is put by a New Testament writer is always unequal to the matter, or that the matter must always be fused again and cast into a new mould before it can be appropriated by us. The higher the reality with which we deal, the less the distinction of matter and form holds. If Christianity brings us into contact with the ultimate truth and reality, we may find that the 'form' into which it was cast at first is more essential to the matter than we had supposed. Just as it would be a rash act to venture to extract the matter of *Lycidas*, and to exhibit it in a more adequate form, it may be a rash act to venture to tell us what Paul and John meant in a form more equal to the meaning than the apostles themselves could supply. It is not necessary to say that it would be, but only that it may be. The mind seems to gain freedom and lucidity by working with such distinctions, but if we forget that they are our own distinctions, and that in the real world, in the very nature of things, a point is reached sooner or later at which they disappear, we are certain to be led astray.

I am not arguing here against drawing or using these distinctions, but against making them so absolute that in the long run one of them must cease to be true, and forfeit all its rights in favour of the other. The chief use, for instance, to which many writers put them is to appeal to the historical against the dogmatic; the historical is employed to drive the dogmatic from the field. To do the reverse would of course be as bad, and my object in these introductory remarks is to deprecate both mistakes. It does not matter, outside the classroom, whether an interpretation is called historical or dogmatic, historico-religious or dogmatico-religious; it does not matter whether we put it under the head of Biblical or of Philosophical theology; what we want to know is whether it is true. In the truth such distinctions are apt to disappear.

Without assuming, therefore, the dogmatic unity of the New Testament, either in its representation of Christianity as a whole, or of the death of Christ in particular, we need not feel precluded from approaching it with a presumption that it will exhibit some kind of coherence. Granting that the Church canonized the books, consciously or unconsciously, it did not canonize them for nothing. It must have felt that they really represented and therefore safeguarded the Christian faith, and as the Church of the early days was acutely conscious of the distinction between what did and what did not belong to Christianity, it must have had some sense at least of a consistency in its Christian Scriptures. They did not represent for it two gospels, or ten, but one. The view Christians took of the books they valued was instinctively dogmatic without ceasing to be historical; or perhaps we may say, with a lively sense of their historical relations the Church had an instinctive feeling of the dogmatic import of the books in its New Testament. It is in this attitude, which is not blind to either side of the distinction, yet does not let either annul the other, that we ought to approach the study of New Testament problems.

It is hardly necessary to prove that in the New Testament the death of Christ is a real subject. It is distinctly present to the mind of New Testament writers, and they have much to say upon it. It is treated by them as a subject of central and permanent importance to the Christian faith, and it is incredible that it should have filled the place it does fill in the New Testament had it ever been regarded as of trifling consequence for the understanding, the acceptance, or the preaching of the gospel. As little is it necessary to say that in using the expression 'the death of Christ', we are not speaking of a thing, but of an experience. Whether we view it as action or as passion, whatever enters into personality has the significance and the worth of personality. The death of Christ in the New Testament is the death of One who is alive for evermore. To every New Testament writer Christ is the Lord, the living and exalted Lord, and it is impossible for them to think of His death except as an experience, the result or virtue of which is perpetuated in His risen life. Nevertheless, Christ died. His death is in some sense the centre and consummation of His work. It is because of it that His risen life is the hope which it is to sinful men; and it needs no apology, therefore, if one who thinks that it has less than its proper place in preaching and in theology endeavours to bring out as simply as possible its place and meaning in the New Testament. If our religion is

to be Christian in any sense of the term which history will justify,
it can never afford to ignore what, to say the least, is the primary
confession of Christian faith.

The starting point in our investigation must be the life and
teaching of Jesus Himself. For this we shall depend in the first
instance on the synoptic Gospels. Next will come an examination
of primitive Christian teaching as it bears on our subject. For
this we shall make use of the early chapters in Acts, and of the
First Epistle of Peter. It will then be necessary to go into greater
detail, in proportion as we have more material at command, in
regard to the teaching of Paul. Of all New Testament writers
he is the one who has most deliberately and continually reflected
on Christ's death; if there is a conscious theology of it anywhere,
it is with him. A study of the Epistle to the Hebrews and of the
Johannine writings—Apocalypse, Gospel, and Epistle—will bring
the subject proper to a close; but two additional chapters will
be added, the first containing some reflections on the importance
of the New Testament conception of Christ's death both to the
evangelist and theologian, and the second dealing with certain
objections which, in modern times, are sometimes brought
against the doctrine of the atonement.

CHAPTER I

THE SYNOPTIC GOSPELS

ALL the Gospels describe the sufferings and death of Christ with a minuteness which has no parallel in their narratives of other events of His life, and they all, to a certain extent, by references to the fulfilment of Old Testament prophecy or otherwise, indicate their sense of its meaning and importance. This, however, reveals the mind of the evangelists rather than that of the Lord. It is in His life, rather than in the record of His death itself, that we must look for indications of His mind. But here we are at once confronted with certain preliminary difficulties. Quite apart from the question whether it is possible at all to know what Jesus thought or spoke about His death—a question which it is taken for granted is to be answered in the affirmative[1] —it has been asserted, largely upon general grounds, that Jesus cannot have entered on His ministry with the thought of His death present to Him; that He must, on the contrary, have begun His work with brilliant hopes of success; that only as these hopes gradually but irrevocably faded away did first the possibility and then the certainty of a tragic issue dawn upon Him; that it thus became necessary for Him to reconcile Himself to the idea of a violent death, and that in various ways, which can more or less securely be traced in the Gospels, He did so; although, as the prayer in Gethsemane shows, there seemed a possibility to Him, even to the last, that a change might come, and the will of the Father be done in some less tragic fashion. This is what is meant by an historical as opposed to a dogmatic reading of the life of Jesus, a dogmatic reading being one which holds that Jesus came into the world in order to die; and it is insisted on as necessary to secure for that life the reality of a genuine human experience. To question or impeach or displace this interpretation is alleged to be docetism; it gives us a phantom as a Saviour instead of the man Christ Jesus.

[1] See the writer's *Jesus and the Gospel*, pp. 320-346.

In spite of its plausibility, I venture to urge that this reading of the Gospels requires serious qualification. It is almost as much an *a priori* interpretation of the history of Jesus as if it were deduced from the Nicene creed. It is derived from the word 'historical', in the sense which that word would bear if it were applied to an ordinary human life, just as abstractly as another reading of the facts might be derived from the words ' ὁμοούσιος τῷ πατρί.' If anyone wrote a life of Jesus, in which everything was subordinated to the idea that Jesus was 'of one substance with the Father', it would no doubt be described as dogmatic, but it is quite as possible to be 'dogmatic' in history as in theology. It is a dogma, and an unreasoned dogma besides, that because the life of Jesus is historical, it neither admits nor requires for its interpretation any idea or formula that cannot be used in the interpretation of the common life of man. The Christian religion rests on the fact that there is not only an identity but also a difference between His life and ours; and we cannot allow the difference (and with it the Christian religion) to be abolished *a priori* by a 'dogmatic' use of the term 'historical'. We must turn to our historical documents—the Gospels—and when we do, there is much to give us pause.

All the Gospels, we remark in the first place, begin with an account of the baptism of Jesus. Whatever may be doubtful about this it cannot be doubtful that it was the occasion of a great spiritual experience to Jesus. Ideas, as Dr. Johnson says, must be given through something; and Jesus, we must believe, gave His disciples an idea of what His experience at baptism was in the narratives which we now read in the Gospels. The sum of that experience is often put by saying that He came then to the consciousness of His Sonship. But the manner in which Jesus Himself puts it is much more revealing. 'A voice came from heaven, Thou art My Son, the Beloved, in Thee I am well pleased.' A voice from heaven does not mean a voice from the clouds, but a voice from God; and it is important to notice that the voice from God speaks in familiar Old Testament words. It does not come unmediated, but mediated through Psalm and prophecy. It is by means of Old Testament Scripture that Jesus expresses His consciousness of what He is; and the Scriptures which He uses to convey His experience to the disciples are the second Psalm, and the forty-second chapter of Isaiah. The first words of the heavenly voice are from the Psalm, the next from the prophet.

Nothing could be more suggestive than this. The Messianic consciousness in Jesus from the very beginning was one with the consciousness of the Servant of the Lord. The King to whom Jehovah says, Thou art My Son, this day have I begotten Thee (Ps. ii. 7),[1] is at the same time (in the mind of Jesus) that mysterious Servant of Jehovah—'My beloved, in whom I am well pleased'—whose tragic yet glorious destiny is adumbrated in Is. xlii. 1 ff. It is not necessary to inquire how Jesus could combine beforehand two lines of anticipation which at the first glance seem so inconsistent with each other. The point is that on the evidence before us, which seems to the writer as indisputable as anything in the Gospels, He did combine them, and therefore cannot have started on His ministry with the cloudless hopes which are sometimes ascribed to Him. However 'unhistorical' it might seem on general grounds, we must hold on the ground of the evidence which is here available that from the very beginning of His public work the sense of something tragic in His destiny—something which in form might only become definite with time, but in substance was sure—was present to the mind of Jesus. When it did emerge in definite form it brought necessities and appeals along with it which were not there from the beginning; it brought demands for definite action, for assuming a definite attitude, for giving more or less explicit instruction; but it did not bring a monstrous and unanticipated disappointment to which Jesus had to reconcile Himself as best He could. It was not a brutal *démenti* to all His hopes. It had a necessary relation to His consciousness from the beginning, just as surely as His consciousness from the beginning had a necessary relation to the prophetic conception of the Servant of the Lord.

This is confirmed if we turn from the baptism to that which

[1] In Lk. iii. 22, *Codex Bezæ* gives the heavenly voice in this form. Probably Jesus told the stories of His baptism and temptation often, giving more or less fully, with brief allusions to Old Testament words or fuller citation of them, such hints of His experience as His hearers could appreciate. Certainly there could be no truer *index* to His life than a combination of Ps. ii. 7 with Is. xlii. 1 ff.—the Son of God as King, and the Servant of the Lord; and this combination, if we go upon the evidence and not upon any dogmatic conception of what is or is not historical, dates from the high hour in which Jesus entered on His public work, and is not an afterbirth of disappointing experiences.

in all the Gospels is closely connected with it, and is of equal importance as illustrating our Lord's conception of Himself and His work—the temptation. Nothing can be more gratuitous than to ascribe this wonderful narrative to the 'productive activity' of the Church, and to allege that the temptations which it records are those which Jesus encountered during His career, and that they are antedated for effect, or for catechetical convenience. Psychologically, the connection of the temptations with the baptism is strikingly true, and two of the three are connected even formally with the divine voice, 'Thou art My Son' (Mt. iii. 17, iv. 3, 6). The natural supposition is that Jesus spoke often to His disciples of a terrible spiritual experience which followed the sublime experience of the baptism—sometimes without detail, as in Mark, who mentions only a prolonged conflict with Satan, during which Jesus was sustained by the ministry of angels; sometimes, as in Matthew and Luke, with details which gave insight into the nature of the conflict. It does not matter that the temptations which are here described actually assailed Jesus at later stages in His life. Of course they did. They are the temptations of the Christ, and they not only assailed Him at particular moments, some of which we can still identify (Mt. xvi. 22 f.; Jn. vi. 15), but must in some way have haunted Him incessantly. They were present to His mind *from the outset of His career*; that is the true meaning of the temptation story, standing where it does. The Christ sees the two paths that lie before Him, and He chooses at the outset, in spiritual conflict, that which He knows will set Him in irreconcilable antagonism to the hopes and expectations of those to whom He is to appeal.

A soul which sees its vocation foreshadowed in the Servant of the Lord, which is driven of the Spirit into the wilderness to face the dreadful alternatives raised by that vocation, and which takes the side which Jesus took in conflict with the enemy, does not enter on its life-work with any superficial illusions. It has looked Satan and all he can do in the face; it is prepared for conflict; it may shrink from death, when death confronts it in the path of its vocation, as hideous and unnatural, but it cannot be startled by it as by an unthought-of, unfamiliar thing. The possibility, at least, of a tragic issue to His work—when we remember the Servant of the Lord—belongs to the consciousness of Jesus from the first. Not that His ultimate triumph is compromised, but He knows before He begins that it will not be attained by any primrose path.

These considerations justify us in emphasizing, in relation to our subject, not merely the fact of Jesus' baptism, but its meaning. It was a baptism of repentance with a view to remission of sins, and there is undoubtedly something paradoxical, at first sight, in the idea of Jesus submitting to such a baptism. Neither here nor elsewhere in the Gospels does He betray any consciousness of sin; for it would be gratuitous to accept the apocryphal Gospel according to the Hebrews as authentic evidence. Jerome tells us that in this Gospel, which in his day was still used by the Nazarenes and could be seen in the library at Caesarea, the narrative ran: 'Behold the mother of the Lord and His brethren said to Him: John Baptist is baptizing with a view to remission of sins: let us go and be baptized by him. But He said to them: "What sin have I done that I should go and be baptized by him? unless, indeed, this very word I have spoken is *ignorantia*," ' i.e. a sin of ignorance or inadvertence (cf. ἀγνόημα, Heb. ix. 7).

If we accepted this account we should have to suppose that Jesus went up to Jordan half reluctantly, His first thought being that a baptism like John's could mean nothing to Him, His next that possibly this proud thought, or the utterance of it, indicated that He might have something, and more perhaps than He knew, to repent of after all. This mingling of what might not unfairly be called petulance with a sudden access of misgiving, as of one who was too sure of himself and yet not quite sure, is as unlike as anything could be to the simplicity and truth of Jesus; and surely it needs no proof that it is another mood than this to which the heavens are opened, and on which divine assurance and divine strength are bestowed. We must abide by the canonical narratives as consistent in themselves, and consistent with the New Testament as a whole. What we see there is Jesus, who, according to all apostolic testimony, and according to the suggestion of the Baptist himself in Mt. iii. 14, knew no sin, submitting to a baptism which is defined as a baptism of repentance. It would not have been astonishing if Jesus had come from Galilee to baptize along with John, if He had taken His stand by John's side confronting the people; the astonishing thing is that being what He

was He came to be baptized, and took His stand side by side
with the people. He identified Himself with them. As far as the
baptism could express it, He made all that was theirs His. It is
as though He had looked on them under the oppression of their
sin, and said: On Me let all that burden, all that responsibility
descend.

The key to the act is to be found in the great passage in Is. liii
in which the vocation of the Servant of the Lord, which, as we
have seen, was present to our Lord's mind at the moment, is
most amply unfolded. The deepest word in that chapter, 'He was
numbered with the transgressors', is expressly applied to our Lord
by Himself at a later period (Lk. xxii. 37). However mysterious
that word may be when we try to define it by relation to the
providence and redemption of God—however appalling it may
seem to interpret it as Paul does, Him who knew no sin, God
made to be sin for us—here in the baptism we see not the word
but the thing: *Jesus numbering Himself with the transgressors*,
submitting to be baptized with their baptism, identifying Himself
with them in their relation to God as sinners, making all their
responsibilities His own. It was 'a great act of loving communion
with our misery', and in that hour, in the will and act of Jesus,
the work of atonement was begun. It was no accident that now,
and not at some other hour, the Father's voice declared Him the
beloved Son, the chosen One in whom His soul delighted. For
in so identifying Himself with sinful men, in so making their
last and most dreadful responsibilities His own, Jesus approved
Himself the true Son of the Father, the true Servant and Representative of Him whose name from of old is Redeemer.[1] It is
impossible to have this in mind, and to remember the career
which the fifty-third chapter of Isaiah sets before the Servant of
the Lord, without feeling that, from the moment He entered on
His ministry, our Lord's thoughts of the future must have been
more in keeping with what eventually happened than those which
are sometimes ascribed to Him as alone consistent with a truly

---

[1] See Garvie's *Studies in the Inner Life of Jesus*, ch. iv. 'The Vocation Accepted',
pp. 117 ff. 'It is in His vicarious consciousness and the sacrifice which this would
ultimately involve that Jesus fulfilled all righteousness. There is a higher righteousness than being justified by one's own works, a higher even than depending on
God's forgiveness; and that belongs to Him who undertakes by His own loving
sacrifice for sinners to bring God's forgiveness to them.'

human career. His career was truly His own as well as truly human, and the shadow of the world's sin lay on it from the first.

Starting from this point, we may now go on to examine the facts as they are put before us in the Gospels.

It is only, indeed, after the great day at Caesarea Philippi, when Jesus accepts from the lips of His disciples the confession of Messiahship, that He begins expressly to teach the necessity of His death. But there are indications earlier than this that it was not alien to His thoughts, and indeed there was much to prompt the thought of it. At the opening of His ministry, in the Sermon on the Mount, He refers to the experience of the ancient prophets (Mt. v. 10-12), a theme to which He returns at the end of His life in His great denunciation of the Pharisees (Mt. xxiii. 37). There was the fate of John the Baptist, which, though the precise date of it is uncertain, was felt by Jesus to be parallel to His own (Mk. ix. 12, 13). There was the sense underlying all His early success, if we may speak of it in such language, of an irreconcilable antipathy in His adversaries, of a temper which would incur the guilt of eternal sin rather than acknowledge His claims (Mk. iii. 20-30). There was the consciousness, going back to very early days, that the most opposite parties were combining to destroy Him (Mk. iii. 6). And there is one pathetic word in which the sense of the contrast between the present and the future comes out with moving power. 'Can the children of the bride-chamber fast while the bridegroom is with them? As long as they have the bridegroom with them they cannot fast. But days will come when the bridegroom shall be taken away from them, and then shall they fast in that day' (Mk. ii. 19 f.).

The force of this exquisite word has been evaded in two ways. It has been argued by some critics that verse 20, in which the taking away of the bridegroom is spoken of, is not really a word of Jesus, but a creation of the Church. It is said to be irrelevant in the circumstances, and made possible only by the parable of Jesus being treated as an allegory. All that is supposed to be apposite to the occasion is the first clause: Can the children of the bride-chamber fast while the bridegroom is with them? But, as has been pointed out, the allegory, which is thus used to discredit verse 20, must be assumed if we are to get any pertinent meaning even for verse 19; and few critics are prepared to expunge both verses.

In the second place it has also been argued that the words do not necessarily refer to a violent or premature or unnatural death, but merely to the parting which is inevitable in the case of all human relations, however joyful, and is perhaps felt more acutely the more joyful they are. But there is nothing elsewhere in the words of Jesus so sentimental and otiose as this. He does not aim at cheap pathetic effects like those romance writers who studiously paint the brightness and gaiety of life against the omnipresent black background of death. The taking away of the bridegroom from the bridal party is *not* the universal experience of man, applied to an individual case; it is something startling, tragic, like sudden storm in a summer sky; and it is as such that it is present to the mind of Jesus as a figure of His own death. Even in the Galilean springtime, when His fortune seems to rise like the rising tide, there is this sad presentiment at His heart, and once at least He suffers it to break through.

The saying about being three days and nights in the heart of the earth, as Jonah was three days and three nights in the whale's belly (Mt. xii. 40), though it does not convey an interpretation of His death, at least suggests that it is not a final defeat, but that the true victory of His cause lies beyond it. What He came to do will be effectively done, not before He dies, but after He has come again through death. And this is the only sign which His enemies can have.

But leaving these somewhat allusive references to His death, let us proceed to those in which it is the express subject of our Lord's teaching.

All the synoptic Gospels introduce it, in this sense, at the same point (Mk. viii. 31; Mt. xvi. 21; Lk. ix. 22). Matthew lays a peculiar emphasis on the date, using it to mark the division of his Gospel into two great parts. 'From that time Jesus began,' he says in iv. 17, 'to preach and to say: Repent, for the kingdom of Heaven is at hand.' 'From that time,' he says in xvi. 21, 'Jesus began to show to His disciples that He must go up to Jerusalem and be killed.' A comparison of the evangelists justifies us in saying broadly that a new epoch in our Lord's ministry has now begun. His audience is not so much the multitudes as the twelve; His method is not so much preaching as teaching; His subject is not so much the kingdom as Himself, and in particular His death.

All the evangelists mention three occasions on which He made deliberate and earnest efforts to initiate the disciples into His thoughts (Mk. viii. 31, ix. 31, x. 32, with parallels in Matthew and Luke). Mark, especially, whose narrative is fundamental, lays stress on the continued and repeated attempts He made to familiarize them with what was drawing near (notice the imperfects ἐδίδασκεν, ἔλεγεν in ix. 31). There is no reason whatever to doubt this general representation. It is mere wantonness to eliminate from the narrative one or two of the three passages on the ground that they are but duplicates or triplicates of the same thing. In Mark, especially, they are distinctly characterized by the varying attitude of the disciples. Further, in the first we have the presumptuous protest of Peter, which guarantees the historicity of the whole. In the second the disciples are silent. They could not make Him out (ἠγνόουν τὸ ῥῆμα), and with the remembrance of the overwhelming rebuke which Peter had drawn down on himself, they were afraid to put any question to Him (ix. 32). The third is attached to that never-to-be-forgotten incident in which, as they were on the way to Jerusalem, Jesus took the lead in some startling manner, so that they followed in amazement and fear. If anything in the Gospels has the stamp of real and live recollection upon it, it is this. It is necessary to insist on this repeated instruction of the disciples by Jesus as a fact, quite apart from what He was able to teach or they to learn. It is often said that the death of Christ has a place in the Epistles out of all proportion to that which it has in the Gospels. This is hardly the fact, even if the space were to be estimated merely by the number of words devoted to it in the Gospels and Epistles respectively. But it is still less the fact when we remember that, according to the Gospels themselves, what characterized the last months of our Lord's life was a deliberate and thrice-repeated attempt to teach His disciples something about His death.

The critical questions which have been raised as to the contents of these passages need not detain us here. It has been suggested that they must have become more detailed in the telling; that unconsciously and involuntarily the Church put into the lips of the Lord words which were supplied to its own mind only by its knowledge of what actually took place; that the references to mocking, scourging, spitting, in particular, could not have been so explicit; above all, that the resurrection on the third day, if spoken of at all, must have been veiled in some figurative form which baffled the disciples at the moment. It has been suggested, on the other hand, that it may have been the idea of a resurrection on the third day, and not on the familiar great day at the end of all things, which bewildered them.

But when these suggestions are carefully examined there seems to be very little in them. Surely we cannot imagine Jesus iterating and reiterating, with the most earnest desire to impress and instruct His followers, the vague, elusive, impalpable hints of what lay before Him which some critics would put in the place of what they regard as impossibly definite predictions. Jesus must have had something entirely definite and sayable to say, when He tried so persistently to get it apprehended. He did not live in cloudland; what He spoke of was the sternest of realities; and for whatever reason His disciples failed to understand Him, it cannot have been that He talked to them incessantly and importunately in shadowy riddles. But, as far as our present purpose is concerned, it is unnecessary to discuss these critical questions. The one point in which all the narratives agree is that Jesus taught that He *must* go up to Jerusalem and die; and the one question it is of importance to answer is, What is meant by this *must* (δεῖ)?

It might obviously have two meanings. It might signify that His death was inevitable, the *must* being one of outward constraint. No doubt, in this sense it was true that He must die. The hostile forces which were arrayed against Him were irreconcilable, and were only waiting their time. Sooner or later it would come, and they would crush Him without remorse. But it might also signify that His death was indispensable, the *must* being one of inward constraint. It might signify that death was something He was bound to accept and contemplate if the work He came to do was to be done, and the vocation to which He was called fulfilled.

These two senses, of course, are not incompatible; but there may be a question as to their relation to each other. Most frequently the second is made to depend upon the first. Jesus, we are told, came to see that His death was inevitable because of the forces arrayed against Him; but being unable, as the well-beloved Son of the Father, merely to submit to the inevitable or to encounter death as a blind fate, He reconciled Himself to it by interpreting it as indispensable, as something which properly entered into His work and contributed to its success. It became not a thing to endure, but a thing to do. The passion was converted into the sublimest of actions.

We need not say that this reasoning has nothing in it; but it is too abstract, and the relation in which the two necessities are put to one another does not answer to the presentation of the facts in the Gospels. The inward necessity which Jesus recognized for His death was not simply the moral solution which He had discovered for the fatal situation in which He found Himself. An inward necessity is identical with the will of God; and the will of God for Jesus is expressed, not primarily in outward conditions, but in Scripture which is for Him the word of God. We have seen already that from the very beginning our Lord's sense of His own vocation and destiny was essentially related to that of the Servant of the Lord in the Book of Isaiah, and it is there that the ultimate source of the δεῖ is to be found. The divine necessity for a career of suffering and death is primary, and it belongs, in however vague and undefined a form, to our Lord's consciousness of what He is and what He is called to do. It is not deduced from the malignant necessities by which He is encompassed, but rises up within Him, in divine power, to encounter these outward necessities and subdue them.

This connection of ideas is confirmed when we notice that what Jesus began to teach His disciples is the doctrine of a suffering *Messiah*. As soon as they have confessed Him to be the Christ, He begins to give them this lesson. The necessity of His death, in other words, is not a dreary, incomprehensible somewhat that He is compelled to reckon with by untoward circumstances; for Him it is given, so to speak, with the very conception of His person and His work. When He unfolds Messiahship it contains death. This was the first and last thing He taught about it, the first and last thing He wished His disciples to learn.

In Mt. xvi. 21, Westcott and Hort read, 'From that time began Jesus *Christ* to show to His disciples that He must go to Jerusalem and suffer many things,' while Mark and Luke, in the corresponding passage, speak of *the Son of Man*. The official expressions, or, to use a less objectionable term, the names which denote the vocation of Jesus, 'the Christ' and 'the Son of Man', show that in this lesson He is speaking out of the sense of His vocation, and not merely out of a view of His historical circumstances. The necessity to suffer and die, which was involved in His vocation, and the sense of which belonged to His very being so that without it He would not have been what He was, was now to form part of His positive teaching. As events brought into the open the forces with which He had to deal, He could point more clearly to the way in which the necessity would work itself out. He could go beyond that early word about the taking away of the bridegroom, and speak of Jerusalem, and of rejection by the elders and chief priests and scribes. And this consideration justifies us in believing that these details in the evangelic narrative are historical. But the manner in which the necessity did work itself out, and the greater or less detail with which Jesus anticipated its course, do not affect in the least the character of that necessity itself. It is the necessity involved in the divine vocation of one in whom the Old Testament prophecy of the Servant of the Lord is to be fulfilled.

It must be admitted that in none of the three summary references which the evangelists make to our Lord's teaching on His death do they say anything of explicitly theological import. They tell us (i) that it was necessary, in the sense which has just been explained; (ii) that it would be attended by such and such circumstances of pain and ignominy; and (iii) that it would be speedily followed by His resurrection. The repeated assurances that His disciples could not understand Him must surely refer to the meaning and necessity which He wished them to see in His death. They must have understood His words about dying and rising, unless, as some have suggested, the date of the rising puzzled them. The only other conclusion is to suppose that the incomprehensible element in the new teaching of Jesus was the truths He wished to convey to them about the necessity, the meaning, the purpose, and the power, of His death. But if we observe the unanimity with which every part of the early Church taught that Christ died for our sins according to the Scriptures, if, as will be shown below, we notice how in Acts, in Peter, in Hebrews, in John, in Paul, passages referring to the Servant of the Lord, and especially to His bearing sin and being numbered with the transgressors, are applied to Christ, it becomes very difficult to believe that this consent in what would seem to be by no means obvious could have any source other than the teaching of Jesus Himself.

Attempts have indeed been made to prove that Jesus never applied the fifty-third chapter of Isaiah to Himself except in Lk. xxii. 37, and that there, when He says with singular emphasis, 'this which is written must be fulfilled in Me, And He was reckoned with transgressors,' He is not at all thinking of His death as having expiatory value in relation to sin: but is thinking only of the dreary fact that His countrymen are going to treat Him as a criminal instead of as the Holy One of God. But there is surely no reason why the most superficial sense of profound words, a sense, too, which evacuates them of all their original associations, should be the only one allowed to Jesus. If there is any truth at all in the connection we have asserted between His own consciousness of what He was and the Old Testament conception of the Servant of the Lord, it is surely improbable that He applied to Himself the most wonderful expression in Isaiah liii in a shallow verbal fashion, and put from Him the great interpretation of the chapter which the New Testament writers embrace with one accord.

On the strength of that quotation and of the consent of the New Testament as a whole which has no basis but in Jesus, we are entitled to argue from the δεῖ of the evangelists—in other words, from the divine necessity Jesus saw in His death—that what He sought in those repeated lessons to induce His disciples to do was to recognize in the Messiah the Person who should fulfil the prophecy of Isaiah liii. The ideal in their minds was something very different; and few things are more difficult to change than an ideal. We do not wonder that at the moment they could not turn, one is tempted to say bodily round, so as to see and understand what He was talking about. And just as little do we wonder that when the meaning of His words broke on them later, it was with that overwhelming power which made the thing that had once baffled them the sum and substance of their gospel. The centre of gravity in their world changed, and their whole being swung round into equilibrium in a new position. Their inspiration came from what had once alarmed, grieved, and discomfited them. The word they preached was the very thing which had once made them afraid to speak.

But in our investigation of our Lord's teaching on His death we are not limited to inferences more or less secure. There are at least two great words in the Gospels which expressly refer to it—the one contained in His answer to James and John when they asked for the places at His right hand and His left in His kingdom, the other spoken at the Supper. We now proceed to consider these.

Part of the difficulty we always have in interpreting Scripture is the want of context; we do not know what were the ideas in the minds of the original speakers or hearers to which the words that have been preserved for us were immediately related. This difficulty has perhaps been needlessly aggravated, especially in the first of the passages with which we are concerned. Yet the context here, even as we have it, is particularly suggestive. Jesus and His disciples are on the way to Jerusalem when Jesus goes on ahead of them, apparently under some overpowering impulse, and they follow in amazement and fear (Mk. x. 32). He calls them to His side once more, and makes the third of those deliberate attempts to which reference has already been made to familiarize them with His death. 'Behold, we go up to Jerusalem; and the Son of Man shall be delivered unto the chief priests and the scribes; and they shall condemn Him to death, and shall deliver Him unto the Gentiles: and they shall mock Him, and shall spit upon Him, and scourge Him, and shall kill Him: and after three days He shall rise again' (Mk. x. 33 f.). It was while Jesus was in the grip of such thoughts—setting His face steadfastly, with a rapt and solemn passion, to go to Jerusalem—that James and John came to Him with their ambitious request. How was He to speak to them so that they might understand Him? As Bengel finely says, He was dwelling in His passion. He was to have others on His right hand and on His left before that. But the disciples' minds were in another world. How, then, was He to bridge the gulf between their thoughts and His? 'Are ye able,' He asks, 'to drink the cup that I drink? or to be baptized with the baptism that I am baptized with?' The cup and the baptism are poetic terms in which the destiny which awaits Him is veiled and transfigured. They are also religious terms, in which that destiny is represented, in all its awfulness, as something involved in the will of God, and involving in itself a consecration. The cup is put into His hand by the Father, and if the baptism is a flood of suffering in which He is overwhelmed, it has also, through the very name which He uses to describe it, the character of a religious act. He goes to be baptized with it as He takes the cup which the Father gives Him to drink.

That the reference in both figures is to His death, and to His death in that tragic aspect which has just been described in the immediately preceding verses, is not open to doubt. And it is as little open to doubt that in the next scene in the Gospel—that in which Jesus speaks to the disciples who were indignant with James and John for trying to steal a march upon them—a reference to His death is so natural as to be inevitable. True greatness, He tells them, does not mean dominance, but service. That is the law for all, even for the highest. It is by supremacy in service that the King in the Kingdom of God wins His place. 'Even the Son of Man came not to be ministered unto, but to minister, and to give His life a ransom for many.'

It is not inept to insist on the sequence and connection of ideas throughout this passage, because when it is really understood it puts the last words—'to give His life a ransom for many'—beyond dispute. It is often asserted that these words are an indication of Pauline influence on the second evangelist. Let us hope that one may be forgiven for saying frankly that this is an assertion which one cannot understand. The words are perfectly in place. They are in line with everything that precedes. They are words in the only key, and of the only fulness, which answer to our Lord's absorption at the time in the thought of His death. A theological aversion to them may be conceived, but otherwise there is no reason whatever to call them in question. There is no critical evidence against them, and their psychological truth is indubitable. So far from saying that Jesus could not have uttered anything so definitely theological, we should rather maintain that in an hour of intense preoccupation with His death no other words would have been adequate to express the whole heart and mind of our Lord.

From this point of view, we must notice a common evasion of their import even by some who do not question that Jesus spoke them. It is pointed out, for instance, that the death is here set in line with the life of our Lord. He came not to be ministered unto but to minister, and in particular, and at last, as His crowning service, to give His life a ransom for many. His death is the consummation of His life, and the consummation of His ministry; but it has no other end than His life, and we must not seek another interpretation for it. We are told that Jesus came into the world to serve men, and especially to serve them by awakening them to that repentance which is the condition of entering the Kingdom of God and inheriting its blessings. So far, His ministry has not been without success; some have already repented, and entered into the Kingdom. But even where He has not proved successful, it is not yet necessary to despair: many will be won to repentance by His death who resisted the appeal of His life.

It is scarcely necessary to point out that the connection of ideas here does not in the least belong to the words of Jesus. Such an interpretation completely leaves out the one thing to which the words of Jesus give prominence—the fact that the Son of Man came expressly to do a service which involved the giving of His life a ransom for many. It is not that Jesus could by faith in the Father reconcile Himself to His death as something which would, in some way at present obscure, contribute to the carrying out of His vocation—something which, in spite of appearances, would not prove inconsistent with it. What the words in the Gospel clearly mean is that the death of Jesus, or the giving of His life a ransom for many, is itself the very soul of His vocation. He does not say that He can bear to die because His death will win many to repentance who are yet impenitent, but that *the object of His coming* was to give His life a ransom for many.

The same consideration discredits any interpretation which finds the key to this passage in Matthew xi. 29 f. This stresses the effect to be produced on human character by the realization of what the death of Jesus is. If men would only put on the yoke of Jesus and learn of Him, if they would drink of His cup and be baptized with His baptism, if, as Paul says, they would be conformed to His death, their souls would be liberated from the restless passions of pride and ambition by which James and John, and the other ten not less than they, were tormented, and death itself would cease to be a terror to them. However true this may be, one cannot look at the text without being impressed by its irrelevance as an interpretation. There is nothing in it to explain the introduction of Christ's death at all as the very end contemplated in His coming. There is nothing in it to explain either λύτρον, or ἀντί, or πολλῶν, or λύτρον ἀντὶ πολλῶν. In spite of the attention it has attracted, it is an ingenious vagary which has surely merited oblivion.

In what direction, then, are we to seek the meaning? The only clue is that which is furnished by the passages in which our Lord Himself speaks of the soul and of the possibility of losing or ransoming it. Thus in Mk. viii. 34 f., immediately after the first announcement of His death, He calls the multitude to Him with His disciples, and says: 'If any man would come after Me, let him deny himself, and take up his cross, and follow Me. For whosoever would save his life (ψυχήν) shall lose it; and whosoever shall lose his life (ψυχήν) for My sake and the gospel's shall save it. For what doth it profit a man, to gain the whole world, and forfeit his life (ψυχήν)? For what should a man give in exchange for his life (ἀντάλλαγμα τῆς ψυχῆς αὐτοῦ)?' It is clear from a passage like this that Jesus was familiar with the idea that the ψυχή or life of man, in the higher or lower sense of the term, might be lost, and that when it was lost there could be no compensation for it, as there was no means of buying it back. It is in the circle of such ideas that the words about giving His life a ransom for many must find their point of attachment, and it is not only far the simplest and most obvious interpretation, but far the most profound and the most consonant with the New Testament as a whole, that Jesus in this passage conceives the lives of the many as being somehow under forfeit, and teaches that the very object with which He came into the world was to lay down His own life as a ransom price that those to whom these forfeited lives belonged might obtain them again. This was the supreme service the Son of Man was to render to mankind; it demanded the

supreme sacrifice, and was the path to supreme greatness. Anything short of this is in the circumstances an anti-climax, and falls
far beneath the passion with which our Lord condenses into a
single phrase the last meaning of His life and death.

It is not quite certain what Old Testament Scriptures lie behind
this passage. It would seem, however, that the world in which
our Lord's mind moved as He spoke was that of Ps. xlix. 7 ff.
and Is. liii. In the Psalm it is asserted that no man can give to
God a ransom for his brother so that he may still live and not
see corruption. What no man can do for his brother the Son of
Man claims to do for many, and to do it by giving His life a
ransom for them. That we are justified also in using the ideas of
the prophecy of Is. liii as a key to the interpretation of the passage
would seem probable from the following points of similarity
which have been noticed. (1) The words δοῦναι τὴν ψυχὴν αὐτοῦ
recall the παρεδόθη εἰς θάνατον ἡ ψυχὴ αὐτοῦ of Is. liii. 12; (2) the
general idea of service pervades both; (3) there is the peculiar use
of the word 'many' in both: My righteous servant shall justify
'many'; He bare the sin of 'many'; to give His life a ransom for
'many'; (4) there is a correspondence in meaning between the
λύτρον as that by which a forfeited life is redeemed, and the giving
of the life or soul as a guilt offering by which legal satisfaction
was rendered for an injury or wrong (Is. liii. 10).

We turn now to consider the account of the institution of the
Lord's Supper. The words which Jesus spoke then throw much
light upon His own conception of His death. The narrative of
Mark begins by saying plainly, 'He took bread, and when He
had blessed, He brake it, and gave to them, and said, Take ye:
this is My body. And He took a cup, and when He had given
thanks, He gave it to them: and they drank *all* of it (πάντες last
and emphatic). And He said unto them, This is My blood of the
covenant, which is shed for many.' This is not qualified by any
other of the New Testament authorities, nor by the practice of
the Church as the New Testament reveals it; and I submit that
it is not open to anyone to go behind it, and to tell us blankly
out of his own head (for that is the only authority left) that the
meaning of what took place was really quite independent of this

giving and taking, eating and drinking; and that while the death of Jesus was the subject of the symbolical actions of breaking the bread and pouring out the wine, and was no doubt meant to benefit some persons, it was a thing in which those who were present, and who at Jesus' word ate and drank the symbols of it, had no interest at all. Jesus made the bread and wine symbols of His death: this is not denied. He handed them to His disciples, pronouncing as He did so the very words in which He conferred on them this symbolical character: this also is not denied. But when He did so, it was not, it is supposed, that the disciples might take them in this character. On the contrary, it was only because they were at their supper anyhow, and because bread and wine are naturally eaten and drunk.

But it is not only necessary to insist on the eating and drinking of the bread and wine, which as broken and outpoured symbolized Christ's death, and as eaten and drunk symbolized the interest of the disciples in that death, and their making it somehow their own; it is necessary to insist on what was further said by Jesus. All the evangelists in their narratives introduce the word 'covenant' (διαθήκη) in some construction or other. Mark has, 'This is My blood of the covenant' (xiv. 24). Matthew, according to some authorities (including that combination of Latin and Syriac versions to which critics are inclined to ascribe a high value) has, 'This is My blood of the new covenant' (xxvi. 28). Luke has what is apparently a Pauline form, 'This cup is the new covenant in My blood' (xxii. 20). Even these words have sometimes been assailed in the determined effort to get behind the Gospels. Three grounds have been assigned for questioning them. The first is that the expression τὸ αἷμά μου τῆς διαθήκης is awkward in Greek; the second, that it is impossible to translate it into Hebrew or Aramaic; and the third, that the conception of the covenant owes its place in Christianity to Paul.

The last of these reasons obviously begs the question. It does not follow that, because Paul makes use of an idea, he originated it. There are very great ideas, indeed, of which Paul says, 'I delivered unto you that which also I received' (1 Cor. xv. 3 f.): why should not this be one of them? Does he not himself declare that it is one, when he prefaces his account of the supper—including in it the idea of the new covenant in the blood of Jesus—with the

words, 'I received of the Lord that which also I delivered unto
you'? (I Cor. xi. 23). The idea of a new covenant, and that of
covenant blood, are Old Testament ideas; and if Jesus was conscious, nay, if it was the very essence of His consciousness, that,
in relation both to law and prophecy, He came not to destroy
but to fulfil, why should not He Himself have spoken the creative
word?

As for the other two reasons, that 'My blood of the covenant'
is awkward in Greek, and that there are persons who cannot
translate it into Hebrew, however true or interesting they may
be, they are obviously irrelevant. It may be awkward in Greek
or in any language to combine in one proposition the two ideas,
'This is My blood', and 'This is covenant blood'. But however
awkward it may be, since they really are ideas which the mind
can grasp, it must be possible to do it, in Greek or in any language. It does not, therefore, seem open to question on any
serious ground whatever that Jesus at the last supper spoke of His
blood as covenant blood. Now, what does this imply? To what
set of ideas in the minds of His hearers, and to what Old Testament associations does it attach itself, so as to be not merely a
word, but an element in a living mind? We get the clue to the
answer when we notice the form in which the words appear in
Matthew, 'This is My blood of the *new* covenant, which is shed
for many *unto remission of sins.*'

The Old Testament twice speaks of 'covenant', in the sense in
which God makes a covenant with His people. There is the
covenant made with sacrifice at Sinai, in the account of which
we have the phrase, 'Behold the blood of the covenant, which
the Lord hath made with you upon all these conditions' (Ex.
xxiv. 8). Here, it is sometimes said, is the original of the words
found in our evangelists; and as nothing is said in Exodus about
the forgiveness of sins, and as the sacrifices mentioned there are
not sin or guilt offerings, but burnt offerings and peace offerings,
it is argued that the insertion in Matthew of the clause 'for forgiveness of sins' is a mistake.[1]

---

[1] Holtzmann, *Neut. Theologie*, i. 302, says: 'The figure of covenant blood,
which alone retains its validity, points, indeed, to a covenant sacrifice, but not
necessarily also to an expiatory sacrifice, with which last alone have been combined the later ideas of exchange and substitution.'

The inference is hasty. Covenant blood is sacrificial blood, and we have every reason to believe that sacrificial blood universally, and not only in special cases, was associated with propitiatory power. 'The atoning function of sacrifice', as Robertson Smith put it, speaking of primitive times, 'is not confined to a particular class of oblation, but belongs to all sacrifices.'[1] Dr. Driver has expressed the same opinion with regard to the Levitical legislation in which the key to the language of our passage must be found. Criticizing Ritschl's explanation of sacrifice and its effect, he says: 'It seems better to suppose that though the burnt-, peace-, and meat-offerings were not offered *expressly*, like the sin- and guilt-offerings, for the forgiveness of sin, they nevertheless (in so far as *kipper* is predicated of them) were regarded as "covering", or neutralizing, the offerer's unworthiness to appear before God, and so, though in a much less degree than the sin- or guilt-offering, as effecting *kappārā* in the sense ordinarily attached to the word, viz. "propitiation".'[2]

Instead of saying 'in a much less degree', I should prefer to say 'with a less specific reference or application', but the point is not material. What it concerns us to note is that the New Testament, while it abstains from interpreting Christ's death by any special prescriptions of the Levitical law, constantly uses sacrificial language to describe that death, and in doing so unequivocally recognizes in it a propitiatory character—in other words, a reference to sin and its forgiveness.

But there is something further to be said. The passage in Exodus is not the only one in the Old Testament to which reference is here made. In the thirty-first chapter of Jeremiah we have the sublime prophecy of a new covenant—a new covenant which is indeed but the efficacious renewal of the old, for there is but one God, and His grace is one—a new covenant, the very condition and foundation of which is the forgiveness of sins. 'They shall all know Me, from the least of them unto the greatest of them, saith the Lord: *for* I will forgive their iniquity, and I will remember their sin no more' (Je. xxxi. 34). It is this which is present to the mind of our Lord as He says of the outpoured wine, 'This is My blood of the covenant.' He is establishing, at

[1] *Religion of the Semites*, p. 219.
[2] Hastings' *Dictionary of the Bible*, s.v. *Propitiation*, p. 132.

the cost of His life, the new covenant, the new religious relation between God and man, which has the forgiveness of sins as its fundamental blessing. He speaks as knowing that that blessing can become ours only through His death; and, as the condition upon which it depends, His death can be presented as a propitiatory sacrifice. It is as though He had pointed to the prophecy in Jeremiah, and said, 'This day is this Scripture fulfilled before your eyes.' He had already, we might think, attached to Himself all that is greatest in the ideals and hopes of the Old Testament —the Messianic sovereignty of Psalms ii and cx, and the tragic and glorious calling of the Servant of the Lord. But there is something which transcends both, and gives the sublimest expression to our Lord's consciousness of Himself and His work, when He says, 'This is My blood of the covenant.' It is a word which gathers up into it the whole promise of prophecy and the whole testimony of the apostles; it is the focus of revelation, in which the Old Testament and the New are one. The power that is in it is the power of the passion in which the Lamb of God bears the sin of the world. The covenant which Jesus inaugurated is therefore essentially 'new' and can be defined only in reference to the remission of sins as, according to Matthew's version, He Himself defines it.

There is really only one objection which can be made, and it is made unceasingly, to this interpretation of the words of Jesus. It is that it is inconsistent with what is elsewhere His unmistakable teaching. The very burden of His message, we are told, is that God forgives unconditionally out of His pure fatherly love. This love reaches of itself deeper far than sin, and bestows pardon freely and joyfully on the penitent. It is nothing less than a direct contradiction of this gospel of the free love of God to make forgiveness dependent upon a sacrificial, that is a propitiary, virtue in the death of Christ. It is to misrepresent God's character, and in so doing to destroy the gospel. We cannot, it is argued, on the strength of one word, and that a dubious word, run counter to the sense and spirit of our Lord's teaching as a whole.

Such a contention can best be answered in the light of what we have already seen to be our Lord's conception of Himself and His calling from the beginning. The love of God, according to Jesus, is no doubt unconditionally free, but it is not an abstraction.

It does not exist *in vacuo*. So far as the forgiveness of sins is concerned, and it is with the love of God in this relation that we have to do, it exists in and is represented by Jesus' own presence in the world; His presence in a definite character, and with a definite work to do, which can be done only at a definite cost. The freeness of God's love is not contradicted by these facts; on the contrary, it is these facts which enable us to have any adequate idea of what that love really is. To say that it is inconsistent with God's free love to make the forgiveness of sins dependent on the death of Jesus is the same as to say with reference to the Christian revelation as a whole, that it is inconsistent with God's free love that entrance into His kingdom and participation in its blessings should be possible only through the presence of Jesus in the world, His work in it, and the attitude which men assume towards Him. Those who accept the latter should not deny the former. If we give any place at all to the idea of mediation, there is no reason why we should reject the idea of propitiation. For propitiation is merely a mode of mediation, a mode of it, no doubt, which brings home to us acutely what we owe to the Mediator, and makes us feel that, though forgiveness is free to us, it does not cost Him nothing.

Of course, if we choose to say that the Son has no place in the gospel at all, but only the Father, we may reject the great word about covenant-blood; or rather, we must reject it. If He has no place in the gospel at all, we do not owe Him anything. Least of all are we indebted to His death for the forgiveness of sins. But there is something in such language which, when confronted with the Gospels, can strike one only as utterly abstract, unconvincing, and unreal. It does not answer to the relation of sinful souls to Jesus, to their devotion, their gratitude, their sense of undying obligation. It was not for a forgiveness with which, in the last resort, He had nothing to do that they poured their precious ointment on His head and wet His feet with tears. In the depths of their being they had the dim sense of what He suffered for their pardon, and were conscious of an obligation for it to Him which they could never repay. The love of God, I repeat, free though it is to sinful men, unconditionally free, is never conceived in the New Testament, either by our Lord Himself or by any of His followers, as an abstraction. Where the forgiveness of sin is concerned, it is not conceived as having reality or as taking effect apart from Christ. It is a real thing to us as it is mediated through Him, through His presence in the world, and ultimately through His death. The love of God by which we are redeemed from sin is a love which we do not know except as it comes in this way and at this cost. Consequently, whatever we owe as sinners to the love of God, we owe to the death of Jesus. It is no more a contradiction of God's free love to the sinful when we say that Christ's death is the ground of forgiveness than it is a contradiction of God's fatherly goodwill to men in general when we admit the word of Jesus, 'No man cometh unto the Father but by Me.' In both cases equally Christ stands between God and man; in both cases equally it is at cost to Him that God becomes our God.

Why should we be loth to become His debtors? The Christian faith is a specific form of dependence on God, and to cavil at the atonement is to begin the process of gradually abandoning that sense of dependence. It is to refuse to allow it to be conditioned by Christ at the central and vital point, the point at which the sinner is reconciled to God; and if we can do without Christ there, we can do without Him altogether. The process which begins with denying that we owe to Him and to His death the forgiveness of sins, ends by denying that He has any proper place in the gospel at all. It is neither from His own lips, nor from the lips of any of the apostles, that we so learn Christ.

CHAPTER II

THE EARLIEST CHRISTIAN PREACHING

THUS far we have confined ourselves to the words of Jesus. The divine necessity of His death, indicated in the Old Testament and forming the basis of all His teaching regarding it, is the primary truth; the nature of that necessity begins to be revealed as the death is set in relation to the ransoming of many, and to the institution of a new covenant—that is, a new religion, having as its fundamental blessing the forgiveness of sins. I do not think this view of our Lord's mind about His own death can be shaken by appealing to His experience in the garden, as though that proved that to the last day of His life the inevitableness of death remained for Him an open question.

The divine necessity to lay down His life for men, which we have been led to regard as a fixed point in His mind, did not preclude such conflicts as are described in the last pages of the Gospel; rather was it the condition of His victory in them. At a distance, it might have been possible for Him to think of death in its heroic and ideal aspects only, as the fulfilment of a divine calling, an infinite service rendered in love to man. But as the fatal hour approached, its realistic and repellent aspects would predominate over everything. It stood out before the mind and imagination of Jesus—we might almost say it obtruded itself upon His senses—as a scene and an experience of treachery, desertion, hate, mockery, injustice, anguish and shame. It is not hard to conceive that in these circumstances Jesus should have prayed as He did in the garden: 'O My Father, if it be possible, let this cup pass from Me,' even though the unmoved conviction of His soul was that He had come to give His life a ransom for many. It is one thing to have the consciousness of so high a calling; it is another to maintain and give effect to it under conditions from which all that is ideal and divine seems to have withdrawn. It is one thing not to count one's life dear, or to make much of it, in comparison with great ends which are to be attained by laying it down; it is

another to lay it down, encompassed not by the gratitude and
adoration of those for whom the sacrifice is made, but by mocking
and spitting and scorn. This was what Jesus did, and He attained
to it through the agony in the garden. The agony does not
represent a doubt as to His calling, but the victorious assertion of
His calling against the dreadful temptation to renounce it which
came in the hour and with the power of darkness.

It is sometimes said that the realization, as they approached, of
the sensible and moral horrors of the death He was to die was
all that wrung from Jesus that last appeal to the Father, made
His soul exceeding sorrowful even unto death, and put Him in
agonia—that is, in deadly fear.[1] I cannot support this view. It does
not answer to what we know of the courage of martyrs. Though
one shrinks from analysing the cry of the heart to God in its
anguish, it is difficult to avoid the impression that both here and
in the experience of being forsaken on the cross, we are in contact with something out of proportion to all that men could do
to Jesus, something that seems to call for connection, if we would
understand it, with realities more mysterious and profound. Language like Calvin's,[2] who says plainly that Jesus endured in His
soul the dreadful torments of a condemned and lost man, may
well be repellent to us; there is something unrealizable and even
impious in such words. But it does not follow that there was
nothing true, nothing in contact with reality, in the state of
mind which inspired them. Not with any logical hardness, not
as carrying out aggressively to its issue any theological theory,
but sensible of the thick darkness in which God is, may we not
urge that these experiences of deadly fear and of desertion are of
one piece with the fact that in His death and in the agony in the
garden through which He accepted that death as the cup which
the Father gave Him to drink, Jesus was taking upon Him the
burden of the world's sin, consenting to be, and actually being,
numbered with the transgressors? They cannot but have some
meaning, and it must be part of the great meaning which makes
the cross of Christ the gospel for sinful men.

No doubt there are those who reject this meaning altogether;

[1] See Field, *Notes on the New Testament*, p. 77, where decisive proof of this is
given; and Armitage Robinson, *Gospel according to Peter*, pp. 84, 87 (ἀγωνιάω).
[2] *Institutio*, II. xvi. 10.

it is dogmatico-religious, not historico-religious, and no more is needed to condemn it. But a dogmatico-religious interpretation of Christ's death—that is, an interpretation which finds in it an eternal and divine meaning, laden with gospel—so far from being self-evidently wrong, is imperatively required by the influence which that death has had in the history of the Christian religion. Such an interpretation carries on, through the experiences of His death, thoughts as to its significance which we owe to Jesus Himself, and connects these thoughts and experiences with the subsequent testimony of the apostles. In other words, to read the accounts of Gethsemane and Calvary in this sense is to read them in line at once with the words of Jesus and with the words of those who were first taught by His Spirit; it is to secure at once the unity of the Gospels with themselves, and their unity, in the main truth which it teaches, with the rest of the New Testament.

To call such an interpretation dogmatico-religious as opposed to historico-religious either has no meaning, or has a meaning which would deny to the person and work of Jesus any essential place in the Christian religion. But if the death of Jesus has *eternal* significance—if it has a meaning which has salvation in it for all men and for all times; a meaning which we discover in Scripture as we look back from it and look forward; a meaning which is the key to all that goes before and to all that comes after (and such a meaning I take it to have, indisputably)—then Gethsemane and Calvary cannot be invoked to refute, but only to illustrate the 'dogmatic' interpretation. They are too great to be satisfied by anything else.

It does not follow, of course, that they were understood at once, even in the light of our Lord's words, by those whom He left as His witnesses. The mind can easily retain words the meaning of which it only imperfectly apprehends. It can retain words by which it is in the first instance moved and impressed, rather than enlightened. It can retain words which are sure, when reflection awakens, to raise many questions, and to ask for definition in a great variety of relations; and it can retain them without at first having any consciousness of these questions whatever. It is in the highest degree probable that it was so with the disciples

of Jesus. We can easily believe that they had right impressions
from our Lord's words, before they had clear ideas about them.
But before proceeding to examine the ideas of the primitive
Christian Church on this subject, it is necessary to give an explicit
utterance on the resurrection, and the presentation of it in the
Gospels.

The resurrection of Jesus from the dead is here assumed to have
taken place, and, moreover, to have had the character ascribed
to it in the New Testament. It is not sufficient to say that there
were appearances to certain persons of the Jesus who had died
—appearances the significance of which is exhausted when we
say that they left on the minds of those who were favoured with
them the conviction that Jesus had somehow broken the bands
of death. It is quite true that Paul, in setting before the Corinthians the historical evidence for the resurrection, enumerates
various occasions on which the Risen Lord was seen, and says
nothing about Him except that on these occasions He appeared
to Peter, to James, to the Twelve, to more than five hundred at
once, and so on: this was quite sufficient for his purpose. But
there is no such thing in the New Testament as an appearance
of the Risen Saviour in which He merely appears. He is always
represented as entering into relation to those who see Him in
ways other than by a flash upon the inner or the outer eye. He
establishes other communications between Himself and His own
besides those which can be characterized in this way. He not only
appeared to them, but spoke to them. He not only appeared to
them, but taught them, and in particular gave them a commission
in which the meaning of His own life and work, and their calling
as connected with it, are finally declared. In every known form
of the evangelic tradition such a charge, or instruction, or commission, is found on the lips of Jesus after the resurrection.

What, then, is the content of this teaching or commission of
the Risen Saviour, which all the evangelists give in one form or
another? Luke has some peculiar matter in which he tells how
Jesus opened the minds of His disciples to understand the Scriptures, recalling the words He had spoken while He was yet with
them, how that all things must be fulfilled which were written
in the law of Moses and in the Prophets and in the Psalms concerning Him. If Jesus spoke to His disciples about what had

befallen Him, all that we have already seen as to His teaching prepares us to believe that it was on this line. Both for Him and for the disciples the divine necessity for His death could be made out only by connecting it with intimations in the Word of God.

But apart from this instruction, which is referred to by Luke alone, it is with the common testimony that we are mainly concerned. In Matthew it runs thus: 'Jesus came to them and spake unto them, saying, All authority hath been given unto Me in heaven and on earth. Go ye therefore, and make disciples of all the nations, baptizing them into the name of the Father and of the Son and of the Holy Ghost: teaching them to observe all things whatsoever I commanded you: and lo, I am with you alway, even unto the end of the world' (Mt. xxviii. 18 ff.). Here we notice as the essential things in our Lord's words (i) the universal mission; (ii) baptism; (iii) the promise of a spiritual presence.

In Mark, as many suppose, the original ending has been lost. The last chapter, however, may have been the model on which the last in Matthew was shaped, and what we have at present instead of it reproduces the same ideas. 'Go ye into all the world, and preach the gospel to the whole creation. He that believeth and is baptized shall be saved; but he that disbelieveth shall be condemned' (Mk. xvi. 15 f.).

In Luke the commission is connected with the teaching referred to above. 'He said unto them, Thus it is written, that the Christ should suffer, and rise again from the dead the third day; and that repentance and remission of sins should be preached in His name unto all the nations, beginning from Jerusalem' (Lk. xxiv. 46 f.). Here again we have (i) the universal commission; (ii) repentance and remission of sins. In John what corresponds to this runs as follows: 'Jesus therefore said to them again, Peace be unto you: as the Father hath sent Me, even so send I you. And when He had said this, He breathed on them and saith unto them, Receive ye the Holy Ghost: whose soever sins ye forgive, they are forgiven unto them; whose soever sins ye retain, they are retained' (Jn. xx. 21 f.). Here once more we have (i) a mission, though its range is not defined; (ii) a message, the sum and substance of which has to do with forgiveness of sins; and (iii) a gift of the Holy Ghost. 'But what', it may be asked, 'has all this to do with the death of Jesus? The death of Jesus is not expressly referred to here, except in what Luke tells about His opening the minds of the disciples to understand the Scriptures, and that simply repeats what we have already had before us.'

The answer is apparent if we consider the context in which the ideas found in this commission are elsewhere found in the New Testament. In all its forms the commission has to do either with baptism (as in Matthew and Mark) or with the remission of sins (as in Luke and John). These are but two forms of the same thing, for in the world of New Testament ideas baptism and the remission of sins are inseparably associated. But the remission of sins has already been connected with the death of Jesus by the words spoken at the supper, or if not by the very words spoken, at least by the significance ascribed to His blood as covenant-blood. And if the Risen Saviour, in giving His disciples their final commission, makes the forgiveness of sins the burden of the gospel they are to preach, which seems to me indubitable, He at the same time puts at the very heart of the gospel His own covenant-founding, sin-annulling death.

This inference from the passages in the Gospels which record the intercourse of the Risen Lord with His disciples may strike some, at the first glance, as artificial. But the air of artificiality will pass away, provided we admit the reality of that intercourse and its relation both to the past teaching of Jesus and to the future work of the apostles. There is a link wanted to unite what we have seen in the Gospels with what we find when we pass from them to the other books of the New Testament, and that link is exactly supplied by a charge of Jesus to His disciples to make the forgiveness of sins the centre of their gospel, and to attach it to the rite by which men were admitted to the Christian society.

In an age when baptism and remission of sins were inseparable ideas, when, so to speak, they interpenetrated each other, it is no wonder that the sense of our Lord's charge is given in some of the Gospels in one form, in some in the other: that here He bids them baptize, and there preach the forgiveness of sins. It is not the form on which we can lay stress, but only the import. The import, however, is secure. Its historicity can be questioned only by those who reduce the resurrection to mere appearances of Jesus to the disciples—appearances which contain nothing but themselves, are unchecked by any other relation to reality, and can therefore be regarded as essentially visionary. And its significance is that it is the very thing which is wanted to evince the unity of the New Testament, and the unity and consistency of the Christian religion, as they have been presented to us in the historical tradition of the Church. Here, where the final revelation is made by our Lord of all that His presence in the world means and involves, we find Him dealing with ideas—baptism and forgiveness—which both in His own earlier teaching, and in the subsequent teaching of the apostles, can be defined only by relation to His death.

There is a general consent that in the early chapters of Acts there is a very primitive type of doctrine and that some source or sources of the highest value underlie the speeches of Peter. They do not represent the nascent catholicism of the beginning of the second century, but the very earliest type of the preaching of the gospel of Jesus Christ by men who had kept company with Him.

It would be out of place here to dwell on the primitive character of the Christology, but it is necessary to refer to it as a guarantee for the historical character of the speeches in which it occurs. Consider, then, passages like these: 'Jesus of Nazareth, a man approved of God unto you by mighty works and wonders and signs which God did by Him in the midst of you, even as ye yourselves know' (ii. 22); 'God hath made Him both Lord and Christ, this Jesus whom ye crucified' (ii. 36); 'Jesus of Nazareth, how that God anointed Him with the Holy Ghost and with power: who went about doing good, and healing all that were oppressed of the devil; for God was with Him' (x. 38). It is impossible to deny that in words like these we have a true echo of the earliest Christian preaching. And it is equally impossible to deny that the soteriology which accompanies this Christology is as truly primitive. What then is it, and what, in particular, is the place taken in it by the death of Jesus?

It is sometimes asserted broadly that the real subject of these early speeches in Acts is not the death of Jesus but the resurrection; the death, it is said, has no significance assigned to it; it is only a difficulty to be got over. But there is a great deal of confusion in this. The apostles were certainly witnesses of the resurrection, and the discourses in these chapters are specimens of their testimony. The resurrection is emphasized in them with various motives. Sometimes the motive may be called apologetic: the idea is that in spite of the death it is still possible to believe in Jesus as the Messiah; God by raising Him from the dead has exalted Him to this dignity. Sometimes it may be called evangelistic. You killed Him, the preacher says again and again (ii. 23 f., iii. 14 f., v. 30 f.), and God exalted Him to His right hand. In these two appreciations of Jesus lies the motive for a great spiritual change in sinful men. Sometimes, again, the resurrection is referred to in connection with the gift of the Spirit; the new life in the Church, with its wonderful manifestations, attests the exaltation of Jesus (ii. 33). Sometimes, once more, it is connected with His return, either to bring times of refreshing from the presence of the Lord (iii. 19 f.), or as Judge of the quick and the dead (x. 42).

This preoccupation with the resurrection in various aspects and relations does not mean, however, that for the first preachers of the gospel the death of Jesus had no significance, or no fundamental significance. Still less does it mean that the death of Jesus was nothing to them but a difficulty in the way of retaining their faith in His Messiahship, a difficulty which the resurrection enabled them to surmount—its sinister significance being discounted, so to speak, by the splendour of this supreme miracle. This last idea, that the cross *in itself* is nothing but a scandal, and that all the New Testament interpretations of it are but ways of getting over the scandal, cannot be too emphatically rejected. It ignores, in the first place, all that has been already established as to our Lord's own teaching about the necessity and the meaning of His death—which has nothing to do with its being a σκάνδαλον. And it ignores, in the second place, the spiritual power of Christ's death in those who believe in Him, both as the New Testament exhibits it, and as it is seen in all subsequent ages of the Church. The gospel would never have been known as 'the word of the cross' if the interpretation of the cross had merely been an apologetic device for surmounting the theoretical difficulties involved in the conception of a crucified Messiah. Yet nothing is commoner than to represent the matter thus. The apostles, it is argued, had to find some way of getting over the difficulty of the crucified Messiah theoretically, as well as practically. The resurrection enabled them to get over it practically, for it annulled the death; and the various theories of a saving significance ascribed to the death enabled them to get over it theoretically—that is all.

Nothing, I venture to say, could be more hopelessly out of touch alike with New Testament teaching and with all Christian experience than such a reading of the facts. A doctrine of the death of Jesus, which was merely the solution of an abstract difficulty —the answer to a conundrum—could never have become what the doctrine of the death of Jesus is in the New Testament—the centre of gravity in the Christian world. It could never have had stored up in it the redeeming virtue of the gospel. It could never have been the hiding-place of God's power, the inspiration of all Christian praise. Whatever the doctrine of Jesus' death may be, it is the feeblest of all misconceptions to trace it to the necessity of saying something about the death which should as far as possible remove the scandal of it. 'I delivered unto you first of all', says Paul to the Corinthians, 'that which also I received, how that Christ died for our sins according to the Scriptures' (1 Cor. xv. 3). Paul must have received this doctrine from members of the primitive Church. He must have received it in the place which he gave it in his own preaching—that is, as the first and fundamental thing in the gospel. He probably received it within seven years of the death of Jesus. Even if the book of Acts were so preoccupied with the resurrection that it paid no attention to the independent significance of the death, it would be perfectly fair, on the ground of this explicit reference of Paul, to supplement its outline of primitive Christian doctrine with some definite teaching on the atonement. But when we look closely at the speeches in Acts, we find that our situation is much more favourable. They contain a great deal which enables us to see how the primitive Church was taught to think and feel on this important subject.

Here we have to consider such points as these. First, the death of Christ is repeatedly presented, as in our Lord's own teaching, in the light of a divine necessity. It took place 'by the determinate counsel and foreknowledge of God' (ii. 23). That His Christ should suffer, was what God foretold by the mouth of all His prophets (iii. 18). In His death, Jesus was the stone which the builders rejected, but which God made the head of the corner (iv. 11). All the enemies of Jesus, both Jew and Gentile, could do to Him only what God's hand and counsel had determined before should be done (iv. 28). A divine necessity, we must remember, is not a blind but a seeing one. To find the necessity for the death of Jesus in the word of God means to find that His death is not only inevitable but indispensable, an essential part of the work He had to do. Not blank but intelligible and moral necessity is meant here.

In the second place we notice the frequent identification, in these early discourses, of the suffering Messiah with the Servant of the Lord in the Book of Isaiah. '. . . The God of our Fathers, hath glorified His Servant Jesus' (iii. 13). 'Of a truth in this city, against Thy holy Servant Jesus . . . both Herod and Pontius Pilate were . . . gathered together' (iv. 27). The same identification is involved in the account of Philip and the Ethiopian eunuch. The place of the Scripture which the eunuch read was the fifty-third chapter of Isaiah, and beginning from the Scripture Philip preached to him Jesus (viii. 35). We cannot forget that the impulse to this connection was given by our Lord Himself, and that it runs through His whole ministry, from His baptism, in which the heavenly voice spoke to Him words applied to the Servant of the Lord in Is. xlii. 1, to the last night of His life when He applied to Himself the mysterious saying, He was numbered with transgressors (Lk. xxii. 37). The divine necessity to suffer is here elevated into a specific divine necessity, namely, to fulfil through suffering the vocation of one who bore the sins of many, and made intercession for the transgressors.

Thirdly, this connection of ideas in the primitive Church is made clearer still, when we notice that the great blessing of the gospel, offered in the name of Jesus, is the forgiveness of sins. This is the refrain of every apostolic sermon. Thus in ii. 38: 'Repent ye, and be baptized every one of you in the name of Jesus Christ unto the remission of your sins.' In iii. 19, immediately after the words, 'the things which God foreshewed by the mouth of all the prophets, that His Christ should suffer, He thus fulfilled,' we read: 'Repent ye therefore, and turn again, that your sins may be blotted out.' In v. 31 Jesus is exalted a Prince and a Saviour to give repentance to Israel and forgiveness of sins. In x. 43, after rehearsing in outline the life, death, and resurrection of Jesus, Peter concludes his sermon in the house of Cornelius: 'To Him bear all the prophets witness, that through His name every one that believeth on Him shall receive remission.'

This prominence given to the remission of sins is not accidental, and must not be separated from the context essential to it in Christianity. It is part of a whole or system of ideas, and other parts which belong to the same whole with it in the New Testament are baptism and the death of Christ. The book of Acts, like all other books in the New Testament, was written within the Christian society, and for those who were at home in it. It was not written for those who had no more power of interpreting what stood on the page than the letter itself supplied. It does not seem to me in the least illegitimate, but on the contrary both natural and necessary, to take all these references to the forgiveness of sins and to baptism as references at the same time to the saving significance 'in relation to sin' of the death of Jesus. This is what is suggested when Jesus is identified with the Servant of the Lord. This is what we are prepared for by the teaching of Jesus, and by the great commission; and we are confirmed in it by what we find in the rest of the New Testament.

It is not a sufficient answer to this to say that the connection of ideas asserted here between the forgiveness of sins or baptism, on the one hand, and the death of Jesus on the other, is not explicit; it is self-evident to anyone who believes that there is such a thing as Christianity as a whole, and that it is coherent and consistent with itself, and who reads with a Christian mind. The assumption of such a connection at once articulates all the ideas of the book into a system, and shows it to be at one with the Gospels and Epistles; and such an assumption, for that very reason, vindicates itself.

Besides the references to baptism and the forgiveness of sins, we ought to notice, in the fourth place, the reference in ii. 42 to the Lord's Supper. 'They continued stedfastly . . . in the breaking of the bread.' The New Testament, it may be pointed out, nowhere gives us the idea of an unbaptized Christian for by one Spirit we were all baptized into one body (1 Cor. xii. 13). Similarly Paul, in regulating the observance of the Supper at Corinth, regulates it as part of the Christian tradition which goes back for its authority through the primitive Church to Christ Himself. 'I received of the Lord that which also I delivered unto you' (1 Cor. xi. 23). In other words, there was no such thing known to Paul as a Christian society without baptism as its rite of initiation, and the Supper as its rite of communion. And if there was no such thing known to Paul, there was no such thing in the world.

There is nothing in Christianity more primitive than the Sacraments, and the Sacraments, wherever they exist, are witnesses to the connection between the death of Christ and the forgiveness of sins. It is explicitly so in the case of the Supper, and the expression of Paul about being baptized into Christ's death (Rom. vi. 3) shows that it is so in the case of the other Sacrament too. The apostle was not saying anything of startling originality, when he wrote at the beginning of Rom. vi: 'Are ye ignorant that all we who were baptized into Christ Jesus were baptized into His death?' Every Christian knew that in baptism what his mind was directed to, in connection with the blessing of forgiveness, was the death of Christ. Both Sacraments, therefore, are memorials of the death, and it is not due to any sacramentalist tendency in Luke that he gives the sacramental side of Christianity the prominence it has in the early chapters of Acts. This particular emphasis only brings out the place which the death of Christ had at the basis of the Christian religion as the condition of the forgiveness of sins. From the New Testament point of view, the Sacraments contain the gospel in brief; they contain it in inseparable connection with the death of Jesus; and as long as they hold their place in the Church the saving significance of that death has a witness which it will not be easy to dispute.

It is natural to link with the Petrine discourses in Acts an examination of the First Epistle of Peter. We shall proceed now, therefore, to examine this Epistle to see what ideas its author connects with the death of Jesus.

To begin with, the death of Jesus has the central place in the writer's mind which it everywhere has in the New Testament. He describes himself as a 'witness of the sufferings of the Christ'

(v. 1). Μάρτυς is to be taken here in its full compass; it means not only a spectator of, but one who bears testimony to. The writer's testimony to the sufferings of the Christ is one in which their significance is brought out in various aspects. But though this sense of 'witness' is emphasized, it by no means excludes the other; rather does it presuppose it. Peter seems to prefer 'sufferings' to 'death' in speaking of the Christ. Perhaps this is because he had been an eye-witness, and 'sufferings' served better than 'death' to recall all that his Lord had endured. Death might be regarded merely as the end of life, not so much a moral reality, as a limit or termination to reality. But sufferings are a part of life, with moral content and meaning, which may make an inspiring or pathetic appeal to men.

In point of fact it is the moral quality of the sufferings of the Christ, and their exemplary character, which first appeal to the apostle. As he recalls what he had seen as he stood by the great Sufferer, what impresses him most is His innocence and patience. He had done no sin, neither was guile found in His mouth: When He was reviled, He reviled not again; when He suffered He did not threaten, but committed himself to Him who judges righteously (ii. 22 f.). In this character of the patient and innocent sufferer Peter commends Jesus to Christians, especially the slaves, who were having their first experience of persecution and finding how hard it was not only to suffer without cause, but actually to suffer for doing well, for loving fidelity to God and righteousness.

It is not necessary to press the parallel unduly, or to argue that the suffering of Christians in imitation of the Christ will have in all respects the same kind of result, or the same kind of influence, as His. Yet Peter identifies the two to some extent when he says, in iv. 13, 'Ye are partakers of Christ's sufferings.' This is a genuinely evangelical point of view. Jesus calls on all His followers to take up their cross, and walk in His steps. The whole mass of suffering for righteousness' sake, which has been since the world began and will be to its close, is 'the sufferings of the Christ'. All who have any part in it are partners with Him in the pain, and will be partners also in the glory which is to be revealed. So far, it may be said, there is no theological reflection in the Epistle; it occupies the standpoint of our Lord's first lesson on the cross: 'I must suffer for righteousness' sake, and so must all who follow Me' (see Mt. xvi. 21-24), with the added admonition, 'Let it be in the same spirit and temper, without amazement, irritation, or bitterness.'

But the Epistle has other suggestions which it is necessary to examine. The first is found in the salutation. This is addressed 'to the elect who are sojourners of the Dispersion in Pontus, Galatia, Cappadocia, Asia, and Bithynia, according to the foreknowledge of God the Father, in sanctification of the Spirit, unto obedience and sprinkling of the blood of Jesus Christ' (i. 1 f.). In this comprehensive address, a whole world of theological ideas is involved. Christians are what they are as elect according to the foreknowledge of God. Their position does not rest on assumptions of their own, or on any movable basis, but on the eternal goodwill of God which has taken hold of them. This goodwill, which they know to be eternal—that is, to be the last reality in the world—has found expression in their consecration by the Spirit.

The word 'Spirit', standing as it does here between God the Father and Christ, must refer to the Holy Spirit, not the spirit of the Christian; the consecration of the believer is wrought by Him. The readers of the Epistle would no doubt connect the words, and be intended by the writer to connect them, with their baptism. It was in baptism that the Spirit was received and that the eternal goodwill of God became a thing which the individual (through faith, of course) grasped in time. But what is in view in this eternal goodwill and its manifestation in time? It has in view 'obedience and the sprinkling of the blood of Jesus Christ'.

We cannot miss the reference here to the institution of the covenant in Ex. xxiv. There we find the same ideas in the same relation to each other. 'Moses took the book of the covenant, and read in the audience of the people: and they said, All that the Lord hath spoken will we do, and be obedient. And Moses took the blood, and sprinkled it on the people, and said, Behold the blood of the covenant, which the Lord hath made with you upon all these conditions.' Such a sprinkling with covenant blood, after a vow of obedience, is evidently in Peter's mind here.

We have already seen, in connection with the institution of

the Lord's Supper, what covenant blood means. As sacrificial, it is sin-covering; it is that which annuls sin as the obstacle to union with God. Within the covenant, God and man have, so to speak, a common life. God is not excluded from human life; He enters into it and achieves His ends in the world through it. Man is not excluded from the divine life; God admits him to His friendship and shows him what He is doing. He becomes a partaker in the divine nature, and a fellow-worker with God. But the covenant is made by sacrifice; its basis and being are in the blood. In this passage, therefore, election and consecration have in view a life of obedience, in union and communion with God; and such a life, it is assumed, is possible only for those who are sprinkled with the blood of Jesus Christ. In other words, it is only this which has abiding power to annul sin as the barrier which comes between God and man. It is sometimes said that the position of the blood in this passage—after obedience—points to its sanctifying virtue, its power to cleanse the Christian progressively, or ever afresh, from all sin; but if we use technical language at all, we should rather say that its character as covenant-blood obviously suggests that on its virtue the Christian is perpetually dependent for his justification before God. With this blood on us we have peace with Him, and the power to live in that peace.

The second express reference to the saving significance of our Lord's death occurs in i. 18 ff. Peter is exhorting those to whom he writes to a life of holiness, and he uses various arguments in support of his plea for sanctification. First, it answers to the essential relations between man and God. 'As He which called you is holy, be ye yourselves also holy in all manner of living' (i. 15). Second, it is required in view of the account they must render. 'If ye call on Him as Father, who without respect of persons judgeth according to each man's work, pass the time of your sojourning in fear' (i. 17). And, third, they have been put in a position to live a holy life by the death of Christ. 'Knowing that you were redeemed, not with corruptible things, with silver or gold, from your vain manner of life handed down from your fathers; but with precious blood, as of a lamb without blemish and without spot, even the blood of Christ' (i. 18 f.).

A lamb without blemish and without spot is a sacrificial lamb, and the virtue here ascribed to the blood of Christ is some sort of sacrificial virtue. The preciousness of the blood cannot be otherwise explained than by saying that it was Christ's blood. But what is the virtue here ascribed to it? By it Christians were ransomed from a vain manner of life handed down from their fathers. The ἐλυτρώθητε of this passage is no doubt an echo of the λύτρον ἀντὶ πολλῶν in Mk. x. 45. The effect of Christ's death was that for Christians a peculiar kind of servitude ended; their life was no longer in bondage to vanity and to custom. The expression ἐκ τῆς ματαίας ὑμῶν ἀναστροφῆς πατροπαραδότου is a very striking one. Life before the death of Christ has touched it is ματαία, or 'futile'. It is a groping or fumbling after something it can never find; it gets into no effective contact with reality; it has no abiding fruit. From this subjection to vanity it is redeemed by the blood of Christ. When the power of Christ's passion enters into any life it is not futile any more: there is no more the need or the inclination to cry ματαιότης ματαιοτήτων, 'vanity of vanities'.

Nothing can be more real or satisfying than the life to which we are introduced by the death of Christ. It is a life in which we can have fruit, much fruit, and fruit that abides. Hence the introduction to it, as ἐλυτρώθητε suggests, is a kind of emancipation. Similarly, life before the death of Christ has touched it is πατροπαράδοτος; it is a kind of tradition or custom, destitute of moral originality or initiative. A man may think he is himself, and that he is acting freely and spontaneously, when he is only indulging self-will, or yielding to impulses of nature in him through which a genuine moral personality has never been able to emerge. But it is the power of Christ's passion descending into the heart which really begets the new creature, to whom moral responsibility—his own—is an original thing, a kind of genius, in virtue of which he does what nobody in the world ever did before, and feels both free and bound to do so. The moral originality of the New Testament life is a miracle that never grows old. And this new life of the Christian, with its satisfying reality, and its wonderful freedom, was bought with the blood of Christ.

It is possible to argue that the new life is called forth *immediately* by the death of Christ—that is, that the impression produced by the spectacle of the cross, if we may so speak, quite apart from its interpretation, emancipates the soul. But there is something

unreal in all such arguments. The death of Christ was never presented to the world merely as a spectacle. It was never presented
by any apostle or evangelist apart from an interpretation. It was
the death of Christ so interpreted as to appeal irresistibly to the
heart, the conscience, the imagination, perhaps we should sometimes add the very senses of men, which exercised the emancipating power. And the only hint which is here given of the line
of interpretation is that which is involved in the reference to the
sacrificial lamb. It was the death of Christ not uninterpreted
(which is really equivalent to non-significant), but interpreted in
some way as a death for our sins which exercised this beneficent
power to liberate and to re-create the soul.

A clearer light is cast on the nature of the connection between
Christ's death and the moral emancipation of believers by the
third passage in which the apostle makes a detailed reference to
the subject. Here the example of Christ in His sufferings is set
before Christian slaves who are called to suffer unjustly. Peter
pleads with them to be patient. 'What glory is it, if, when ye
sin, and are buffeted for it, ye shall take it patiently? but if, when
you do well, and suffer for it, ye shall take it patiently, this is
acceptable with God. For hereunto were ye called: because Christ
also suffered for you (ὑπὲρ ὑμῶν ἔπαθεν), leaving you an
example, that ye should follow His steps' (ii. 20 f.). It is the exemplary character of the sufferings of Christ that is in view when
the writer goes on: 'Who did no sin, neither was guile found in
His mouth: who, when He was reviled, reviled not again; when
He suffered, threatened not; but committed Himself to Him that
judgeth righteously.'

In these words the appeal of the example is clear. It is equally
clear that in what follows the exemplary character of Christ's
sufferings is left behind, or transcended, and that they are considered in another aspect. It is as though the apostle could not
turn his eyes to the cross for a moment without being fascinated
and held by it. He saw far more in it habitually, and he saw far
more in it now, than was needed to point his exhortation to the
wronged slaves. It is not *their* interest in it, as the supreme example
of suffering innocence and patience, but the interest of all sinners
in it as the only source of redemption, by which he is ultimately
inspired: 'Who His own self bare our sins in His body upon the

tree, that we, having died unto (the) sins, might live unto right-eousness; by whose stripes ye were healed.' The enlargement of view is shown by the change to the first person (He bore *our* sins, that *we* might live, etc.), the writer including himself and all Christians with those whom he addresses in the benefits of Christ's death. It is only in the last clause—'by whose stripes ye were healed'—that he returns to his immediate subject, the slaves who were buffeted for doing well. What precisely is it, then, which is here affirmed of Christ in His death?

Literally, it is that He Himself bore our sins in His body on to the tree. The use of ἀναφέρειν with ἁμαρτίαν is not common: it occurs only in Is. liii. 12 and Nu. xiv. 34, the more usual expression being λαμβάνειν. But it seems absurd for this reason, and also for the reason that ἀναφέρειν τι ἐπὶ τὸ θυσιαστήριον is a common expression, to argue that here the tree or cross is regarded as an altar, to which sin was literally carried up to be slain.[1] That which is slain at the altar is always regarded as a gift acceptable to God: the slaying is only the method in which it is irrevocably made His. Nothing is more perverse than the attempt to present sin in this light. The words of the apostle must be interpreted as the common sense of Christians always has interpreted them: that Christ bore our sins in His body as He ascended the Cross, or ascended to it.

There is something in the words ἐν τῷ σώματι and ἐπὶ τὸ ξύλον which leaves a singular and even poignant impression of reality on the mind. To us the passion is idealized and transfigured; 'the tree' is a poetic name for the cross, under which the hard truth is hidden. But σῶμα implies flesh and blood, and ξύλον means timber. We may have wondered that an apostle and eye-witness should describe the sinlessness and the suffering of Jesus, as the writer of this Epistle does, almost entirely in words quoted from the Old Testament. But even as we wonder, and are perhaps visited with misgivings, we are startled by these words in which the passion is set before us as a spectacle of human pain which the writer had watched with his own eyes as it moved to its goal at the cross. But this reminiscent, pictorial turn which he has given to his expression does not alter the meaning of the principal

[1] See, for instance, Alford's note on the passage, and the qualified support given to it in Bigg's *Commentary*.

words—'Who His own self bore our sins.'[1] This is the interpretation of the passion: it was a bearing of sin.

Now, to bear sin is not an expression for which we have to
invent or excogitate a meaning: it is a familiar expression, of
which the meaning is fixed. Thus, to take the instance referred
to above (Nu. xiv. 34): 'After the number of the days in which
ye spied out the land, even forty days, for every day a year, shall
ye bear your iniquities': the meaning clearly is, bear the consequences of them, take to yourselves the punishment which they
involve. Or again, in Lv. v. 17: 'If any one sin, and do any of
the things which the Lord hath commanded not to be done;
though he knew it not, yet is he guilty, and shall bear his iniquity':
the meaning is as clearly, he shall lie under the consequences
attached by the law to his act. Or again, in Ex. xxviii. 43, it is
stated that the sons of Aaron are to observe punctiliously the laws
about their official dress, 'that they bear not iniquity, and die'.
To die and to bear iniquity are the same thing, death being the
penalty here denounced against impiety.

Expressions like these indicate the line on which we are to fill
out the meaning of the words, 'Who His own self bare our sins.'
They are meant to suggest that Christ took on Him the consequences of our sins, that He made our responsibilities, as sin
had fixed them, His own. He did so when He went to the cross,
that is, in His death. His death, and His bearing of our sins, are
not two things, but one. It may be true enough that He bore
them on His spirit, that He saw and felt their exceeding sinfulness,
that He mourned over them before God. But however true and
moving such considerations may be, they are not what the apostle
means in the passage before us. He means that all the responsibilities in which sin has involved us, responsibilities which are
summed up in that death which is the wages of sin, have been taken
by Christ upon Himself. His interpretation of the passion is that it
is a bearing of sin or, more precisely, that it is the bearing of others'
sin by one who is Himself sinless. (Nu. xxx. 15; Heb. ix. 28.)

---

[1] In his *Bible Studies* (E. Tr. p. 88 ff.) Deissmann argues that there is no suggestion here of the special ideas of substitution or sacrifice: all that is meant is
that when Christ *bears up to the cross* the sins of men, then men have their sins no
more: the *bearing up to* is a *taking away*. In view of the other references in the
Epistle and of the Old Testament parallels, this is rather a refusal to think out
the apostle's thoughts than a stricter interpretation of his words.

The apostle does not raise the question whether it is possible for one to assume the responsibilities of others in this way. He assumes (and the assumption, as we shall see, is common to all the New Testament writers) that the responsibilities of sinful men have been taken on Himself by the sinless Lamb of God. This is not a theorem he is prepared to defend; it is the gospel he has to preach. It is not a precarious or a felicitous solution of an embarrassing difficulty—the death of the Messiah; it is the foundation of the Christian religion, the one hope of sinful men. It may involve a conception of what Christ is, which would show the irrelevance of the objection just referred to, that one man cannot take on him the responsibilities of others; but leaving that apart for the moment, the idea of such an assumption is unquestionably that of this passage. It is emphasized by the very order of the words—ὃς τὰς ἁμαρτίας ἡμῶν αὐτὸς ἀνήνεγκεν; it was *not His own* but *our* sins that were borne at Calvary.

Having stated clearly what was done by Christ in His death, Peter goes on to speak of its aim. *He* bore *our* sins, that having died to the sins, we might live to righteousness. It is not possible to argue from ἀπογενόμενοι that our death was involved in His— that we actually or ideally died when He did, and so have no more relation to sins. It is quite fair to render, 'that we might die to our sins and live to righteousness.' A new life involves death to old relations, and such a new life, involving such death, is the aim of Christ's bearing of our sins.

How this effect is mediated the apostle does not say. Once we understand what Christ's death means—once we receive the apostolic testimony that in that death He was taking all our responsibilities upon Him—no explanation may be needed. The love which is the motive of it acts immediately upon the sinful; gratitude exerts an irresistible constraint. His responsibility means our emancipation; His death our life; His bleeding wound our healing. Whoever says 'He bore our sins' says substitution; and to say substitution is to say something which involves an immeasurable obligation to Christ, and has therefore in it an incalculable motive power. This is the answer to some of the objections which are commonly made to the idea of substitution on moral grounds. They fail to take account of the sinner's sense of debt to Christ for what He has done, a sense of debt which it is not too much to designate as the most intimate, intense, and uniform characteristic of New Testament life. It is this which bars out all ideas of being saved from the consequences of sin, while living on in sin itself. It is so profound that the whole being of the Christian is changed by it. It is so strong that it extinguishes and creates at one and the same time. Under the impression of it, to use the apostle's words here, the aim of Christ's bearing of our sins is fulfilled in us—we die to the sins and live to righteousness.

This interpretation of the passage in the second chapter is confirmed when we proceed to the one in the third. The subject is still the same, the suffering of Christians for righteousness' sake. 'It is better', says the apostle in iii. 17, 'if the will of God should will, that ye suffer for well-doing than for evil-doing. Because Christ also suffered for sins once, the righteous for the unrighteous, that He might bring us to God.' Here, as in the previous passage, an exemplary significance in Christ's sufferings is assumed, and to it, apparently, the writer reverts in iv. 1, 'as Christ suffered in the flesh, arm ye yourselves also with the same mind'; but it is not this exemplary significance on which he enlarges. On the contrary, it is a connection which the death of Christ, or His passion, has with sins. Christ, he says, died in connection with sins once for all (ἅπαξ); His death has a unique significance in this relation.

What the special connection was is indicated in the words δίκαιος ὑπὲρ ἀδίκων. The obvious implication of these words is that the death on which such stress is laid was something to which the unrighteous were liable because of their sins, and that in their interest the Righteous One took it on Himself. When He died for them, it was *their* death which He died. His death has to be defined by relation to sin, but it is the sin of others, not His own. The writer no more asks here than he asked in the previous case, How can such things be? He does not limit the *will* of love —he does not, in a world made and ruled by God, limit beforehand the *power* of love—to take on it to any extent the responsibility of others. This is his gospel, that a Righteous One has once for all faced and taken up and in death exhausted the responsibilities of the unrighteous, so that they no more stand between them and God; his business is not to prove this, but to preach it. The only difference is that whereas in the second chapter, if we can draw such a distinction in the New Testament, the aim is a *moral* one 'that we may die to sin and live to righteousness', in the present case it is *religious* 'that He might conduct us to God'.

The word προσάγειν has always a touch of formality in it; it is a great occasion when the Son who has assumed our responsibilities for us takes us by the hand to 'bring' us to the Father. We find the same idea of the προσαγωγή as the great Christian privilege in Rom. v. 2 and Eph. ii. 18. Sin, it is implied, keeps man at a distance from God; but Christ has so dealt with sin on man's behalf that its separative force is annulled. Those who commit themselves to Christ and to the work which He has done for them in His passion, are now able to draw near to God and to live in His peace. This is the end contemplated in His dying for sins once, the righteous for the unrighteous. We can only repeat here what has just been said in connection with the previous passage. If Christ died the death in which sin had involved us, if in His death He took the responsibility of our sins upon Himself, no word is equal to this which falls short of what is meant by calling Him our substitute. Here also, as in the second chapter, the substitution of Christ in His death is not an end in itself: it has an ulterior end in view. And this end is not attained except for those who, trusting in what Christ has done, find access to God through Him.

Such access, we must understand, is not a thing which can be taken for granted. It is not for the sinful to presume on acceptance with God whenever they want it. Access to God is to the apostle the most sublime of privileges, purchased with an unspeakable price. For such as we are it is possible only because Christ died for our sins. And just as in the ancient tabernacle every object used in worship had to be sprinkled with atoning blood, so all the parts of Christian worship, all our approaches to God, should consciously rest on the atonement. They should be felt to be a privilege beyond price; they should be penetrated with the sense of Christ's passion, and of the love with which He loved us when He suffered for sins once for all, the just for the unjust, *that He might conduct us to God*.

There is no other passage in the First Epistle of Peter which speaks with equal explicitness of the saving significance of Christ's death. But the passages which have just been reviewed are all the more impressive because of the apparently incidental manner in which they present themselves to us. The apostle is not avowedly discussing the theology of the passion. There is nothing in his Epistle like that deliberate grappling with the problem of the justification of the ungodly which we find, for example, in the third and fourth chapters of the Epistle to the Romans. His general purpose, indeed, is quite different. It is to exhort to patience and constancy Christians who are suffering for the first time severe persecution, and who are disposed to count it a strange thing that has befallen them. To all such the suffering Christ is held up as an example. He is the first of martyrs, and all who suffer for righteousness' sake, as they share the suffering which He endured, should confront it in the same spirit which He displayed.

The imitation of Jesus, however, is not an independent thing for the apostle; at least he never speaks of it by itself. It is the sense of obligation to Christ which enables us to lift our eyes to so high an example; and Peter glides insensibly, on every occasion, from Christ the pattern of innocence and patience in suffering to Christ the sacrificial lamb, Christ the bearer of sin, Christ who died, righteous for unrighteous men. It is here the inspiration is found for every genuine *imitatio Christi*; and the unforced, inevitable way in which the apostle falls back regularly on the profounder interpretation of the death of Christ, shows how central and essential it was to him. He does not dwell anywhere of set purpose on the attitude of the soul to this death, so as to make clear the conditions on which it becomes effective for the Christian's emancipation from a vain and custom-ridden life, for his death to sin, or for his introduction to God. As has been already remarked, the sense of obligation to Christ, the sense of the love involved in what he has done for men, may produce all these effects immediately.

There are two particulars in which the First Epistle of Peter makes a near approach to other New Testament books, especially to Pauline ones, in their conception of the conditions on which the blessings of the gospel are enjoyed, and it may not be out of place to refer to them here. The first is the emphasis it lays on faith. The testing of the Christian life is spoken of as 'the trying of your faith' (i. 7); the salvation of the soul is 'the end of your faith' (i. 9); Christians are those 'who through Him'—that is, through Christ—'have faith in God' (i. 21). The other is the formula 'in Christ', which has sometimes been treated almost as if it were the signature of Paul. It occurs in the last verse of the Epistle: 'Peace be unto you all that are in Christ.' Probably it is not too bold to suggest that in these two ideas—that of 'faith' and that of being 'in Christ'—we have here, as elsewhere in the New Testament, a clue to the terms on which all the Christian facts, and most signally the death of Christ, as the apostle interprets it, have their place and efficacy in the life of men.

The Second Epistle of Peter does not contain much that is directly relevant to our subject. There is one expression, however, which should be noted. It comes in the description of certain false teachers in ii. 1, who are spoken of as 'denying the Master who bought them' (τὸν ἀγοράσαντα αὐτοὺς δεσπότην ἀρνούμενοι). The idea of ἀγοράζειν is akin to that of λυτροῦσθαι, and the New Testament in other places emphasizes the fact that we are bought with a price (1 Cor. vi. 20, vii. 23), and that the price is the blood of Christ (Rev. v. 9). But though these ideas no doubt underlie the words just quoted, there is no expansion or application of them in the context. The passage takes for granted the common faith of Christians in this connection, but does not directly contribute to its elucidation.

CHAPTER III

THE EPISTLES OF PAUL

WHEN we pass from primitive Christian preaching to the Epistles of Paul, we are embarrassed not by the scantiness but by the abundance of our materials. It is not possible to argue that the death of Christ has less than a central, if not the central and fundamental place, in the apostle's gospel. But before proceeding to investigate more closely the significance he assigns to it, there are some preliminary considerations to which it is necessary to attend.

Attempts have often been made, while admitting that Paul teaches what he does teach, to evade it, either (i) because it is a purely individual interpretation of the death of Jesus which has no authority for others; or (ii) because it is speculative theology, and not a part of the apostolic testimony; or (iii) because it is not a fixed thing, but a stage in the development of apostolic thought, which Paul was on the way to transcend, and would eventually have transcended, and which we by his help can quite well leave behind us; or (iv) because it is really inconsistent with itself, a bit of patchwork, pieced out here and there with incongruous elements, to meet the exigencies of controversy; or (v) because it unites, in a way inevitable for one born a Pharisee, but simply false for those who have been born Christian, conceptions belonging to the imperfect as well as to the perfect religion—conceptions which it is our duty to abandon.

I do not propose to consider such criticisms of Paul's teaching on the death of Christ directly. For one thing, abstract discussion of such statements, apart from their application to given cases, never leads to any conclusive results. For another, when we do come to the actual matters in question, it often happens that the distinctions just suggested disappear, for the apostolic words have a virtue in them which enables them to combine in a kind of higher unity what might otherwise be distinguished as testimony and theology. But while this is so it is relevant, and one may think important, to point out certain characteristics of Paul's presentation of his teaching which constitute a formidable difficulty in the way of those who would evade it.

The first is, the assurance with which he expresses himself. The doctrine of the death of Christ and its significance was not Paul's theology, it was his gospel. It was all he had to preach. It is with it in his mind—immediately after the mention of our Lord Jesus Christ, *who gave Himself for our sins, that He might deliver us out of this present evil world*—that he says to the Galatians: 'Though we, or an angel from heaven, should preach unto you any gospel other than that which we preached unto you, let him be anathema. As we have said before, so say I now again, If any man preacheth unto you any gospel other than that which ye received, let him be anathema' (Gal. i. 4, 8 f.). I cannot agree with those who disparage this, or affect to forgive it, as the unhappy beginning of religious intolerance. Neither the Old Testament nor the New Testament has any conception of a religion without this intolerance. The first commandment is, 'Thou shalt have none other gods beside Me,' and that is the foundation of the true religion. As there is only one God, so there can be only one gospel. If God has really done something in Christ on which the salvation of the world depends, and if He has made it known, then it is a Christian duty to be intolerant of everything which ignores, denies, or explains it away. The man who perverts it is the worst enemy of God and men. It is not bad temper or narrowmindedness in Paul which explains this vehement language; it is the jealousy of God which has kindled in a soul redeemed by the death of Christ a corresponding jealousy for the Saviour. It is intolerant only as Peter is intolerant when he says, 'Neither is there salvation in any other' (Acts iv. 12), or John, when he says, 'He that hath the Son hath the life; he that hath not the Son of God hath not the life' (1 Jn. v. 12); or Jesus Himself when He says that no man knoweth the Father 'save the Son, and he to whomsoever the Son willeth to reveal him' (Mt. xi. 27).

Intolerance like this is, indeed, an essential element in the true religion. It is the instinct of self-preservation in it; the unforced and uncompromising defence of that on which the glory of God and the salvation of the world depends. If the evangelist has not something to preach of which he can say, 'If any man makes it his business to subvert this, let him be anathema,' he has no gospel at all. Intolerance in this sense has its counterpart in comprehension; it is when we have the only gospel, and not till then, that we have the gospel for all. It is a great argument, therefore, for the essential as opposed to the casual or accidental character of Paul's teaching on Christ's death—for it is with this that the Epistle to the Galatians is concerned—that he displays his intolerance in connection with it. To minimize his teaching here is not to do something which leaves his gospel unaffected; as he understands it, it is to wound his gospel mortally.

Another consideration of importance in this connection is Paul's relation to the common Christian tradition. No doubt the apostle was an original thinker, and in the Epistle to the Galatians he is concerned to vindicate his originality, or at least his independence; but his originality is sometimes exaggerated. He did not invent Christianity. There were apostles and preachers and men in Christ before him. And he tells us expressly that in the fundamentals of Christianity he not only agreed with them, but was indebted to them. 'I delivered unto you first of all that which also I *received*, how that Christ died for our sins according to the Scriptures; and that He was buried; and that He hath been raised on the third day according to the Scriptures' (1 Cor. xv. 3). It is impossible to suppose that the tradition which Paul had himself received, and which he transmitted to the Corinthians, contained no reference to the meaning of Christ's death such as is implied in the words—'He died *for our sins* according to the Scriptures.' It is the meaning of the event for sinners which constitutes a gospel, and this, he wishes to assert, is the only gospel known. 'Whether it be I or they—whether it be I or the twelve apostles at Jerusalem—this is the way we preach, and it was thus that you became believers' (see 1 Cor. xv. 11).

This doctrinal tradition of Christianity, if we may call it so, was supplemented and guaranteed by the ritual one. In the same Epistle to the Corinthians Paul says again, speaking of the Supper, 'I received of the Lord that which also I delivered unto you' (1 Cor. xi. 23). Since an immediate supernatural revelation of what took place on the last night of our Lord's life has no affinity to anything we know of revelations, we must understand Paul

to mean that what he had handed on to the Corinthians had
before been handed on to him, and went back originally to the
Lord Himself.

But Paul could not receive this ritual tradition, and we know
he did not, without receiving at the same time the great interpretative words about the new covenant in Christ's blood, which
put the death of Christ, once for all, at the foundation of the
gospel. It is not Paulinism which does this, it is the Christianity
of Christ. The point at issue between the apostle and his Jewish
Christian adversaries was not whether Christ had died for sins;
every Christian believed that. It was rather how far this death
of Christ reached in the way of producing or explaining the
Christian life. To Paul it reached the whole way. It explained
everything; it supplanted everything he could call a righteousness
of his own; it inspired everything he could call righteousness at
all. To his opponents, it did not so much supplant as supplement.
They agreed that but for the atoning death the sinner is hopeless;
but even when he has believed in it, he has much to do, they
insisted, on his own account, much which is not generated in
him by the sense of obligation to Christ, but must be explained
on other principles, for example, that of the authority of the
Jewish law.

It is not necessary to enter into this controversy here, but what
may fairly be insisted upon is the fact, which is evident in all
the Epistles, that underneath the controversy Paul and his opponents agreed in the common Christian interpretation of Christ's
death as a death in which sin had been so dealt with that it no
longer barred fellowship between God and those who believed
in Jesus. This, again, should make us refuse to reject anything
on this subject in Paul as being merely Pauline—an idiosyncrasy
of an individual. We must remember that his great argument
against Judaizing Christians is that they are acting inconsistently:
they are unwittingly doing something which contravenes, not
Paulinism, but the gospel they have already received of redemption through the death of Christ.

Again, the perception of Paul's place in Christian tradition, and
of his debt to it, should make us slow to lay stress on the development which has been discovered in his writings. Leaving out the
Pastorals, Paul wrote his other Epistles within the space of ten

years. But he had been preaching the gospel, in which the death of Christ had from the beginning the place and significance which we have just seen, at least fifteen years before any of the extant Epistles were written. Is it credible that he had no intellectual life at all for those fifteen years, and that then, all of a sudden, his brain began to work at high pressure, and continued so to work till the end of his life? It is true that in the Epistles of the imprisonment, as they may be conveniently called—Colossians, Ephesians, Philippians—we see the whole gospel in relations other than those in which it is exhibited in the Epistles of the great missionary period—Thessalonians, Corinthians, Galatians, Romans. But this is something quite different from a development in the gospel itself; and in point of fact we cannot discover in Paul's interpretation of Christ's death anything which essentially distinguishes his earliest Epistles from his latest. To suppose that a great expansion of his thought took place between the letters to the Thessalonians and those to the Corinthians is to ignore at once the chronology, the nature of letters, and the nature of the human mind. Paul tells us himself that he came to Corinth determined to know nothing among the Corinthians but Jesus Christ and Him crucified. But he came in that mood straight from Thessalonica, and in that mood he wrote from Corinth the letters to Thessalonica, in which, nevertheless, there is, as we shall see, only a passing allusion to Christ's death.

Nothing could demonstrate more clearly how entirely it depends upon conditions which we may or may not have the means of discovering whether any particular part of the apostle's whole conception of Christianity shall appear in any given Epistle. If development might be asserted anywhere, on general grounds, it would be in this case and on this subject. There is far more about Christ's death, and far more than is explicit, in the First Epistle to the Corinthians than in the First to the Thessalonians. Yet precisely at this point our knowledge of Paul's mind when he reached Corinth (1 Cor. ii. 1 f.), and of the brief interval which lay between this and his visit to Thessalonica, puts the idea of development utterly out of the question. As far as the evidence goes—including the evidence of Paul's Epistles on the one hand, and of his admitted relation to the doctrinal and ritual tradition of Christianity on the other—the apostle had one message on Christ's death from first to last of his Christian career. His gospel, and it was the only gospel he knew, was always 'the word of the cross' (1 Cor. i. 18), or 'the word of reconciliation' (2 Cor. v. 19). The applications might be infinitely varied, for, as has been already pointed out, everything was involved in it, and the whole of Christianity was deduced from it; but this is not to say that it was in process of evolution itself.

There are two other sets of questions which might be raised here, either independently or in relation to each other, concerning first the experimental and then the controversial or apologetic aspects of Paul's theology. How much of what he tells us of the death of Christ is the interpretation of experience, and has value as such? How much is mere fencing with opponents, or squaring of accounts with his own old ways of thinking about God and the soul, without value now because the conditions to which it is relative no longer exist?

These questions, as has been already remarked, are not to be discussed abstractly, because taken abstractly the antitheses they present are inevitably tainted with falsehood. They assume an opposition which does not exist, and they ignore the capacity of the truth to serve a variety of intellectual and spiritual purposes. Paul could use his gospel, no doubt, in controversy and in apology, but it was not devised for controversial or apologetic ends. The truth, by virtue of what it is, can always be its own vindication and defence. It can define itself in all relations, against all adversaries. But it is not constituted truth when it does so; it is only exhibited as truth. The fact that Christ died for our sins, that His death is an atoning death, is a magnificent apology for the cross, turning its shame into glory. But it is mere unintelligence, and not philosophy or criticism, to maintain that it was invented or believed just in order to remove the offence of the cross.

The gospel which Paul preached is not an apologetic or a controversial truth, or a truth relative to the exigencies of Jewish prejudice; it is an independent, eternal, divine truth, the profoundest truth of revelation, which for that very reason contains in it the answer to all religious questions whether of ancient or of modern times. So far from its being a truth which only a mind of peculiar antecedents or training could apprehend it is of all truths the most universal. It was his understanding of it as such that made Paul a missionary to all men. When he thought of what it meant, it made him exclaim, 'Is God the God of Jews only?' (Rom. iii. 29.) Is the God who is revealed in the death of Christ for sin a God who speaks a language that only one race can understand? Incredible. The atoning death of Christ, as a revelation of God, is a thing in itself so intelligible, so correspondent to a universal need, so direct and universal in its appeal, that it must be the basis of a universal religion. It is so far from being a truth (if we can speak of truth on such terms) relative only to one race, or one upbringing, or one age, or one set of prejudices, that it is the one truth which for all races and in all ages can never admit of any qualification. In itself true, it can be used as a weapon, but it was no necessity of conflict which fashioned it. It is the very heart of revelation itself.

The same attitude of mind to the Pauline teaching which would discount some of it as controversial or apologetic, as opposed to experimental or absolute, is seen in the disposition to distinguish in that teaching, as the expression is, fact from theory. In all probability this also is a distinction which it will not repay us to discuss *in vacuo*. Everything depends on the kind of fact which we are supposed to be theorizing. The higher we rise in the scale of reality the more evanescent becomes the distinction between the thing itself and the theory of it. A fact like the one with which we are here concerned, a fact in which the character of God is revealed, and in which an appeal is to be made to the reason, the conscience, the heart, the whole moral being of man, is a fact which must be, and must be seen to be, full of rational, ethical, and emotional content. If instead of 'theory' we use an equivalent word, say 'meaning', we discover that the absolute distinction disappears. The fact is not known to us at all unless it is known in its meaning, in that which constitutes it a revelation of God and an appeal to man. And to say that we know it in its meaning is to say that we know it theoretically, or in or through a theory of it. A fact of which there is no theory is a fact in which we can see no meaning; and though we can apply this distinction so far when we are speaking of physical facts, and argue that it is fire which burns and not the

theory of heat, we cannot apply it at all when we are speaking
of a fact which has to make impact upon us in other than physical
ways, through conscience, through the heart, through the intelligence, and therefore in a manner to which the mind can really
respond.

Paul's own words in Romans v. 11 enable us to illustrate this.
We have received, he says, or taken, the reconciliation. If we
could take it physically, as we take a doctor's prescription which
would affect us all the same whatever our spiritual attitude to
it might be, then we might distinguish clearly between the fact
and the theory of it, and argue that as long as we accepted the
fact, the theory was neither here nor there. If, however, the fact
with which we are dealing cannot be physically accepted at all
—if it addresses itself to a nature which is higher than physical, a
nature of which reason, imagination, emotion, conscience, are
the elements—then the fact itself must be seen to be one which
appeals to all these elements; that is, it must be an interpreted
fact, something in which fact and theory are indissolubly one.
The cross must be exhibited in ὁ λόγος τοῦ σταυροῦ, the reconciliation in ὁ λόγος τῆς καταλλαγῆς; and λόγος is always a rational,
a theoretical word.

It is much easier to say there is a distinction of fact and theory,
a distinction between the testimony and the theology of Paul,
than to prove it. It is much easier to imagine that one can preach
the gospel without any theory of the death of Christ than, knowing what these words mean, to do so. The simplest preacher,
and the most effective, is always the most absolutely theoretical.
It is a theory, a tremendous theory, that Christ's death is a death
for sin. But unless a preacher can put some interpretation on the
death, unless he can find a meaning in it which is full of appeal,
why should he speak of it at all? Is it the want of a theory that
deprives it of its place in preaching?

There is one other subject to which it is necessary to refer before considering Paul's teaching in detail, the connection between
Christ's death and His resurrection. The tradition of Protestant
theology undoubtedly tends to isolate the death, and to think of
it as a thing by itself, apart from the resurrection; sometimes,
one is tempted to say, apart even from any distinct conception

of Him who died. But we know that Paul himself puts an extra-ordinary emphasis on the resurrection. Sometimes it is co-ordi-nated with the death. 'If we believe that Jesus died and rose again,' he writes to the Thessalonians, including in this the whole of the Christian faith (1 Thes. iv. 14). He 'was delivered for our offences, and was raised again for our justification,' he says to the Romans, making the resurrection as essential as the death (Rom. iv. 25, A.V.). It is the same with the summary of funda-mental truths, which constituted the gospel as he preached it at Corinth, and which has been repeatedly referred to already: 'first of all . . . that Christ died for our sins according to the Scrip-tures; and that He was buried; and that He hath been raised on the third day according to the Scriptures' (1 Cor. xv. 3 f.). But there are passages in which he gives a more exclusive emphasis to the resurrection. Thus in Rom. x. 9 he writes: 'If thou shalt confess with thy mouth Jesus as Lord, and shalt believe in thy heart that God raised Him from the dead, thou shalt be saved'; and in 1 Cor. xv. 17: 'If Christ hath not been raised, your faith is vain; ye are yet in your sins.'

It is possible, however, to do full justice to all such expressions without qualifying in the slightest the prominence given in Paul to Jesus Christ as crucified. It was the appearance of the risen One to Paul which made him a Christian. What was revealed to him on the way to Damascus was that the crucified One was the Son of God, and the gospel that He preached afterwards was that of the Son of God crucified. There can be no salvation from sin unless there is a living Saviour: this explains the emphasis laid by the apostle on the resurrection. But the living One can be a Saviour only because He has died: this explains the emphasis laid on the cross. The Christian believes in a living Lord, or he could not believe at all; but he believes in a living Lord who died an atoning death, for no other can hold the faith of a soul under the doom of sin.

The importance of Paul's teaching, and the fact that dissent from any specifically New Testament interpretation of Christ's death usually begins with it, may justify these preliminary obser-vations. We now go on to notice more precisely what the apostle teaches. What then, let us ask, are the relations in which Paul

defines the death of Christ? What are the realities with which
he connects it, so that in these connections it becomes an intelligible thing, not a brute fact like the facts of physics before their
laws are known, but a significant, rational, ethical, appealing fact,
which has a meaning, and can act not as a cause but as a motive?
In other words, what is the doctrinal construction of this fact in
virtue of which Paul can preach it to man as a gospel?

To begin with, he defines it by relation to *the love of God*. The
death of Christ is an illustration or rather a demonstration of that
love. It is a demonstration of it which can never be surpassed.
There are great, though rare examples of love among men, but
nothing which could give any suggestion of this. 'Scarcely for a
righteous man will one die: for the good man possibly one might
dare even death: but God commends *His* love to us in that while
we were yet sinners Christ died for us' (see Rom. v. 7 f). We
shall return to this, and to Paul's inferences from it, when the
teaching of his Epistle to the Romans is considered;[1] but meanwhile we should notice that the interpretation of Christ's death
through the love of God is fundamental in Paul. In whatever
other relations he may define it, we must assume, unless the contrary can be proved, that they are consistent with this. It is the
commonest of all objections to the propitiatory doctrine of the
death of Christ that it is inconsistent with the love of God. Not
only amateur, but professional theologians of all grades have
rejected Paul's doctrine of propitiation as inconsistent with Jesus'
teaching on the love of the Father. But if a mind like Paul teaches
both things, if he makes the death of Christ in its propitiatory
character the supreme demonstration of the Father's love, is there
not an immense probability that there is misunderstanding some-
where? It may be a modern idea that a death for sins, with a
view to their forgiveness, is inconsistent with God's love. It is
certainly not Paul's. Whatever the process, he related that death
to God's love as the supreme proof of it.

Secondly, the apostle defines Christ's death by relation to *the
love of Christ*. The Son of God, he says, 'loved me, and gave
Himself up for me' (Gal. ii. 20). 'The love of Christ constraineth

[1] See p. 104.

us; because we thus judge, that one died for all' (2 Cor. v. 14).
'Walk in love, as Christ also hath loved us and hath given Himself for us an offering and a sacrifice to God for a sweet-smelling
savour' (Eph. v. 2, A.V.). 'Christ also loved the church, and gave
Himself for it' (Eph. v. 25, A.V.). Christ is not an instrument,
but the agent, of the Father in all that He does. The motive in
which God acts is the motive in which He acts: the Father and
the Son are at one in the work of man's salvation. It is this which
is expressed when the work of Christ is described, as it is in
Phil. ii. 8 and Rom. v. 19, as obedience—obedience unto death,
and that the death of the cross. The obedience is conceived as
obedience to the loving will of the Father to save men—that is,
it is obedience in the vocation of Redeemer, which involves death
for sin. It is not obedience merely in the sense of doing the will
of God as other men are called to do it, the everyday keeping
of God's commandments; it is obedience in this unique and
incommunicable, yet moral, calling to be at the cost of life the
Saviour of the world from sin. Hence it is in the obedience of
Christ to the Father that the great demonstration of *His* love to
men is given; 'He loved me,' the apostle says, 'and gave Himself
for me.' In His obedience, in which He makes His great sacrifice,
Christ is fulfilling the will of God; and the response which He
evokes by His death is a response toward God. It is at this point,
in the last resort, that we become convinced of the deity of
Christ. It is a work of God which He is working, and the soul
that is won for it is won for God in Him.

The relation of Christ's death to the love of God and of Christ
is its fundamental relation on one side. On the other side, and
this is our third point, Paul relates it essentially *to sin*. It is a death
for sin, whatever else may be said of it. 'First of all, Christ died
for our sins.' It was sin, and not something else, which made
death necessary as a demonstration of God's love and Christ's.
Why was this so? The answer of the apostle is that it was so
because sin had involved *us* in death, and there was no possibility
of Christ's dealing with sin effectually except by taking *our*
responsibility in it on Himself—that is, except by dying for it.
It is assumed in this, of course, that there is an ethical connection of some kind between death and sin, and that such a

connection of words as, 'The wages of sin is death' (Rom. vi. 23),
really has meaning. No doubt this has been denied. Death, it is
argued, is the debt of nature, not the wages of sin; it has no moral
character at all. The idea of moral liability to death, when you
look at the universality of death quite apart from moral considerations, is a piece of pure mythology. In spite of the assurance
with which this argument is put forward it is not difficult to
dissent from it. What it really does is to treat man abstractly, as
if he were no more than a physical being; whereas, if we are
to have either religion or morality preserved in the world, it is
essential to maintain that he is more. The argument is one of the
numberless class which proves nothing, because it proves too
much. It is part of a vaster argument which would deny at the
same time the spiritual nature and the immortality of man.

It is obviously right to say that death comes physically, that
through disease, or accident, or violence, or mere physical
exhaustion, it subdues to itself everything that lives. But this does
not touch the profounder truth with which Paul is dealing, that
death comes from God, and that it comes in man to a being
who is under law to Him. Man is not like a plant or an animal,
nor is death to him what it is at the lower levels of life. Man
has a moral nature in which there is a reflection of the holy law
of God, and everything that befalls him, including death itself,
must be interpreted in relation to that nature. *Conscience*, quickened by the law of God, has to look at death, and to become
alive, not to its physical antecedents, but to its divine meaning.
What does God say through conscience to a spiritual being about
death? He says what the apostle says—death is the wages of sin.
It is in the fact of death that the divine judgment on sin comes
home to the conscience. The connection between sin and death
is real, though it is not physical; and because it is what it is,
because death by God's ordinance has in the conscience of sinful
men the tremendous significance which it does have, because it
is a power by which they are all their lifetime held in bondage,
because it is the expression of God's implacable and final opposition to evil, He who came to bear our sin must also die our death.
Death is the word which sums up the whole liability of man in
relation to sin, and therefore, when Christ came to give Himself
for our sins, He did it by dying.

It does not occur to Paul to ask how Christ could die the death which is the wages of sin, any more than it occurred to Peter to ask how He could bear the sins of others. If any one had argued that the death which Jesus died, since it had not the shadow of a bad conscience cast upon it, was not the death which is the wages of sin, can we not conceive him asking, 'What death, then, was it? Is there any other? The death He died was the only death we know; it was death in all that tragic reality that we see at Calvary. And the sinlessness of Jesus, when we take His love along with it, so far from making it impossible for Him to know and feel it as all that it was, may have actually enabled Him to realize its awful character as no sinful soul had ever done or could do. Instead of saying, *He* could not die the death which is the wages of sin, it may be far truer to say, None *but* He could.'

With these general remarks on the different relations in which Paul defines the death of Christ, we may now proceed to consider the teaching of the Epistles in detail, keeping as far as possible to chronological order.

THE EPISTLES TO THE THESSALONIANS

The only indisputable relevant passage in these Epistles is 1 Thes. v. 9 f., 'God appointed us not unto wrath, but unto the obtaining of salvation through our Lord Jesus Christ, who died for us, that, whether we wake or sleep, we should live together with Him.' If the question is raised, What did Christ do for us with a view to our salvation, Paul has only one answer: He died for us. There is nothing in the Epistles like the language of the hymn:

'For us despised, for us He bore
His holy fast, and hungered sore;
For us temptations sharp He knew,
For us the Tempter overthrew.'

The only thing He is said to have done for us is to die, and this He did, because it was determined for Him by sin. In the nature of things the relation of sin and death made it binding on Him to die if He was to annul sin. The purpose here assigned

to Christ's death, that whether we wake or sleep we should live
together with Him, suggests that His power to redeem is dependent on His making all our experiences His own. If we are to
be His in death and life, then He must take our death and life to
Himself. If what is His is to become ours, it is only on the condition that what is ours He first makes His. There is the same
suggestion in Romans xiv. 9: 'To this end Christ died, and lived
again, that He might be Lord of both the dead and the living.'
Not as though death made Him Lord of the dead, and rising
again, of the living; but as One to whom no human experience
is alien, He is qualified to be Lord of men through all. The particular character elsewhere assigned to death as the doom of sin
is not here mentioned, but it does not follow that it was not felt.
On the contrary, we should hold rather that Paul could never
allude to the death of Christ without becoming conscious of its
propitiatory character and of what gave it that character. The
word would inevitably assume the meaning which it bears when
he says, 'First of all, Christ died for our sins.'

THE FIRST EPISTLE TO THE CORINTHIANS

Here we have much fuller references to the subject. For one thing,
its supreme importance is insisted on when we find the gospel
described as 'the word of *the cross*' (i. 18), and the apostle's
endeavours having as their aim that *the cross* of Christ should
not be made void (see i. 17). In the same spirit he contrasts the
true gospel with the miracles claimed by the Jews, and the
wisdom sought by the Greeks: 'We preach *Christ crucified*, . . .
the power of God, and the wisdom of God' (i. 23 f.). So again
in the second chapter he reminds the Corinthians how he came
to Achaia determined to know nothing among them but Jesus
Christ and Him crucified: his whole gospel, the testimony of
God, as he calls it, was in this (ii. 1 f.). In other passages he refers
to the death of Christ in general terms which suggest the cost at
which man's redemption was achieved. Twice over, in vi. 20,
and vii. 23, he writes, 'Ye were bought *with a price*'; making it
the basis, in the first instance, of an exhortation to glorify God
in the nature He had made His own at so dear a rate, and, in the
other, of an exhortation to assume all the responsibilities of that

freedom for which they had been so dearly ransomed, and not to become servants of men, that is not to let the conventions, or judgments, or consciences of others invade a responsibility which had obligations to the Redeemer alone.

It may not be possible to work out in detail the symbolism of the idea of a price which is found in these passages. We may not be able to say what it answered to, who got it, how it was fixed, and so on. But what we may legitimately insist upon is the idea that the work of man's salvation was a costly work, and that the cost, however we are to construe it, is represented by the death of Christ. 'Ye were bought with a price,' means, 'Ye were not bought for nothing.' Salvation is not a thing which can be assumed, or taken for granted; it is not an easy thing, about which no difficulty can possibly be raised by anyone who has any idea of the goodness of God. The point of view of the New Testament is the very opposite. Salvation *is* a difficult thing, an incredible thing, an impossible thing; it is the miracle of miracles that such a thing should be; the wonder of it never ceases, and it nowhere finds a more thrilling expression than in Paul's words, 'Ye were bought with a price.' Paul will show us in other ways why cost, and in particular the cost of Christ's death, was necessary. But it is a great step in initiation into the gospel he preached to see that cost had to be incurred, and actually was incurred, that men might be redeemed for God.

There is another passage in the First Epistle to the Corinthians on which I propose to lay stress greater than is usually done in connection with the apostle's teaching on Christ's death. I refer to the tenth and eleventh chapters in which Paul speaks of the Sacraments. He is concerned about the recrudescence of immorality among the saints, about the presumptuous carelessness with which they go into temptation, relying, apparently, on their sacramental privileges to ensure them against peril. He points out that God's ancient people had had similar privileges, indeed identical ones, yet had fallen in the wilderness owing to their sins. You are baptized into Christ? Yes, and all our fathers were baptized into Moses in the cloud and in the sea; they formed one body with him, and were as sure as you are of God's favour. You have supernatural meat and supernatural drink in the Lord's Supper, meat and drink which have the assurance of a divine and immortal life in them? So had they in the manna and the water from the rock. They all ate the same supernatural meat as you do, they all drank the same supernatural drink; they drank of a supernatural rock which followed them, and the rock was Christ.[1]

It is obvious from this passage (1 Cor. x. 1-4) as well as from the references to baptism in i. ff. and xii. 13, and from the full explanation of the Supper in xi. 23 ff., that the Sacraments had a large place in the church at Corinth; and not only a large place, but one whose significance can hardly be exaggerated. And, as has been pointed out already, there is no true interpretation of the Sacraments except by reference to the death of Christ. Baptism has always in view, as part at least of its significance, the forgiveness of sins; and, as the rite which marks the believer's initiation into the new covenant, it is essentially related to the act on which the covenant is based, namely, that which Paul delivered first of all to this Church, 'that Christ died for our sins'. When, in Romans vi, Paul argues that baptism into Christ means baptism into His death, he is not striking out a new thought, of a somewhat venturesome originality, to ward off a shrewd blow suddenly aimed at his gospel. He is bringing out only what was always to him the essential meaning of this ordinance. The Supper, again, of which he speaks at length in 1 Cor. x and xi, bears an unmistakable reference to Christ's death. The cup is specially defined as the new covenant in His blood, and the apostle sums up the meaning of the Sacrament in the words, 'As often as ye eat this bread, and drink the cup, ye proclaim the Lord's death till He come' (1 Cor. xi. 26). In all probability καταγγέλλετε ('proclaim' or 'publish') implies that the Sacrament

[1] I have rendered πνευματικὸν here 'supernatural' rather than 'spiritual', because it suggests better the element of mystery, or rather of divineness, which all through this passage is connected with the Sacraments. Baptism is not a common washing, nor is the Supper common meat and drink; it is a divine cleansing, a divine nourishment, with which we have to do in these rites. There is a mysterious power of God in them, which the Corinthians were inclined to conceive as operating like a charm for their protection in situations of moral ambiguity or peril. This is so far suggested to the Greek reader by πνευματικὸν, for πνεῦμα and its derivatives always involve a reference to God; but as it is not necessarily suggested to the English reader by 'spiritual', I have ventured on the other rendering. The indefiniteness of 'supernatural' is rather an advantage in the context than a drawback. Moffatt and the A.R.S.V. also translate 'supernatural'. For a recent full discussion see The First Epistle of Peter, E. G. Selwyn, pp. 281-4.

was accompanied by words in which its significance was expressed; it was not only a picture in which the death of Christ was represented and its worth to the Church declared; there was an articulate confession of what it was, and of what the Church owed to it.

If we compare Rom. vi with I Cor. x and xi, it seems obvious that some modern theology tries to draw a broader line of distinction between the Sacraments than really exists. No doubt, this is partly due to the fact that in our times baptism is so often that of infants, while the Supper is partaken of only by adults, whereas, in New Testament times, the significance of both was defined in relation to conscious faith. But it would not be easy to show from Paul's Epistles that in content and meaning, in the blessings which they represented and which were conveyed through them, there is any very great distinction. The truth seems rather to be that both the Sacraments are forms into which we may put as much of the gospel as they will carry; and Paul, for his part, puts practically the whole of his gospel into each. If baptism is relative to the forgiveness of sins, so is the Supper. If baptism is relative to the unity of the Church, so is the Supper. We are not only baptized into one body (I Cor. xii. 13), but because there is one bread, we are one body, many though we be who partake of it (I Cor. x. 17). If baptism is relative to a new life in Christ (Rom. vi. 4 f.), in the Supper Christ Himself is the meat and drink by which the new life is sustained (I Cor. x. 3 f.). And in both the Sacraments, the Christ with whom we enter into relation is the Christ who died. We are baptized into His death in the one; we proclaim His death till the end of time in the other.

It is hardly possible to exaggerate the significance of these facts, though it is possible enough to ignore them altogether. The superstition that has gathered round the Sacraments, and that has tempted even good Christians to speak of abolishing them, probably showed itself at a very early date. There are unmistakable traces of it in the First Epistle to the Corinthians itself, especially in the tenth chapter. But instead of lessening, it increases our assurance of the place which these ordinances had in Christianity from the beginning. And although the rationale of the connection between the death of Christ and the blessings of the gospel is not elucidated by them, it is presupposed in them. In ordinances with which every Christian was familiar, and without which a place in the Christian community could neither be acquired nor retained, the death of Christ was perpetually kept before all as a death essentially related in some way to the forgiveness of sins.

Not much light falls on our subject from the one sacrificial allusion to Christ's death in 1 Cor. v. 7: 'For our passover also hath been sacrificed, even Christ.' No doubt τὸ πάσχα here, as in Mk. xiv. 12, means the paschal lamb, and the apostle is thinking of Christ as the Lamb of God, by whose sacrifice the Church is called and bound to a life of holiness. It is because of this sacrifice that he urges the Corinthians to keep festival, not in old leaven, nor in leaven of malice and wickedness, but in the unleavened bread of sincerity and truth. It is implied here certainly that there is an entire incongruity between a life of sin, and a life determined by a relation to the sacrificial death of Christ; but we could not, from this passage alone, make out what, according to Paul, was the ground of this incongruity. It would be wrong, in a passage with this simply allusive reference to the passover, to urge the significance of the lamb in the twelfth and thirteenth chapters of Exodus, and to apply this to interpret the death of Christ. There is no indication that the apostle himself carried out his thought on these lines.

THE SECOND EPISTLE TO THE CORINTHIANS

This Epistle is of supreme importance for our subject. From one point of view, it is a defence of Paul's apostleship, and of his work in the apostolic office. The defence rests mainly on two pillars; first, his comprehension of the gospel; and second, his success in preaching it. There are one or two references in the earlier chapters to the sufferings and even the death of Jesus in an aspect with which we are not here specially concerned. Thus in i. 5, Paul says: 'The sufferings of Christ abound unto us', meaning by this that in his apostolic work he suffered abundantly just as Christ had suffered; the weariness and peril from which Jesus could not escape haunted him too; the Lord's experience was continued in him. Similarly, in iv. 10, when he speaks of always bearing about in the body τὴν νέκρωσιν τοῦ Ἰησοῦ, 'the dying of Jesus', he means that his work and its attendant sufferings are killing him as they killed his Master; every day he feels his strength lessen, and the outer man perish.

But the great revelation of what Christ's death is in relation to sin is made not in these passages but in chapter v, in which he is defending his conduct in the apostolic office against the assaults of his enemies. Extravagant or controlled, the motive of his conduct was always the same. 'The love of Christ constrains us,' he writes, 'because we thus judge, that one died for all (so then all died), and died for all that they who live should no longer live for themselves, but for Him who died for them, and rose again' (see verses 14 and 15). The importance of this passage is that it connects the two relations in which Paul is in the habit of defining Christ's death, that is its relation to the love in which it originated, and to the sin with which it dealt. It shows us also how to construe these two things in relation to each other. Christ's death, we are enabled to see, was a loving death so far as men are concerned only because in that death He took the responsibilities of men upon Himself. Deny that, and it will be impossible to show any ground on which the death can be construed as a loving death at all. It is necessary to examine the passage in detail.

The love of Christ, the apostle argues, constrains us, because we thus judge—i.e. because we put a certain interpretation on His death. Apart from this interpretation, the death of Christ has no constraining power. Here we find in Paul himself a confirmation of what has been said above about the distinction of fact and theory. It is in virtue of a certain theory of Christ's death that the fact has its power to constrain the apostle. If it were not susceptible of such an interpretation, if this theory were inapplicable to it, it would cease to constrain.

What, then, is the theory? It is that one died for all; ὑπὲρ πάντων means that the interest of all was aimed at and involved in the death of the one. How it was involved in it these words do not enable us to say. They do not by themselves show the connection between Christ's death and the world's good. But Paul draws an immediate inference from them: 'so then all died'. In one sense, it is irrelevant and interrupts his argument. He puts it into a hurried parenthesis, and then eagerly resumes what it had suspended. 'One died for all (so then all died), and died for all that they who live should no longer live to themselves, but to Him who died for them and rose again.' Yet it is in this immediate inference —that the death of Christ *for* all involved the death *of* all—that the missing link is found. It is because Christ's death has this inclusive character, because, as Athanasius puts it, 'the death of all was fulfilled in the Lord's body',[1] that His death has in it a power which puts constraint on men to live for Him.

I cannot agree with the view that the words can be understood only in connection with the apostle's declaration elsewhere, that he has been 'crucified with Christ'. That declaration is a declaration of Christian experience, the fruit of faith. But what the apostle is dealing with here is something antecedent to Christian experience, something by which all such experience is to be generated and which, therefore, is in no sense identical with it. The problem before us is to discover what it is in the death of Christ which gives it its power to generate such experience, to exercise on human hearts the constraining influence of which the apostle speaks. And this is precisely what we discover in the inferential clause: 'so then all died'. This clause puts as plainly as it can be put the idea that His death was equivalent to the death of all. In other words, it was the death of all men which was died by Him. Were this not so, His death would be nothing to them. It is beside the mark to say that His death is died by them rather than theirs by Him. The very point of the apostle's argument may be said to be that in order that they may die His death He must first die theirs. Our dying His death is not, in the New Testament, a thing which we achieve on our own initiative or out of our own resources. It is the fruit of His dying ours. If it is our death that Christ died on the cross, there is in the cross the constraint of an infinite love. But if it is not our death at all, if it is not our burden and doom that He has taken to Himself there, what then is it to us? The death of all was died by Him. His death can put the constraint of love upon all men, only when it is thus judged.

When the apostle proceeds to state the purpose of Christ's death for all—'that they which live should not henceforth live to themselves, but to Him who died for them and rose again'—he does it at the psychological and moral level suggested by the

[1] *De Incarnatione*, c. xx, § 5.

words, 'The love of Christ constrains us.' He who has done so tremendous a thing as to take our death to Himself has established a claim upon our life. We are not in the sphere of mystical union, of dying with Christ and living with Him, but in that of love transcendently shown, and of gratitude profoundly felt. But it will not be easy for anyone to be grateful for Christ's death, especially with a gratitude which will acknowledge that his very life is Christ's, unless he understands the cross in the sense that Christ there made the death of all men His own.

It is in this same passage that Paul gives the fullest explanation of what he means by reconciliation (καταλλαγή), and an examination of this idea will also illustrate his teaching on the death of Christ. Where reconciliation is spoken of in Paul, the subject is always God, and the object is always man. The work of reconciling is one in which the initiative is taken by God, and the cost borne by Him; men are reconciled in the passive, or allow themselves to be reconciled, or receive the reconciliation. We never read that God has been reconciled. God does the work of reconciliation in or through Christ, and especially through His death. In Christ He was engaged in reconciling the world—or rather, nothing less than a world—to Himself (2 Cor. v. 19). He reconciled us to Himself through Christ (2 Cor. v. 20). When we were enemies, we were reconciled to God by the death of His Son (Rom. v. 10). Men who once were alienated, and enemies in mind through wicked works, yet now He has reconciled in the body of His flesh through death (Col. i. 21 f.).

It is very unfortunate that the English word reconcile diverges seriously, though in a way of which it is easy to be unconscious, from the Greek καταλλάσσειν. We cannot say in English, God reconciled us to Himself, without conceiving the persons referred to as being actually at peace with God, as having laid aside all fear, distrust and love of evil, and entered, in point of fact, into relations of peace and friendship with God. But καταλλάσσειν, as describing the work of God, or καταλλαγή, as describing its immediate result, do not necessarily carry us so far. The work of reconciliation, in the sense of the New Testament, is a work which is *finished*, and which we must conceive to be finished, *before the gospel is preached*. It is the good tidings of the gospel, with which the evangelists go forth, that God has wrought in

Christ a work of reconciliation which avails for no less than the world, and of which the whole world may have the benefit. The summons of the evangelist is—'*Receive* the reconciliation; consent that it become effective in your case.' The work of reconciliation is not a work wrought upon the souls of men, though it is a work wrought in their interests, and bearing so directly upon them that we can say that God has reconciled the world to Himself. It is a work—as Cromwell said of the covenant—*outside of us*, in which God so deals in Christ with the sin of the world, that it shall no longer be a barrier between Himself and men.

From this point of view we can understand how many modern theologians, in their use of the word reconciliation, come to argue at cross purposes, as it were, with the apostle. Writers who do not think of the work of Christ as anything else than the work which Christ is perpetually doing in winning the souls of men for God, and who describe this as the work of reconciliation, though they may seem to the practical modern intelligence to be keeping close to reality, are doing all that can be done to make the Pauline, or rather the New Testament point of view, bewildering to a modern reader. Reconciliation, in the New Testament sense, is not something which is being done; it is something which is done. No doubt there is a work of Christ which is in process, but it has as its basis a finished work of Christ. It is in virtue of something already consummated on His cross that Christ is able to make the appeal to us which He does, and to win the response in which we *receive* the reconciliation. A finished work of Christ and an objective atonement—a καταλλαγή in the New Testament sense—are synonymous terms; the one means exactly the same as the other. And it seems to me self-evident, as I think it did to Paul, that unless we can preach a finished work of Christ in relation to sin, a καταλλαγή or reconciliation or peace which has been achieved independently of us at an infinite cost and to which we are called in a word or ministry of reconciliation, we have no real gospel for sinful men at all. It is not in something Christ fain would do that we see His love; it is in something He has done already. Indeed, it is only through what He has done already that we can form any idea, or come to any conviction, of what He fain would do. He has died for us all, and by that death (not His own, properly speaking, but

the death of the sinful race taken to Himself) He has so demonstrated the reality and infinity of the love of God to the sinful as
to make it possible for apostles and evangelists to preach peace
to all men through Him.

In the passage with which we are dealing Paul appends to the
apostolic message, abruptly and without any conjunction, the
statement of the great truth of Christ's finished work which
underlies it. 'We are ambassadors therefore on behalf of Christ,
as though God were intreating by us: we beseech you on behalf
of Christ, *be* ye reconciled to God. Him who knew no sin He
made to be sin on our behalf; that we might become the righteousness of God in Him' (2 Cor. v. 20 f.). The want of a conjunction here does not destroy the connection; it makes the appeal of
the writer more solemn and thrilling. There need not be any misunderstanding as to what is meant by the words, 'Him who knew
no sin He made to be sin on our behalf.' To everyone who has
noticed that Paul constantly defines Christ's death, and nothing
but His death, by relation to sin, and who can recall similar
passages in the Epistles to the Galatians and to the Romans, to
which we shall presently come, it is obvious that these tremendous
words cover precisely the same meaning as 'He died for our sins.'
When the sinless one, in obedience to the will of the Father,
died on the cross the death of all, the death in which sin had
involved all, then, and in that sense, God made Him to be sin
for all.

But what is meant by saying, 'in that sense'? It means, 'in the
sense of His death'. And what that means is not to be answered
a priori, or on dogmatic grounds. It is to be answered out of the
gospel history, out of the experience of our Lord in the Garden
and on the cross. It is there we see what death meant for Him,
what it meant for Him to make our sin, and the death in which
God's judgment comes upon sin, His own. And it is the love
which, in obedience to the Father, did not shrink from *that* for
us which gives power and urgency to the appeal of the gospel.

We ought to feel that moralizing objections here are beside
the mark, and that it is not for sinful men who do not know
what love is to tell beforehand whether, or how far, the love of
God can take upon itself the burden and responsibility of the
world's sin, or, if it does so, in what way its reality shall be made

good. The premise of the gospel is that we cannot bear that responsibility ourselves; if we are left alone with it, it will crush us to perdition. The message of the gospel, as it is here presented, is that Christ has borne it *for* us. If we deny that He *can* do so, is it not tantamount to denying the very possibility of a gospel? Christ bore our sins. Mysterious and awful as this thought is, it is the key to the whole of the New Testament. The phrase 'God made Him to be sin on our behalf' is merely another equivalent of this; it means neither more nor less. The end contemplated—that we might become the righteousness of God in Him—is here stated religiously or theologically. Christ takes our place in death, and in so doing is identified with the world's sin. The end in view in this is that we should take His place in life and in so doing stand justified in God's sight.

By what psychological process this change in our position is mediated Paul does not here tell. What he does is to give a religious equivalent for the ethical and psychological representation of verse 15: 'He died for all, that they which live should no longer live unto themselves, but unto Him who for their sakes died and rose again.' It took no less than His death on their behalf to bring into their life a motive of such creative and recreative power; and it takes no less than His being made sin for them to open for them the possibility of becoming God's righteousness in Him. To say so is not to bring different things into an artificial correspondence. The two statements are but the ethical and the theological representation of one and the same reality; and it confirms our interpretation of the passage and our conviction of the coherence of the apostolic gospel that under various and independent aspects we are continually coming on the same facts in the same relation to each other.

THE EPISTLE TO THE GALATIANS

The verses in the Second Epistle to the Corinthians which we have just discussed may fairly be called the *locus classicus* on the death of Christ in Paul's writings. Yet in proceeding to the Epistle to the Galatians we are introduced to a document which, more exclusively than any other in the New Testament, deals with this subject and its significance. Even in the salutation, in which the

apostle wishes his readers grace and peace from God the Father
and the Lord Jesus Christ, he expands the Saviour's name by
adding, in a way unexampled in such a connection elsewhere,
'who gave Himself for our sins that He might redeem us from
the present world with all its ills, according to the will of our
God and Father' (see i. 4). Reference has already been made to
the vehement words in which he anathematizes any man or angel
who shall preach a different gospel. At the end of the second
chapter he puts again, in the strongest possible form, his conviction that Christianity, the new and true religion, is a thing
complete in itself, exclusive of everything else, incapable of compromise or of supplement, and that it owes this completeness,
and if we choose to call it so, this intolerance, to the supreme
significance and power which belong in it to the death of Christ.
'I have been crucified with Christ; my life is no longer mine, it
is Christ who lives in me; the life I now live in flesh I live in
faith, faith in the Son of God who loved me and gave Himself
up for me' (see ii. 20).

The whole of the Christian religion lies in that. The whole of
Christian life is a response to the love exhibited in the death of
the Son of God for men. No one can become right with God
except by making the response of faith to this love, that is, except
by abandoning himself unreservedly to it as the only hope for
sinful men. To trust it wholly and solely is the only right thing
a man can do when confronted with it. And when he does so
trust it he is completely, finally, and divinely right. According
to Paul, to supplement it is to frustrate the grace of God; it is to
compromise the Christian religion in its very principle. To such
a sin he will be no party. If righteousness is by law, as he sums it
up in one of his passionate and decisive words, then Christ died
for nothing (ii. 21). Paul knew by experience that all he was, or
could ever become as a Christian, came out of the cross. This is
why he could say to the Corinthians, 'I determined not to know
anything among you, save Jesus Christ, and Him crucified' (1 Cor.
ii. 2), and why he repeats it in other words to the Galatians,
'God forbid that I should glory, save in the cross of our Lord
Jesus Christ, whereby the world is crucified unto me and I unto
the world' (Gal. vi. 14, A.V. mg.).

Put positively, then, we may say that the aim of the Epistle to the Galatians is to show that all Christianity is contained in the cross, which is the generative principle of everything Christian in the life of man. Put negatively, we may say its aim is to show that law, and especially, as it happened, the ritual side of the Jewish law, contributes nothing to that life. Now Paul, it might be argued, had come to know this experimentally and independently of any theory. When it had dawned on his mind what the cross of Christ was, when he saw what it signified as a revelation of God and His love, everything else in the universe faded from his view.

Newman speaks, in a familiar passage of the *Apologia*, of resting in 'the thought of two, and two only, absolute and luminously self-evident beings, myself and my Creator'. In the relations and interaction of these two his religion consisted. A religion so generated, though it may be very real and powerful, is, of course, something far poorer than Christianity. Yet in a somewhat similar way we might say of Paul that for him the universe of religion consisted of the soul and the Son of God giving Himself up for it. All that God meant for him, all that he could describe as revelation, all that begot within him what was at once religion, life, and salvation, was included in this act of Christ. No law, however venerable, no customs, however dear to a patriotic heart, no traditions of men, however respectable in effect or intention, could enter into competition with this. To mention them alongside of it was dishonouring to Christ, was an annulling of the grace of God, and betrayed such a radical misapprehension of Christ's death, that, for those who so misapprehended it, it was made entirely ineffective. 'Ye are severed from Christ,' Paul cries, 'ye who would be justified by the law; ye are fallen away from grace' (v. 4).

But though Paul had learned this by experience, he does not, in point of fact, treat this subject of law empirically. He does not content himself with saying, 'I tried the law till I was worn out, and it did nothing for me. I made an exhaustive series of experiments with it, fruitless experiments, and so I am done with it. Through the law I have died to the law (ii. 19); it has itself taught me, by experience under it, that it is not the way to life, and so it is to me now as though it were not.' He does not content himself with giving this as his experience of the law. Nor does he, on the other hand, content himself with giving us simply and empirically his experience of Christ. He does not say, 'Christ has done everything for me and in me. The constraint of His love is the whole explanation of my whole being as a Christian. By the grace of God, and by nothing else, I am what I am, and therefore the law is nothing to me. I am so far from finding myself obliged to acknowledge its claims still that it is my deepest conviction that to acknowledge its claims at all is to frustrate the grace of God, to make void the cross of Christ.'

If he had written thus, and he might truly have written thus, it would probably have seemed attractive and convincing to many who have misgivings about what he actually has written. But Paul could not, and did not, remain at this empirical standpoint. He has a theory again, or let us say an understanding, of the relations of Christ and law which enables him to justify and comprehend his experience. Apart from the truths of which this theory is the vehicle, the death of Christ would not be what it is, or exercise over the soul the power which it does. It is some dim sense of these truths, truths which the theory does not import but only unfolds, which in every case gives the death of Christ its constraining influence upon sinful men. What, then, is the theory?

Briefly, it is summed up in the words, *Christ under the law*. This is the expression used in Galatians iv. 4, and its indefiniteness, in this form, makes it seem unobjectionable enough. It signifies that when He came into the world Christ came under the same conditions as other men. All that a Jew meant when he said 'Law' had significance for Him; the divine institutions of Israel had a divine authority which existed for Him as well as for others. To say that the Son of God was made 'under the law' would thus mean that He had the same moral problem in His life as other men; that He identified Himself with them in the spiritual conditions under which they lived; that the incarnation was a moral reality and not a mere show.

It is certain, however, that this is not all that Paul meant, and to the writer, at least, it is not certain that Paul ever had this as a distinct and separate object of thought present to his mind at all. What he really means by 'Christ under the law' comes out in its full meaning in Gal. iii. 13: Christ redeemed us from the curse of the law, having become a curse for us. 'Under the law', in short, is an ambiguous expression, and it is necessary to be clear as to which of two possible interpretations it bears in this case. In relation to man in general, the law expresses the will of God. It tells him what he must do to please God. It is imperative, and nothing more. We may say, of course, that Christ was under the law in this sense; it is self-evident. But as has just been hinted, it is doubtful whether Paul ever thought of this by itself. To him at least, to be under the law in this sense did not yield the explanation of Christ's redeeming power. In the mere fact that Christ came to keep the law which was binding on all, there was no demonstration of love to sinners sufficient, of itself, to make them new creatures.

But this is not the only sense which can be assigned to the words, 'under the law'. The law has not only a relation to man as such, in which it expresses the will of God; it has a relation to men as sinners, in which it expresses the condemnation of God. Now Christ is our Redeemer, according to the apostle, because He was made under the law in this sense. He became not only *man*, bound to obedience (and it is not easy to say where the omnipotent loving constraint is to be discovered in this), but He became *curse* for us. He made our *doom* His own. He took on Him not only the calling of a man, but our responsibility as sinful men. It is in this that His work as Redeemer lies, for it is in this that the measure, or rather the immensity, of His love is seen. To say, 'He became a curse for us', is exactly the same as to say, 'He was made sin for us', or 'He died for us'. But it is infinitely more than to say, 'He was made man for us', or even, 'As a man He was bound to obedience to the law'—a proposition to which there is nothing analogous in the New Testament.

The conception of obedience, as applicable to the work of Christ, will recur in other connections. Here it is enough to say that if we wish to put the whole work of Christ under that heading, we must remember that what we have to do with is not the ordinary obedience of men, but the obedience of a Redeemer. Christ had an ethical vocation, as Paul reminds us in the very first reference to His death in this Epistle: He 'gave Himself for our sins, that He might deliver us out of this present evil world, *according to the will of our God and Father*'. But His vocation, in carrying out that redeeming will, was a unique one, and, according to Paul, its uniqueness consisted in this. One who knew no sin had, in obedience to the Father, to take on Him the responsibility, the doom, the curse, the death of the sinful.

If it is maintained that this was morally impossible, may we not ask again, What is the alternative? Is it not that the sinful should be left alone with their responsibility, doom, curse, and death? And is not that to say that redemption is impossible? The obedience of the Redeemer transcends morality, if we will; it is something to which morality is unequal; from the point of view of ordinary ethics, it is a miracle. But it is the very function of the Redeemer to do the thing which it is impossible for sinful men to do for themselves or for each other; and Paul's justification of the miracle is that it creates all the genuine and victorious morality, all the keeping of God's commandments in love, which the world can show.

There have been many attempts to find something quite different in Galatians. If the aim has not been to evade this line of argument and this connection of ideas, it has at least been to dispense with the necessity of considering it. Thus it is argued that Paul in the whole Epistle is dealing with Jews, or with people who wanted to be Jews, and with their relation to the ceremonial law—a situation which no longer has reality for us. But this is hardly the case. Paul nowhere draws any distinction in the law between ceremonial and moral precepts. The law for him is one, and it is the law of God. It is owing to accidental circumstances that the ceremonial aspect of it is more prominent in this Epistle, as the ethical aspect is in Romans. But we shall find the same line of argument repeated in Romans, where it is the moral law which is at stake. And when the apostle tells us that through the law he has died to the law (Gal. ii. 19), or that we have died to the law through the body of Christ (Rom. vii. 4), or that we are not under law but under grace (Rom. vi. 14), he has not the moral law any less in view than the ceremonial. He means that *nothing* in the Christian life is explained by *anything* statutory, and that everything in it is explained by the inspiring power of that death in which Christ made all our responsibilities to the law His own.

There is a sense, of course, in which the law is Jewish, but Paul had generalized it in order to be able to preach the gospel

to the Gentiles. He had found analogies to it in every society
and in every conscience; in his evangelistic preaching he defined
all sin by relation to it. In the fullest possible meaning of the
term, 'law' had significance for all men; and it was a gospel for
all men that Paul preached when he declared that Christ redeemed
us from the curse of the law, by becoming a curse for us. No
doubt when he wrote these words he was thinking, as his antecedents and circumstances compelled him to think, of himself
and his fellow countrymen who had known so well the yoke of
bondage. That is, primarily ἡμᾶς means *us Jews*. But that does
not alter the fact that the universal gospel underlies the expression,
and is conveyed by it; it means only that here a definite application is made of that gospel in a relevant case.

The same considerations dispose of the attempts that are made
to evacuate the 'curse' of meaning by identifying it with the
'cross'. No doubt Paul appeals in support of his idea that Christ
became a curse for us to the text in Dt. xxi. 23, which he quotes
in the form 'Cursed is every one that hangeth on a tree.' No
doubt he avoids applying to Christ the precise words of the text
as found in the LXX, 'Accursed of God' (κεκατηραμένος ὑπὸ τοῦ θεοῦ).
So do we, because the words would be false and misleading.
Christ hung on the tree in obedience to the Father's will, fulfilling
the purpose of the Father's love, doing a work with which the
Father was well pleased, and on account of which the Father
highly exalted Him. Hence to describe Him as accursed of God
would be absurd. It is not because Paul shrinks from his own
logic that he says He became a curse for us, instead of saying
He became a curse of God, or accursed of God, for us; it is because
he is speaking in truth and soberness. Death is the curse of the
law. It is the experience in which the final repulsion of evil by
God is decisively expressed; and Christ died. In His death everything was made His that sin had made ours—everything in sin
except its sinfulness. There is no *essential* significance in the
crucifixion, as though it would have been impossible to say that
Christ became a curse for us if He had died in any other way.
The curse, in truth, is only one of Paul's synonyms for the death
of Christ—one which is relative, no doubt, to the conception
of Christ as 'under the law', but which for its meaning is entirely
independent of the passage in Deuteronomy.

The New Testament has many analogies to this use of the Old. Christ rode into Jerusalem on an ass, and declared Himself a King in doing so. But no one supposes that His sovereignty is constituted or exhausted in this; it is entirely independent of it, though in connection with a certain prophecy (Zc. ix. 9) it can be identified with it. So again He was crucified between two thieves, and an evangelist says that there the Scripture, 'He was numbered with transgressors', was fulfilled. But we know that the Scripture was fulfilled in another and profounder sense, and would have been fulfilled all the same though Jesus had been crucified alone (Lk. xxii. 37 and some MSS. of Mk. xv. 28). And so also with the Deuteronomic quotation in Gal. iii. 13. The Old Testament here gave Paul an expression—an *argumentum*, if we will; it did not give him his gospel. He had said already, for example, in 2 Cor. v. 21, and will say again in other forms, all he has to say here: that in His death Christ was made under the law, not merely as that which laid its imperative, but as that which laid its sentence, upon man; that He took to Himself in His death our responsibility, our doom, our curse, as sinful men, and not merely our obligation to be good men. And though it is Christian, it is not illogical, to avoid such an expression as accursed of God. For in so making the doom of men His own in death Christ was doing God's will.

The other passages in Galatians which deal with our subject bring to view the ethical rather than the theological import of the death of Christ. 'They that are of Christ Jesus', writes Paul in v. 24, 'have crucified the flesh with the passions and lusts thereof.' Ideally, we must understand, this crucifixion of the flesh is involved in Christ's crucifixion; really, it is effected by it. Whoever sees into the secret of Calvary, whoever is initiated into the mystery of that great death, is conscious that the doom of sin is in it. To take it as real and to stand in any real relation to it is death to the flesh with its passions and desires. So with the last passage in the Epistle where the subject recurs (vi. 14): 'Far be it from me to glory, save in the cross of our Lord Jesus Christ, through which the world hath been crucified unto me, and I unto the world.' Here the apostle reiterates with new emphasis at the end of his letter what he has enforced from the beginning, that the cross is the explanation of everything Christian. Of course it is the cross interpreted as he has interpreted it. Apart from this interpretation, which shows it to be full of a meaning that appeals irresistibly to man, it can have no rational or moral influence at all. But with this interpretation it is the annihilative and the creative power in Christianity; the first commandment of the new religion is that we shall have no God but Him who is fully and finally revealed there.

THE EPISTLE TO THE ROMANS

In this Epistle, Paul is not so directly controversial as in the Epistle to the Galatians, and he has no specific opponents in mind. But the gospel is defined in it in relation to law, in very much the same sense as in Galatians. The completeness of the Christian religion, its self-containedness, its self-sufficiency, and the impossibility of combining it with or supplementing it from anything else, are assumed or proved in much the same way.

The question of religion for Paul is, How shall a man, a sinful man, be righteous with God? The gospel brings the answer to that question. It is because it does so that it is a gospel. It tells sinful men of a righteousness which is exactly what they need. It preaches something on the ground of which God the Judge of all can receive them, sinners as they are. 'A righteousness of God,' Paul calls it, naming it after Him who is its source, and at the same time characterizing it as divinely perfect and adequate, a righteousness of God which is somehow identified with Jesus Christ (iii. 22; cf. 1 Cor. i. 30). In particular it is identified somehow with Jesus Christ in His death (iii. 25), and therefore in Romans as in Galatians this death of Christ is the source of all that is Christian. All Christian inferences about God are deduced from it. Once we are sure of it and of its meaning, we can afford a great deal of ignorance in detail. We know that it covers everything and guarantees everything in which we are vitally interested. We know that it disposes of the past, creates the future, and is a security for immortal life and glory (v. 9 ff., viii. 31 ff.). What, then, does Paul say of the righteousness of God, and of the death of Christ in relation to it?

The critical passage is iii. 21 ff. To give a detailed exegesis of it would be to do what has been perhaps too often done already, and would raise questions to distract as well as to aid intelligence. As is well known, there are two principal difficulties in the passage. The one is the meaning of ἱλαστήριον (propitiation) in verse 25. The other is raised by the question whether the right-eousness of God has the same meaning throughout, or whether it may not have in one place, say in verse 22, the half-technical sense which belongs to it as a summary of Paul's gospel, and in another, say in verse 26, the larger and more general sense which might belong to it elsewhere in Scripture as a synonym for God's character, or at least for one of His essential attributes. Not that these two principal difficulties are unrelated to each other. On the contrary, they are inextricably intertwined, and cannot be discussed apart. It is an argument for distinguishing two senses of δικαιοσύνη θεοῦ (the righteousness of God) that when we do so we are enabled to see more clearly the meaning of ἱλαστήριος. It is the very function of Jesus Christ set forth by God as a propitiation in His blood to exhibit these two senses (which are equally indispensable if there is to be a religion for sinful men) in their unity and consistency with each other. And, on the other hand, the term ἱλαστήριος, to say the least, is relative to some problem created by sin for a God who would justify sinners; and the distinction of two senses in which δικαιοσύνη θεοῦ is used enables us to state this problem in a definite form.

Assuming, then, that both difficulties will come up for con-sideration, there is a certain convenience in starting with the second—that which is involved in the use of the expression 'the righteousness of God'. It is used in verses 21, 22, 25, and 26; and the use of it is implied in verse 24: 'being justified freely by His grace'. It seems to me a strong argument for the double sense of this expression that when the apostle brings his argument to a climax the two senses have sifted themselves out, so to speak, and stand distinctly side by side. The end of all God's action in His redeeming revelation of Himself to men is 'that He might Himself be just, and the justifier of him that hath faith in Jesus' (εἰς τὸ εἶναι αὐτὸν δίκαιον καὶ δικαιοῦντα τὸν ἐκ πίστεως Ἰησοῦ, verse 26). The first part of this end—God's being righteous Him-self—might quite fairly be spoken of as δικαιοσύνη θεοῦ (God's righteousness); it is, indeed, what under ordinary circumstances is meant by the words. Compare, for example, the use of them in verse 5 of this same chapter. But God's appearance in the character of ὁ δικαιῶν (He who justifies) is also the manifestation of a righteousness of God, and indeed of the righteousness of God in the sense in which it constitutes Paul's gospel—a righteousness of God which is related to the good of the believing sinner. Both things are there: a righteousness which comes from God and is the hope of the sinful, and God's own righteousness, or His character in its self-consistency and inviolability. In virtue of the first, God is ὁ δικαιῶν, the Justifier; in virtue of the second, He is δίκαιος, Just.

What Paul is concerned to bring out, and what by means of the conception of Christ in His blood as ἱλαστήριος (endued with propitiatory power) he does bring out, is precisely the fact that both things *are* there, and there in harmony with each other. There can be no gospel unless there is such a thing as a righteousness of God for the ungodly. But just as little can there be any gospel unless the integrity of God's character be maintained. The problem of the sinful world, the problem of all religion, the problem of God in dealing with a sinful race, is how to unite these two things. The Christian answer to the problem is given by Paul in the words: 'Jesus Christ whom God set forth a propitiation (or, in propitiatory power) in His blood.' In Jesus Christ so set forth there is the manifestation of God's righteousness in the two senses, or, if we prefer it, in the complex sense, just referred to. Something is done which enables God to justify the ungodly who believe in Jesus, and at the same time to appear signally and conspicuously a righteous God. What this something is we have still to consider. But meanwhile it should be noted that this interpretation of the passage agrees with what we have already seen, that justification of the ungodly, or forgiveness of sins, or redemption, or whatever we are to call it, is a real problem for Paul. *Gospel* is the last thing in the world to be taken for granted. Before there can be any such thing a problem of tremendous difficulty has to be solved, and according to the apostle of the Gentiles it has received at God's hands a tremendous solution.

Before entering into this, it is only fair to refer to the interpretations of the passage which aim at giving the righteousness of

God precisely the same force all through. In this case, of course, it is the technical, specifically Pauline sense which is preferred; the δικαιοσύνη θεοῦ is to be read always as that by which sinful man is justified. This is done by different interpreters with very various degrees of insight.

There are those who seem unconscious that there is any problem, any moral problem, in the situation at all. The righteousness of God, they argue, is essentially self-imparting; it 'goes out' and energizes in the world; it takes hold of human lives and fills them with itself; it acts on the analogy of a physical force, like light or heat, diffusing itself and radiating in every direction, indiscriminately and without limit. Legal religion, no doubt, conceives of it otherwise; to legalism, God's righteousness is a negative attribute, something in which God, as it were, stands on the defensive, maintaining His integrity against the sin of the world; but that is only a mistake. God's righteousness is effluent, overflowing, the source of all the goodness in the world; and we see in Jesus Christ that this is so.

The truth in all this is as obvious as the irrelevance. Of course all goodness is of God; no man would less have wished to question this than Paul. But Paul felt that the sin of the world made a difference to God; it was a sin against His righteousness, and His righteousness had to be vindicated against it; it could not ignore it, and go on *simpliciter* 'justifying' men as if nothing had happened. Such an interpretation of the passage ignores altogether the *problem* which the sin of the world (as Paul looked at it) presented to God. It makes no attempt whatever to define the relation, on which everything in the passage turns, between the divine righteousness and the death of Christ as a ἱλαστήριον. And in missing altogether the problem, it misses as completely the solution; that is, it misses the gospel. We cannot keep Christianity, or any specifically Christian truth, if we deny its premises, nor can we either state or solve a moral problem if we confine ourselves to physical categories.

Secondly, there are those who assimilate the righteousness of God in this passage to the δικαιοσύνη θεοῦ of the Psalms and the later chapters of Isaiah, those familiar passages in which it is so

often found as a parallel to σωτηρία (salvation). It is in these, they
argue, that the real antecedents are found both of Paul's thoughts
and of his language. What, for instance, could be closer to his
mind than Ps. xcviii. 2: 'The Lord hath made known His salvation; His righteousness hath He openly shewed in the sight of
the heathen'? In the gospel we have the manifestation of the
righteousness of God in this sense, a righteousness which is indistinguishable from His grace, and in which He shows Himself
righteous by acting in accordance with His covenant obligations
—receiving His people graciously, and loving them freely.

There is something attractive in this, and something true; but
it is as completely irrelevant to Paul's thought in the passage
before us as the more superficial view already referred to. For
one thing, Paul never refers to any of these passages in connecting
his gospel with the Old Testament. He must have been perfectly
aware that they were written on a plane other than that on which
he stood as a sinful man and a preacher to sinners. They were
written for God's covenant people, to assure them that God
would be true to the obligations of the covenant, and would
demonstrate His righteousness in doing so. God's righteousness,
in all these passages, is that attribute to which His people appeal
when they are wronged. The situation which Paul has before
him, however, is not that of God's people, wronged by their
enemies and entitled to appeal to His righteousness to plead their
cause and put them in the right; it is that of people who have no
cause, who are all in the wrong with God, whose sins impeach
them without ceasing, to whom God as Righteous Judge is not,
as to a wronged covenant people, a tower of hope, but a name
which sums up all their fears. The people for whom Isaiah and
the Psalms were written were people who, being put in the
wrong by their adversaries on earth, had a supreme appeal to
God, before whom they were confident they should be in the
right. The people to whom Paul preaches are people who before
God have no case, so that the assurances of the prophet and the
psalmists are nothing to them.

There is, of course, such a thing as a 'new covenant', and it is
possible for those who are within it to appropriate these Old
Testament texts. We have, for example, a clear instance of such
appropriation in 1 Jn. i. 9: 'If we confess our sins, He is faithful

and righteous to forgive us our sins, and to cleanse us from all unrighteousness.' In other words, He is true to the obligations of His covenant with us in Christ. These glorious Old Testament Scriptures, therefore, are not without their meaning for the New. But it is a complete mistake, and it has been the source of the most far-reaching and disastrous confusion, to try to deduce from them the Pauline conception of the righteousness of God. And it must be repeated that in such interpretations, as in others already referred to, there is again wanting a sense of the *problem* with which Paul is undoubtedly grappling. Nor is any attempt made to define explicitly and intelligibly the relation between the righteousness of God, conceived as it is here conceived, and the propitiation in the blood of Christ. Indeed, it is not too much to say that for Paul there is no such thing as a δικαιοσύνη θεοῦ except through the propitiation; whereas here the δικαιοσύνη θεοῦ is fully explained, with no reference to the propitiation whatever.

It is worth while to refer, in the third place, to one particular construction of the passage, in which an attempt is made to keep the same sense of δικαιοσύνη θεοῦ throughout, and at the same time to do justice to the problem which is obviously involved. In the interpretation righteousness means acting according to one's proper norm, doing what one ought to do. God's proper norm, the true rule of action for Him, is that He should institute and maintain fellowship with men. He would not be righteous if He did not do so; He would fail to act in His proper character. Now, in setting forth Christ as a propitiation, God does what the circumstances require if fellowship is to be instituted and maintained between Himself and sinful men; and it is in this sense that the propitiation manifests or demonstrates His righteousness. It shows God not unrighteous, not false to Himself and to the true norm of His action (as He would have been if in the face of sin He had simply let the idea of fellowship with man go), but manifesting Himself as a righteous God, who is true to Himself and to His norm most signally and conspicuously in this, that in spite of sin He takes means to secure that fellowship between Himself and men shall not finally lapse.

This is ingenious and attractive, though whether the conception of the righteousness of God from which it starts would have been recognized by Paul or by any Scripture writer is another matter. But apart from this, it obviously leaves unanswered the question, What is the means which God takes to secure fellowship with *sinful* men, that is to act toward *them* in a way which does justice to Himself? On the answer given to this a great deal depends. It is implied in this whole argument that sin does create a problem for God; that something has to be *done*, where sinful men are concerned, before fellowship with God can be taken for granted; and that God actually *does* what has to be done when He sets forth Christ as a propitiation, through faith, in His blood. The question is, therefore, if we are going to think seriously at all, What is the propitiation? or more precisely, How is the propitiation to be defined in relation to the sin of the world, in view of which God provided it, that He might be able still to maintain fellowship with man?

In reply, it is not enough to say that the suffering of death is what God in His grace is pleased to claim from the sinful race as the condition of restored fellowship, and that He has been further pleased to accept as satisfying this condition that particular suffering of death which Christ endured, and which can be reproduced in individuals through faith, *if everything is of mere good pleasure and there is no rational necessity at any point*. It was not an arbitrary appointment of God that made the death of Christ ἱλαστήριον; it was the essential relation, in all human experience, of death and sin. Christ died for our sins, because it is in death that the divine judgment on sin is finally expressed. Once we put law and necessity out of the relation between Christ's death and our sin, we dismiss the very possibility of thinking on the subject; we may use words about it, but they are words without meaning.

It is a significant feature of all such 'explanations' of Christ's death, that they do not bring it into any real relation to the Christian's freedom from the law, or to the controversies which raged round this in the Pauline churches; and this is only one of the ways in which it appears that, though using certain Pauline words, they have gone off the rails of Pauline thought. The passage in Romans becomes simple as soon as we read it in the light of those we have already examined in 2 Corinthians and in Galatians. It is Christ set forth in His blood who is a propitiation; that is, it is Christ who died. In dying, as Paul conceived it, He made our sin His own. He took it on Himself as the reality which it is in God's sight and to God's law. He became sin, became a curse for us. It is this which gives His death a propitiatory character and power, which makes it possible, in other words, for God to be at once righteous and a God who accepts as righteous those who believe in Jesus. He is righteous, for in the death of Christ His law is honoured by the Son who takes the sin of the world to Himself as all that it is to God; and He can accept as righteous those who believe in Jesus, for in so believing sin becomes to them what it is to Him. I do not know any word which conveys the truth of this if 'vicarious' or 'substitutionary' does not. Nor do I know any interpretation of Christ's death which enables us to regard it as a demonstration of love to sinners, if this vicarious or substitutionary character is denied.

There is much preaching *about* Christ's death which fails to be a preaching of Christ's death, and therefore to be in the full sense of the term 'gospel preaching'. The simplest hearer feels that there is something irrational in saying that the death of Christ is a great proof of love to the sinful, unless there is shown at the same time a rational connection between that death and the responsibilities which sin involves, and from which that death delivers. Perhaps one should apologise for using so simple an illustration, but the point is a vital one, and it is necessary to be clear. If I were sitting on the end of the pier on a summer day enjoying the sunshine and the air, and some one came along and jumped into the water and got drowned 'to prove his love for me', I should find it quite unintelligible. I might be much in need of love, but an act in no rational relation to any of my necessities could not prove it. But if I had fallen over the pier and were drowning, and some one sprang into the water, and at the cost of making my peril, or what but for him would be my fate, his own, saved me from death, then I should say, 'Greater love hath no man than this.' I should say it intelligibly, because there would be an intelligible relation between the sacrifice which love made and the necessity from which it redeemed.

Is it making any rash assumption to say that there must be such an intelligible relation between the death of Christ, the great act in which His love to sinners is demonstrated, and the sin of the world for which in His blood He is the propitiation? I do not think so. Nor have I yet seen any intelligible relation established between them except that which is the key to the whole of New Testament teaching. This bids us say, as we look at the cross, *He* bore *our* sins, *He* died *our* death. It is *so* His love constrains us.

Accepting this interpretation, we see that the *whole* secret of Christianity is contained in Christ's death, and in the believing abandonment of the soul to that death in faith. It is from Christ's death, and the love which it demonstrates, that all Christian inferences are drawn. Once this is accepted, everything else is easy and is secure. 'While we were yet sinners, Christ died for us. *Much more* then, being now justified by His blood, shall we be saved from the wrath of God through Him. For if, while we were enemies, we were reconciled to God through the death of His Son, *much more*, being reconciled, shall we be saved by His life' (Rom. v. 8 ff.). The *much more* implies that in comparison with this primary, this incredibly great proof of God's love, everything else may be taken for granted. It is the same argument which is employed again in viii. 32: 'He that spared not His own Son, but delivered Him up for us all, how shall He not also with Him freely give us all things?' And as it includes everything else on the part of God, so does it also on the part of man. The propitiatory death of Christ, as an all-transcending demonstration of love, evokes in sinful souls a response which is *the whole of Christianity*. The love of Christ constraineth us: whoever can say that can say all that is to be said about the Christian life.

But this is not the way in which Paul's gospel is usually represented now. It has become almost an axiom with many writers on this subject, that the apostle has two doctrines of reconciliation —one juridical and the other ethico-mystical. There is, on the one hand, the doctrine that Christ died for us, in a sense like that which has just been explained; and on the other, the doctrine that in a mystical union with Christ effected by faith we ethically die with Him and live with Him, this dying with Christ and living with Him, or in Him, being the thing we call salvation. What the relation of the two doctrines is to each other is variously represented. Sometimes they are added together as though in spite of their independence justice had to be done to both in the work of man's salvation, a doctrine of justification by faith alone in Christ who died for us finding its indispensable supplement in a doctrine of spiritual regeneration through baptism, in which we are vitally united to Christ in His death and resurrection. It has been held that it is not Pauline to say that the fellowship of life with Christ is established by faith; it is established only by baptism. But Paul, it is safe to say, was incapable of divorcing his thoughts so completely from reality as to represent the matter thus. He was not pedantically interpreting a text, but expounding an experience. And there is nothing in any Christian experience answering to this dead or inert justification by faith which has no relation to the new life; nor again is there anything in Christian experience like this new life which is added by baptism to the experience of justification by faith but does not spring out of it. It is morally wrong to any serious-minded person to construe his words in this way.

The other interpretation does not add the two sides of the Pauline gospel together. On this view they stand side by side, and though salvation is made equally dependent on both they are never combined. Romans vi has nothing to do with Romans iii. The conception of the new life, derived from union with Christ in His death and resurrection, is just as indifferent to justification by faith as the representation of Christ's death in Romans vi is to the sacrificial representation of the same thing in Romans iii.

In opposition to these views I venture to put in a plea for the coherence of Paul. If we found the one theory, as it is called, at one period of his life, and the other at another, there might be a *prima facie* case for inconsistency. But when both are set out in full detail, in a definite sequence, in the same letter, and that the most systematic of all the apostle's writings, and one which aims unambiguously at exhibiting his gospel as a whole, the presumption is all the other way. There are cases in which it is fallacious to say *post hoc, ergo propter hoc*, but this is not one. There could not be a greater mistake than to assume that in the sixth chapter of Romans Paul makes a new beginning, forgetting all that he has said, and meeting objections to that gospel which we have been expounding by introducing ideas which have no relation to it, and which may indeed be described as a correction of it, or a supplement to it, or a substitute for it, but which are in no sense whatever a vindication of it. A vindication of it is clearly what Paul means to give, and we are bound to assume that he saw what he was doing. He had preached that sinful men are justified freely through faith in Jesus set forth by God as a propitiation in His blood, and his adversaries had brought against this gospel the accusation that it tempted to and even justified continuance in sin. What is his answer?

To begin with, it is an expression of moral horror at the suggestion. μὴ γένοιτο! But, in the next place, it is a demonstration of the *inconsistency* of such a line of action with what is involved in justification. 'Men who like us *died* to sin, how shall we still live in it?' (Rom. vi. 2.) Why should it be taken for granted that 'dying to sin' is a new idea here, on a new plane, an idea which startles one who has been following only that interpretation of justification which we find in Rom. iii-v? It may be a new idea to a man who takes the point of view of Paul's opponents, and who does not know what it is to be justified through faith in the propitiation which is in Christ's death. But it is not a new idea to the apostle, nor to anyone who has received the reconciliation he preaches; nor would he be offering any logical defence of his gospel if it *were* a new idea. But it is no new idea at all. It is Christ dying for sin, Paul reminds the objectors to his doctrine, it is Christ dying our death on the tree, who evokes the faith by which we become right with God. And the faith which He evokes answers to what He is and to what He does: it is faith which has a death to sin in it.

Of course, if Christ's death were not what it has been described to be, it would be nothing to us; it would evoke no faith at all; but being what it has been described to be, the faith which is the response to it is a faith which inevitably takes moral content and quality from it. The very same experience in which a man becomes right with God, that is, the experience of faith in Christ who died for sins, is an experience in which he becomes a dead man so far as sin is concerned and a living man (though this is but the same thing in other words) so far as God is concerned. As long as faith is at its normal tension the life of sin is inconceivable. For faith is an attitude and act of the soul in which the whole being is involved, and it is determined through and through by its object.

This, I repeat, is what is given in experience to the man who believes in Christ as Paul preaches Him in Rom. iii. 25 f., and this is the ethical justification of his gospel. What is fundamental here is Christ in the character of propitiation, Christ bearing our sin in His death. It is this Christ and no other who draws us in faith to Himself, so that in and through faith His death and life become ours. The forensic theory of atonement, as it is called, is not unrelated to the ethico-mystical; it is not parallel to it; it is not a mistaken *ad hominem* or rather *ad Pharisaeum* mode of thought which ought to be displaced by the other. It has the essential eternal truth in it by which *and by which alone* the experiences are generated in which the strength of the other is supposed to lie.

I do not much care for the expression 'mystical union' with Christ, for it has been much abused, and in Paul especially has led to much hasty misconstruction of the New Testament. But if we are to use it at all, we must say that it is something which is not a substitute for, but the fruit of, the vicarious death of Christ. It owes its very being to that atonement outside of us, that finished work of Christ, which some would use it to discredit. Because this is so, Paul can use it, so far as he does so, not to replace, or to supplement, or to correct, but to vindicate and show the moral adequacy of his doctrine of justification.

Of course, in the last resort, the objection brought against Paul's gospel can be refuted only practically. It must be lived down, not argued down; hence the hortatory tone of Romans vi. But the new life is involved in the faith evoked by the sin-bearing death of Christ, and in nothing else; it is involved in this, and this is pictorially presented in baptism. Hence the use which Paul makes of this sacrament in the same chapter. He is able to use it in his argument in the way he does because baptism and faith are but the outside and the inside of the same thing. If baptism, then, is symbolically inconsistent with continuance in sin, as is apparent to everyone, faith is really inconsistent with it. But faith is relative to the δικαιοσύνη θεοῦ, the divine justification which is Paul's gospel, and therefore that gospel in turn is beyond moral reproach. The true connection of the apostle's ideas is perfectly put in the glorious lines of that great mystic, St. Bernard:

Propter mortem quam tulisti
Quando pro me defecisti;
Cordis mei cor dilectum
In te meum fer affectum!

As a comment on the connection between Romans iii-v and Romans vi-viii, or, in other words, on the relation of the substitution of Christ to ethical identification with Him, of Christ for us to Christ in us or we in Him, this will never be surpassed for truth and power. But blot out the first two lines, and the inspiration of the third and fourth is gone. Precisely so, if we blot out the 'forensic' gospel of Paul we shall find that the 'ethico-mystical' one has the breath of its life withdrawn.

It is possible to go more into detail here on lines suggested by Paul himself. Christ died our death on the cross, and the faith which that death evokes has a death in it also. But how are we to interpret this? By relation to what are we to define the death which is involved in faith? We may define it by relation to anything by relation to which *Christ's* death has been defined. Thus, following the apostle, we can say that the death involved in faith is, in the first place, a *death to sin*. Christ's death on the cross was a death to sin, the apostle tells us, in the sense that it introduced Him to a condition in which He had no longer any responsibility in relation to it (Rom. vi. 10). He had assumed the responsibility of it in love, but He had also discharged it, and sin had no claim on Him further. For us, dying to sin may seem to have a different meaning; it is not only a discharge from its responsibilities that is wanted, but a deliverance from its power. But this can come only on the foundation of the other; it is the discharge from the responsibilities of sin involved in Christ's death and appropriated in faith, which is the motive power in the daily ethical dying to sin. It really is such a motive power, and the only one in the world, when we realize what it is.

Now just as death to the law—to anticipate for a moment another experience involved in faith in the death of Christ—needs to be realized by ceaseless vigilance against all that would enslave the conscience and against everything in our nature that makes us seek external supports and authorities to relieve us of the responsibility of becoming a law to ourselves under the constraint of the cross, so must death to sin also be realized by moral effort. It is involved in faith, so far as the principle and the motive power are concerned. The man who plants his whole hope in the revelation of God made in Christ who is the propitiation is a man who is taking sin, death, the law and the judgment of God as all that they are to Christ. In other words, he is owning sin, and disowning it utterly; acknowledging it in all its responsibility as unreservedly, and separating himself from it as entirely, as Christ did when He died. Such faith, involving such a relation to sin as can be called a death to it, covers the whole life, and is a moral guarantee for it. Yet the death to sin which is lodged in it has to be carried out in a daily mortification of evil; the initial crucifixion with Christ must become a daily crucifixion of the passions and lusts.

Secondly, it may be said even more specifically that the death involved in faith is a *death to the flesh*. This is the point of the difficult passage in Rom. viii. 3 f. Paul is there describing the way of salvation from sin, and says that the law was impotent in the matter owing to the flesh. The flesh virtually means sin in its constitutional and instinctive character, sin as the nature or the second nature of man, it does not here matter which. What the law could not do God took another way of doing. He sent His Son in the likeness of flesh of sin, and as a sin-offering, and in so doing condemned sin in the flesh. ὁμοίωμα here no doubt emphasizes Christ's likeness to us: it is not meant to suggest difference or unreality in His nature. He was all that we are, short of sin. Yet He came in connection with sin, or as a sin-offering, and it is through this that we must interpret the expression 'condemned sin in the flesh'. It does not mean that Christ showed sin to be inexcusable by Himself leading a sinless life; there is no salvation, no emancipation from sin in that. The condemnation is the act of God, and in sending His own Son in connection with sin—which must mean in the one connection to which Paul ever refers, that is as a propitiation for it—God condemned it in the flesh. His judgment came on it in the death which Christ died in our nature, and with that judgment its right and its power in our nature came to an end. I say its right and its power, for the things are related. Until the responsibilities involved in sin have been fully acknowledged and met, as they are acknowledged and met in the death of Christ, its power remains. To express the truth psychologically, until sin is expiated the sinner has a bad conscience, and as long as a man has a bad conscience he cannot begin to be a good man. It is because Christ's death deals effectually with the responsibility of sin and puts right with God the man who believes in Him that it can do for our nature what law could never do—break sin's power.

It has been argued that it is a mistake to find here the idea of expiation: the context shows that the writer is interested only in the moral deliverance from evil. But from the point of view of Paul, this is not a reasonable objection: it is setting the end against the means. He knew by experience that sin could have its power broken only by being expiated, and that is precisely what he teaches here. Only, he gives it a peculiar turn. The fact that expiation has been made through Christ's death for sin in the very nature which we wear, is used to bring out the idea that in that nature, at all events, sin can have no indefeasible right and no impregnable seat. The death involved in faith in Christ is a death not only to sin generally, but to sin in the constitutional and virulent character suggested by the flesh. But like the other 'deaths', this one too needs to be morally realized. 'Mortify therefore your members which are upon the earth.'

Thirdly, the death involved in faith is repeatedly defined by Paul as a *death to the law*, or to law in general (Gal. ii. 19; Rom. vi. 14, vii. 4). There is undoubtedly something paradoxical in this, and it is the point at which, from the beginning, Paul's gospel was most misunderstood and most assailed. On the one hand, when Christ died, justice was done to the law of God, both as an imperative and as a condemning law, as it had never been done before. The will of God had been honoured by a life of perfect obedience, and the awful experience of death in which God's inexorable judgment on sin comes home to the conscience had been borne in the same obedience and love by His sinless Son. On the other hand, when this death evokes the faith for which it appeals, the righteous requirement of the law is fulfilled in the believer; the law gets its due in his life also, or, as the apostle puts it, it is established by faith. How is it, then, that faith involves a death to the law? It is through the assurance, given to faith at the cross, that so far as doing the will of God is concerned a new and living way has been found. It is not the law in its old legal form, the law of statutory injunctions and prohibitions, which is to generate goodness in sinful man; it is the law glorified in the atonement. The whole inspiration of the

Christian life lies here, and it *is* an inspiration, not a statutory requirement. Nothing is to count in the life of a Christian which does not come with perfect freedom from this source.

This explains the extraordinary emphasis which Paul everywhere lays on liberty. Liberty is the correlative of responsibility. Man must be perfectly free so that the whole weight of his responsibilities may come upon him. But this weight of responsibility cannot be faced, and would not sanctify even if it could be faced, *in vacuo*. It can be faced only when we know God in Christ crucified. And it does sanctify when the constraint of the atonement, with its awful homage to the holiness of God, descends upon the heart. But this is all that is required, for this is too great to be compromised by alliance with anything else. Perfect freedom with entire responsibility to the Redeemer, the obligation to be a law to oneself with the power of Christ's passion resting upon the spirit, that is the death to law which Paul contemplates. No statutes, no traditions of men, no dogmas, intellectual or moral, no scruples in the consciences of others, are to have *legal* obligations for us any longer. Not even the letters written by the finger of God on the tables of stone constitute a legal obligation for the Christian. *All* that he is to be must come freely out of the atoning death of Christ. He is dead to the law—in the widest sense of the word, he is dead to law— through the body of Christ.

From this freedom we are always being tempted to relapse. We are always establishing for ourselves, or letting others impose upon us, customs, whether intellectual, as creeds, or ethical, as the conventional ways of being charitable or of worshipping God, which, though good in themselves, tend to corrupt the world just because they are customs. In other words, we are always tacitly denying that the death of Christ does full justice to law in every sense of the term, and that for those who believe in it law exists henceforth only in the divine glory of the atonement, and in the life which it inspires.

It may seem astonishing that in all this no reference has been made to the Spirit, but the omission, I think, can be justified. For one thing, Paul himself discusses the whole subject of the Christian's death with Christ without reference to the Spirit. The Spirit is not mentioned in the sixth chapter of Romans. I do not say it is not implied—for instance, in the allusions to baptism; but it is implied *in* all that the apostle says; it is not implied as something to be *added* to it. Theologically, the Spirit is the divine correlative of faith and of the dying with Christ and living with Christ of which we have been speaking. His work is manifested in every Christian experience. It is not something specifically divine which comes in through baptism and has no relation to faith and justification; it is related in the same way to all. He is the divine factor in all that restores man to, and maintains him in, the life of God. But the Spirit does not work *in vacuo*. He glorifies Christ. He works through the propitiation, interpreting, revealing, applying it.

If we think of the Spirit as an abstractly supernatural power, a power of God not working through the gospel and its appeal to the reason, conscience, and will of man, we are not on Christian ground. Without the Spirit, that is, without God, all that has been said about the meaning of Christ's death could not prevail over men. But just because the action of the Spirit is implied as the correlative of faith at every point, it is illegitimate to call it in to explain one Christian experience more than another. For instance, we must not derive regeneration from it, or the new life, and then leave out justification. Either Spirit or faith may truly be said to be co-extensive with Christianity, and therefore they are co-extensive with each other. But if we are speaking of the new moral life of the Christian, and ask what we mean by the Spirit psychologically, that is, what form the experience of His work takes, I should say it is indistinguishable from that infinite assurance of God's love, given in Christ's death, through which the Christian is made more than conqueror in all the difficulties of life, inward or external. It is with this assurance that the Spirit is connected when Paul opens his discussion of the subject in Rom. v. 5: 'The love of God hath been shed abroad in our hearts through the Holy Spirit which was given unto us.' With this same assurance he concludes his discussion in Rom. viii. 35: 'Who shall separate us from the love of God?' The triumphant certainty of this love, a certainty always recurring to and resting on that miracle of miracles, the sin-bearing death of Christ, is the same thing as joy in the Holy Spirit, and it is this joy which is the Christian's strength. From the Spirit, then,

or from the love of God as an assured possession, the Christian
life may equally be explained. And it is not another, but the
same explanation, when we say that it is begotten and sustained
from beginning to end by the virtue which dwells in the propitiatory death of Jesus.

V. THE EPISTLES OF THE IMPRISONMENT

In these Epistles a new range seems to be given to Christ's death
and to the work of reconciliation which is accomplished in it.
This holds good, at least, for the Epistles to the Colossians and
Ephesians; so far as Philippians is concerned, we find ourselves
in the same circle of ideas as in Galatians and Romans. The close
parallel, indeed, of Phil. iii. 9 f. with the exposition of the apostolic gospel in these earlier letters is a striking proof of the tenacity
and consistency of Paul's thought. But in Colossians we are
confronted with a new situation. 'The world' which is the object
of reconciliation is no longer, as in 2 Cor. v. 19 or Rom. iii. 19,
the world of sinful men; it is a world on a grander scale. God
has been pleased 'through Him to reconcile all things unto Himself, having made peace through the blood of His cross; through
Him, I say, whether things upon the earth, or things in the
heavens' (Col. i. 20). The reconciliation of sinful men is represented as though it were only a part of this vaster work. 'And
you,' it is added, 'who were once estranged, and enemies in mind
by wicked works, He has now reconciled in the body of His
flesh through death' (see verses 21 f.).

The same ideas are found in the Epistle to the Ephesians (i. 7 ff.).
Here we start with the historical Christ, in whom we have our
redemption through His blood, the forgiveness of our trespasses.
But when the mystery of Christ's work is revealed to the Christian
intelligence, it is seen to have as its end 'the gathering together
in one of all things in Him, both things in [or above] the heavens
and things on the earth' (see verse 10).

This enlargement of the scope of Christ's death, or, if we prefer
to call it so, this extension of its virtue into regions where we
cannot speak of it from experience, has sometimes had a discon-
certing effect, and the bearings of it are not quite clear. It is argued
by some, who naturally wish to be as precise as possible in inter-

preting their author, that 'the things in heaven and the things on earth', which are referred to in the passages just quoted, must be spiritual beings. Only such can be the objects of reconciliation, for only such can have estranged themselves from God by sin. But where do we find the idea of any such estrangement in Scripture except in the case of disobedient angels to whom the idea of reconciliation is never applied?

For answer we are pointed to various passages in the Old and New Testaments, not to mention Jewish rabbinical literature, in which there is the conception of spiritual beings whose fortunes are somehow bound up with those of men. Thus in Is. xxiv. 21, a passage in which apocalypse begins to displace prophecy, we read: 'It shall come to pass in that day, that the Lord shall punish the host of the high ones on high, and the kings of the earth upon the earth.' The two sets of persons here referred to somehow correspond to each other; there is a counterpart in the unseen world of the characters and fortunes visible on earth. Again, in the book of Daniel we hear of 'the prince of the kingdom of Persia' (x. 13), 'the prince of Greece' (x. 20), and 'your prince' (x. 21), meaning the prince of the children of Israel. These princes, as the name Michael in x. 21 shows, were in all cases angelic beings who in some way or other were identified with the nations representing them in the unseen world, pleading their cause, fighting their battles, and mysteriously involved in their fortunes. In the early chapters of Revelation we find something quite analogous to this. Here the epistles of the risen Lord are addressed to the angels of the churches. The angel is not a bishop, but the personification, so to speak, of the church in the world unseen, the spiritual counterpart of it conceived as a person on whom its character and responsibilities will be visited somehow. The same idea, with an individual application, is also found in our Lord's word about the angels of the little ones, who in heaven do always behold the face of His heavenly Father (Mt. xviii. 10), and again in Acts xii. 15, where the people who would not believe that Peter had been released from prison said, 'It is his angel.'

On such a background of Jewish belief the interpretation of these passages has been essayed. It is not man only, we are asked to believe, who has been involved in sin, and in the alienation

from God which is its consequence. The sin of man has consequences which reach far beyond man himself. It stretches down-
ward through nature, which has been made subject to vanity
because of it, and it stretches upward into a spiritual world
which we may not be able to realize, but which, like nature, is
compromised somehow by our sin, and entangled in our responsibility to God. For these higher beings, then, as well as for
man, Christ has done His reconciling work, and when it is
finished they as well as we will be gathered together in one in
Him.

It would perhaps be going too far to say that there is nothing
in this, and that no such ideas were ever present in the apostle's
mind. The people to whom he wrote believed in 'thrones and
dominions and principalities and powers'; and although there
may be a touch of indifference, not to say scorn, in some of his
own allusions to the high-sounding names—for instance, in Eph.
i. 21 f.—they had some sort of reality for him too. There are
passages like Col. ii. 15, or those in which he refers to τὰ στοιχεῖα
τοῦ κόσμου (Gal. iv. 3; Col. ii. 8), where he seems to connect
the spiritual beings in question with the angels through whom
the law was given (Gal. iii. 19, Acts vii. 53), and to represent
the superseding of Judaism by Christianity as a victory of Jesus
over these inferior but refractory powers to whom for a while
the administration of human affairs, and especially of the im-
mature, materialistic and legal stages of religion had been committed. But if he had definitely held such a view as has just been
expounded, the probabilities are that it would have told more
decidedly on his thinking, and found less ambiguous expression
in his writings. He could not, in Rom. i-viii, for example, have
given that complete account of his gospel, of the need for a
righteousness of God, of the provision of it, and of the vindication
of it, without so much as alluding to these vaguely conceived
beings.[1] At best they could belong only to the quasi-poetical
representation of his faith, not to the gospel which he preached

---

[1] Rom. viii. 38 f. does not refute this, for the apostle's exposition of his thoughts
is already complete, and this is an emotional utterance in which there is no more
need or possibility of defining Christ's death by relation to angels and principalities and powers, than by relation to abstractions like height and depth. The
only *thought* in the passage is that God's love in Christ is the final reality from
which nothing can separate the believer.

on the basis of experience, nor to the theology or philosophy which was its intellectual expression.

When we look at the Epistles of the Imprisonment generally, our minds are drawn rather in another direction. The enlarged scope of the work of reconciliation is part of that expansion, so to speak, of Christ's person from a historical to a cosmical significance which is characteristic of these Epistles as a whole. Christ is no longer a second Adam, the head of a new humanity, as in the earlier letters (Rom. v. 12 ff.; 1 Cor. xv. 45 ff.); He is the centre of the universe. He is a person so great that Paul is obliged to reconstruct His whole world around Him. He is the primary source of all creation, its principle of unity, its goal (Col. i. 15 ff.). In consistency with this, the meaning and efficacy of what He has done extends through it all. His Person and work have absolute significance. Wherever we have to speak of revelation or of reconciliation, in whatever world, in whatever relations, it is of Him we have to speak.

Whether Paul would have presented this genuinely Christian truth to his imagination in the somewhat fantastic fashion just explained may be more or less doubtful; in any case it is of little consequence. What is of consequence is his conviction that in Jesus Christ dwelt all the fulness of the Godhead—all that makes God in the full sense of the term God—bodily, that is, in organic unity and completeness; and that the same completeness and finality belong to His reconciling work. 'The blood of His cross': it is in this we find the resolution of all discords, not only in the life of man, but in the universe at large. It is in this we see a divine love which does not shrink from taking on itself to the uttermost the moral responsibility for the world it has made, for all the orders of being in it, and all their failures and fortunes. Different ages and circumstances will picture to themselves the eternal truth of this in different ways. We must take care that ways of picturing it which are uncongenial to our way of thinking do not deprive us of the truth itself.

It is a more limited, but not less wonderful, illustration of the reconciliation accomplished by Christ's death that the apostle gives in Eph. ii. 11-22 when he tells how Jew and Gentile have been reconciled in the one body of Christ. This is one of the great thoughts of Paul. 'Is God the God of Jews only?' he asks in Rom. iii. 29 as he contemplates Christ set forth as a propitiation in His blood. Is the great appeal of the cross one which is intelligible only to men of a single race, or to which only those who have had a particular training can respond? On the contrary, there is nothing in the world so universally intelligible as the cross. Hence it is the meeting-place not only of God and man, but of all races and conditions of men with each other. There is neither Greek nor Jew, male nor female, bond nor free, there. The cross is the basis of a universal religion, and has in it the hope of a universal peace. But of all Christian truths which are confessed in words, this is most outrageously denied in deed. There is not a Christian church nor a Christian nation in the world which believes heartily in the atonement as the extinction of privilege, and the levelling up of all men to the same possibility of life in Christ, to the same calling to be saints. The spirit of privilege, in spite of the cross, is obstinately rooted everywhere even among Christian men.

The Pastoral Epistles do not introduce us to any new ideas on the subject of the atonement, but there are a number of statements which are linked closely with passages we have already noticed in the earlier Epistles. For example, we read in 1 Tim. ii. 5, 'There is one God, one Mediator also between God and men, Himself man, Christ Jesus, who gave Himself a ransom for all (ἀντίλυτρον ὑπὲρ πάντων).' It is in virtue of that ransoming death that Jesus mediates between God and sinners. Apart from it, He would not be a mediator in any sense relevant to man's situation. This is in harmony with the use of 'mediator' in the Epistle to the Hebrews. There also Jesus is Mediator, but it is of a covenant which is characterized as κρείττων, καινή, and νέα; He is the means through which, at the cost of His death, sinners enter into the perfect religious relation to God. But though this idea is found in Hebrews, it does not follow that in itself it is not Pauline, nor even (though ἀντίλυτρον is found only here in the New Testament) that it is not Pauline in expression. The dying with Christ, referred to in 2 Tim. ii. 6, is more akin to what we have found in 2 Cor. i and iv than to Rom. vi: it is a share in martyr sufferings which is meant, not formally the mortification of the old man.

In Titus there are two passages which should be mentioned. The first is in ii. 14, where we read of our Saviour Jesus Christ, 'who gave Himself for us, that He might redeem us from all iniquity (ἀνομίας, lawlessness), and purify unto Himself a people for His own possession, zealous of good works'. It is somewhat peddling to suggest that Paul would rather have said we were redeemed from νόμος than from ἀνομία, and that even in touching on a Pauline thought an expression which is not Pauline is used (λυτρώσηται for 'redeem'). The whole expression, λυτροῦσθαι as well as ἀνομία, comes from Ps. cxxx. 8, and Paul might be allowed the liberty to quote the Old Testament as well as anybody else.

The general impression we receive from the Pastoral Epistles is of a maturity and completeness in the expression given to the data relevant to the atonement. The apostle can now state in more summary and concise fashion the main aspects of the subject upon which he has dwelt at greater length in his previous letters. Hence we find in Tit. iii. 4 ff. the comprehensive statement, 'When the kindness of God our Saviour, and His love toward man, appeared, not by works done in righteousness, which we did ourselves, but according to His mercy He saved us, through the washing of regeneration and renewing of the Holy Ghost, which He poured out upon us richly, through Jesus Christ our Saviour; that, being justified by His grace, we might be made heirs according to the hope of eternal life.'

CHAPTER IV

THE EPISTLE TO THE HEBREWS

THE Epistle to the Hebrews is in many ways one of the most independent books of the New Testament; yet it has affinities with almost every strain of thought to be found elsewhere in primitive Christianity.[1] Of all New Testament writers its author is the most theological, that is, he is most exclusively occupied with presenting Christianity as the final and absolute religion; not *a* religion, in the sense in which it might concede a legitimate place to others, but religion *simpliciter*, because it does perfectly what all religion aims to do. This is what is expressed in his favourite word αἰώνιος (eternal). John in his Gospel and Epistles uses this word twenty-three times, but invariably to qualify *life*, and with him it is rather the combination than the adjective which is characteristic. But in Hebrews αἰώνιος is used far more significantly, though less frequently. Jesus is author of 'eternal' salvation (v. 9), that is, of final salvation, which has no peril beyond. All that salvation can mean is secured by Him. The elements of Christianity include preaching on eternal' judgment (vi. 2), that is, a judgment which has the character of finality, from which there is no appeal, and beyond which there is no fear or no hope. Christ has obtained 'eternal' redemption for us (ix. 12). Not a redemption like that which was annually achieved for Israel, and which had to be annually repeated, as though its virtue faded away, but a redemption the validity of which abides for ever. Christ has offered Himself through 'eternal' spirit (ix. 14). In Christ's sacrifice we see the final revelation of what God is, that behind which there is nothing in God, so that the religion which rests on that sacrifice rests on the ultimate truth of the divine nature, and can never be shaken. Those who are called receive the promise of the 'eternal'

---

[1] For a discussion of the Epistle which brings it into line with primitive Christianity as a whole, see *The Gospel in the Epistle to the Hebrews*, R. V. G. Tasker (Tyndale Press, 1950).

inheritance (ix. 15), not an earthly Canaan in which they are strangers and pilgrims and from which they may be exiled, but the city which has the foundations, from which God's people go out no more. And finally, the blood of Christ is the blood of an 'eternal' covenant (xiii. 20). In the death of Christ a religious relation is constituted between God and men which has the character of finality. God, if it may be so expressed, has spoken His last word; He has nothing in reserve. The foundation has been laid of the kingdom which can never be removed. It is this conception of absoluteness or finality in everything Christian which dominates the book.

Speaking generally, the Epistle may be said to give a description of the person and work of Christ as constituting the perfect religion for men, and to define this religion in relation to the ancient religion of the Jews as embodied in the tabernacle service.

Curiously enough, the person and work of Christ thus interpreted have been looked at, so to speak, from both ends. Some theologians, of whom Westcott may be taken as a type, begin at the beginning, or rather at i. 3. They start with the pre-existent, the eternal Son of God. They point to what He essentially is—the brightness of the Father's glory and the express image of His substance. They point to His providential action—He bears or guides all things by the word of His power. They point to the work He did as incarnate—He made purgation of sins. They point to the exaltation which followed—He sat down on the right hand of the Majesty in the Heavens. And then they draw the general conclusion that what Christ did, according to the Epistle, was to fulfil man's destiny under the conditions of the fall. That destiny, it is assumed, He would have fulfilled in any case. The incarnation is part of the original plan of the world. But, in the peculiar circumstances of the case in hand (that is, under the conditions of the fall), the incarnation had to be modified into an atonement.

Other theologians begin, if one may say so, at the end. Their Christ is essentially Christ the High Priest, in the heavenly sanctuary, mediating between God and men, securing for sinful men access to God and fellowship with Him. Christ exercises His High Priestly function in heaven, but it rests upon the death which He died on earth. This argument runs in exactly the opposite direction from Westcott's. Christ is essentially a Priest, the work of bringing sinners into fellowship with God is essentially the work He has to do, and the work He does. It is in that work alone that we know Him. But to do it He had to die, and in order to die He had to have a body prepared for Him, that is, He had to become incarnate (x. 5). It is not the incarnation which is taken for granted, and the atonement which in the peculiar circumstances of man's case is wrought into it or wrought out of it to meet an emergency. It is the actual fact of an atonement and a reconciling priestly ministry which is made the foundation of everything; the incarnation is defined solely by relation to it. The atonement, and the priestly or reconciling ministry of Christ, are the end to which the incarnation is relative as the means.

That this last view is the view of the Epistle and of the New Testament in general I do not doubt: it is the only view which has an experimental, as opposed to a speculative, basis. And I venture to say that the other shifts the centre of gravity in the New Testament so disastrously as to make great parts of it, and these the most vital parts, unintelligible. One could not go to the New Testament with a more misleading schematism in his mind than that which is provided by the conception of the incarnation and its relation to the atonement to which Westcott's influence has given currency in many circles.

But leaving this larger question on one side, we may start with the fact that both schools of interpreters meet in the middle and find the real content of the Epistle, religious and theological, in what it has to say of the historical Christ. And that, beyond a doubt, is concentrated in what it has to say of His death. It was with 'the suffering of death' in view that He became incarnate; it is because of 'the suffering of death' that He is crowned with that glory and honour in which He appears in the presence of God on our behalf. Here then we come to our proper subject again, and may ask, as in the case of Paul, in what relations the death of Christ is defined by the writer so as to bring out its meaning.

In the first place, it is defined by relation to God, and especially, as in Paul, by relation to His love. It is by the grace of God that Jesus tastes death for every man (ii. 9). God is not conceived in this Epistle, or in any part of the New Testament, as a malignant or hostile Being who has to be won by gifts to show His good-will to man. Whatever the death of Christ is or does, it is and does in the carrying out of His purpose. It is the grace of God to sinners which is demonstrated in it. This is involved also in two other ideas emphasized in the Epistle. One is the idea that no man takes the honour of priesthood to himself of his own accord. He must be called of God, as Aaron was (v. 4). Christ has had this call; we hear it in Ps. cx, which He Himself applied to Him-self (Mk. xii. 35 ff.). 'Thou art a priest for ever, after the order of Melchisedec.' It is true that the priest represents the people toward God, but he can do so only by God's appointment. Con-sequently it is a work of God which he does, a gracious work, in which he is not persuading God, as it were, against His will, but on the contrary carrying out His will for the good of men.

The other idea used in the interpretation of Christ's work, and especially of His death, which connects them in a similar way with God, is the idea of obedience. Jesus, though He was a Son, yet learned obedience through the things which He suffered (v. 8). When He appeared in the body which God had prepared for Him, it was with the words on His lips, 'Lo, I am come . . . to do Thy will, O God' (x. 7). There is nothing of irresponsibility or adventure in Christ's life and death. It is all obedience, and therefore it is all revelation. We see God in it because it is not His own will but the will of the Father which it accomplished. Even when we come to consider its relation to sin, this must be borne in mind. Atonement is not something contrived, as it were, behind the Father's back; it is the Father's way of making it possible for the sinful to have fellowship with Him.

In this connection the author introduces one idea, not very easy to define. In speaking of the actual course of Christ in life and death, he says, 'It became Him (ἔπρεπεν γὰρ αὐτῷ) for whom are all things, and through whom are all things, in bringing many sons unto glory, to make the author of their salvation perfect through sufferings' (ii. 10). What ἔπρεπεν suggests is not so much the kind of necessity we have found in other places in the New Testament, as moral congruity or decorum. Suffering and death are our lot. It is congruous with God's nature, we can feel, so to speak, the moral propriety of it, when He makes suffering

and death the lot of Him who is to be our Saviour. He would
not be perfect in the character or part of Saviour if He did not
have this experience. What this suggests is the interpretation of
Christ's death by moral aesthetics rather than by moral law, by
a rule to be apprehended in feeling rather than in conscience. It
is moving and impressive, an action in congruity with God's
nature and our state, whether we see a more inevitable necessity
for it or not. In all these ways, at all events, the writer attaches
Christ's death to the grace, the will, and the character of God;
and in all these ways, therefore, he warns us against setting that
death and God in any antagonism to each other.

But besides defining it by relation to God, the writer defines
Christ's death also by relation to sin. At the very beginning, in
the sublime sentence in which he introduces the Son, His earthly
work is summed up in the phrase: 'having made purgation of
sins' (i. 3). How this is done, he does not tell at this point, but
the sequel makes it indubitable. It was done by His sacrificial
death. So, again, he speaks of Christ as being once offered to
bear the sins of many (ix. 28); as having been once manifested
at the end of the world to put away sin by the sacrifice of Himself (ix. 26); as being a merciful and faithful high priest in our
relations to God to make propitiation for the sins of the people
(ii. 17); as having offered one sacrifice for sins for ever, and
having perfected for ever by that sacrifice those who are being
sanctified (x. 12-14). There is the same sacrificial conception in
all the references in the Epistle to the blood of Christ. He entered
into the most holy place through (the shedding of) His own
blood (ix. 12). The blood of Christ shall 'cleanse your conscience
from dead works' (ix. 14). We have 'boldness to enter into the
holy place by the blood of Jesus' (x. 19). His blood is the blood
of the covenant with which we are sanctified, and to lapse from
the Christian religion is to be guilty of the inconceivable, the
unpardonable sin, of counting that blood a profane thing (x. 29).
In all these ways the death of Christ is defined as a sacrificial
death, or as a death having relation to sin: the two things are
one.

It is quite possible to lose ourselves here by trying to give to
details in the sacrificial language of the Epistle an importance

which they will not bear. The writer refers to sacrifices of different kinds in his interpretation of the death of Christ. Sometimes he speaks of it in connection with the Old Testament sin offerings; at others in connection with the covenant sacrifices at Sinai, on which the ancient relation of God to His people was based. More than all, he thinks of it in terms of the annual sacrifices on the great day of atonement, when the earthly sanctuary was purged of its defilement, and the high priest entered into the most holy place, representing and embodying Israel's access to God and fellowship with Him. But no emphasis is laid on the distinguishing features of these various sacrifices. They are looked at simply in the expiatory or atoning significance which is common to them all. They represent a divinely appointed way of dealing with sin, in order that it may not bar fellowship with God; and the writer thinks of them broadly in this light.

Important, however, as his reference to sacrifice may be, it is not so much through the idea of sacrifice as through the idea of priesthood that we are initiated into the writer's mind. In relation to the priest, indeed, the various conceptions of sacrifice are unified. The distinctions of sin offerings, burnt offerings, peace offerings, and so forth, disappear; sacrifice is reduced to this—it is the characteristic function of the priest, the indispensable means to the fulfilment of his calling. A priest is the essential figure in religion as it is conceived in the Epistle to the Hebrews. When the priesthood is changed there is necessarily also a change of law, the whole religious constitution is altered (vii. 12). In other words, the priest determines what the religion is. Hence if we wish to know what Christianity is, in which Christ is Priest, we must investigate the priesthood as it is discharged by Him.

The priest's function, speaking generally, is to establish and to represent the fellowship of God and man. That fellowship must exist, it must be incorporated and made visible, in the priest's own person; and through his ministry it must be put within reach of the people for whom he acts as priest. Through his ministry they must be put in a position to draw near to God themselves, to worship, to have fellowship with God, in a word, to become God's people. If we ask why a priest and a priestly work of mediation are necessary, why men cannot immediately and in their own right, as it were, draw near to God, the answer is self-evident. It is because their sin stands in the way, and cannot be ignored. In the Epistle to the Hebrews, as everywhere in the New Testament, sin is a problem, and the burden of the book is that God has dealt with the problem in a way answering to its magnitude. He has instituted a priesthood to deal with it. He has appointed His Son a Priest with this very end in view, that He should make propitiation for the sins of the people (ii. 17).

If we ask how this Priest deals with sin in order to make propitiation for it, the answer, as has already been observed, is given in Old Testament terms. He deals with it by the way of sacrifice. This is the only method of propitiation known to the Old Testament which is of a piece with the idea of priesthood. It is irrelevant to argue, as is sometimes done by persons who are anxious that the grace of the gospel should not be abused, that the Old Testament provides propitiation only for certain kinds of sin, and these not the more serious. Such thoughts are not present to the writer's mind. Propitiation must be made for sin if sinful men are to have fellowship with God at all. The only propitiation known to Scripture, as made by a priest, is that which is made through sacrifice. Apart from shedding of blood there is no remission (ix. 22). The writer has no conception beforehand of sins with which the Priest and the sacrifice present to his mind are unable to deal. He does recognize the possibility that men may despise the gospel altogether and, even after they have known its power, may trample under foot the blood of the covenant with which they were sanctified, and so commit a sin for which in the nature of the case there can be no further propitiation, or as he puts it, for which there is no more a sacrifice in reserve (x. 26). But that is another matter. His position, speaking generally, is that in Christ and His death we have a Priest and a sacrifice capable of dealing effectively with sin as the barrier between God and man, and actually dealing with it in such a way that, in spite of it, God has a worshipping people among sinful men.

Can we, now, get any way under the surface here? Sacrifice is not a familiar nor a self-interpreting idea to us, whatever it may have been to the author and to those whom he addressed. Can we penetrate or explain it at all, so as to make intelligible to ourselves any relation which the death of Christ had to sin, or to the will of God in regard to sin?

Sometimes the attempt is made to do this by looking immediately at the effect of Christ's work in the souls of men, and deducing its relation to sin, as a secondary thing, from this. The Epistle, of course, does not ignore the effect of Christ and His sacrifice upon men: it has, indeed, a variety of words to describe it. Sometimes the word employed is ἁγιάζειν (to sanctify). The priestly Christ and His people are He who sanctifies, and they who are sanctified (ii. 11). Christians have been sanctified through the offering of the body of Jesus Christ once for all (x. 10). By one offering He has perfected for ever those who are being sanctified (x. 14). It was Christ's object in dying to sanctify the people through His own blood (xiii. 12).

There has been much discussion as to what sanctification in such passages means, and especially as to whether the word is to be taken in a religious or an ethical sense. Probably the distinction would not have been clear to the writer. One thing is certain, however; it is not to be taken in the sense of some Protestant theology. The people were sanctified, not when they were raised to moral perfection—a conception utterly strange to the New Testament as to the Old—but when, through the annulling of their sin by sacrifice, they had been constituted into a people of God and, in the person of their representative, had access to His presence. In short, in the Epistle to the Hebrews, the word ἁγιάζειν, corresponds as nearly as possible to the Pauline δικαιοῦν. The sanctification of the one writer is the justification of the other; and the προσαγωγή or access to God, which Paul emphasizes as the primary blessing of justification (Rom. v. 2; Eph. ii. 18, iii. 12), appears everywhere in Hebrews as the primary religious act of 'drawing near' to God through the great High Priest (iv. 16, vii. 19-25, x. 22). It seems fair, then, to argue that the immediate effect of Christ's death upon men is religious rather than ethical. In technical language, it alters their relation to God, or is conceived as doing so, rather than their character. Their character, too, alters eventually, but it is on the basis of that initial and primary religious change. The religious change is not a result of the moral one, nor an unreal abstraction from it.

A similar result follows if we consider another of the words used to explain the effect of Christ's priestly and sacrificial work upon men—the word τελειοῦν, rendered 'to make perfect'. It is widely used in the Epistle in other connections. Christ Himself was made perfect through sufferings (ii. 10); that is, He was made all that a High Priest, or an author of salvation, ought to be. It does not mean that suffering cured Him of moral faults, but that, apart from suffering and what He learned in it, He would not have been completely fitted for His character of representing and succouring mortal men. So again, when we read that the law made nothing perfect (vii. 19), the meaning is that, under the ancient religion of Israel, nothing reached the ideal. The sanctuary was a worldly or material sanctuary (ix. 1). The priests were sinful mortal men, ever passing on their unsatisfactory functions to their successors (vii. 23). The sacrifices were of irrational creatures, 'the blood of bulls and goats', which could never make the worshipper perfect as touching the conscience (ix. 9), that is, they could never completely lift the load from within and give him boldness and joy in the presence of God. The access to the holiest of all was not abiding. As represented in the High Priestly ministry of the day of atonement, the way to God was open only for a moment and then shut again (ix. 7 f.).

There was nothing perfect there, nothing in that religious constitution which could be described as τέλειον or αἰώνιον. But with Christ, all this is changed. By one offering He has perfected for ever those who are being sanctified (x. 14). The word cannot mean that He has made them sinless, in the sense of having freed them completely from all the power of sin, from every trace of its presence. It means obviously that He has put them into the ideal religious relation to God. Because of His one offering, their sin no longer comes between them and God in the very least. It does not exclude them from His presence or intimidate them. They come with boldness to the throne of grace; they draw near with a true heart and in full assurance of faith; they have an ideal, an unimpeachable standing before God as His people (iv. 16, x. 22). In Pauline language, there is now no condemnation. Instead of standing afar off, in fear and trembling, they have access to the Father. They joy in God through the Lord Jesus

Christ, through whom they have received the atonement (Rom. viii. 1, v. 2–11).

Once more, if we examine the passage (ix. 13, 14) in which the verb καθαρίζειν is used to express the result of Christ's work in relation to man, we shall be led to the same conclusion. In the sentence in which it occurs the writer is contrasting the efficacy of the ancient sacrifices with that of the sacrifice of Christ. 'For if the blood of goats and bulls, and the ashes of a heifer sprinkling them that have been defiled, sanctify unto the cleanness of the flesh: how much more shall the blood of Christ, who through the eternal Spirit offered Himself without blemish unto God, cleanse your conscience from dead works to serve the living God.' The Old Testament sacrifices had an outward efficacy; they removed such defilements as excluded a man from the communion of Israel with God in its national worship. The New Testament sacrifice has an inward efficacy; it reaches right to the conscience and puts the man in a position to offer religious service (λατρεύειν) to a living God. In some way it neutralizes or annuls sin so that religious approach to God is possible in spite of it.

The examination of these words justifies us in drawing one conclusion. The writer of the Epistle to the Hebrews does not conceive of a regenerating, or, in the modern sense of the term, sanctifying, effect of Christ's death upon the soul as immediate or primary. He does not conceive it as directly emancipating the soul from sin, nor does he regard this experience of emancipation as the only reality with which we have to deal. It is often argued that the idea of an antecedent relation of Christ's death to sin—antecedent, that is, to the emancipation of the soul from sin's power—is essentially unreal. This is certainly not the view of the writer to the Hebrews. On the contrary, he has, like Paul and others to whom reference has been, and will yet be made, the conception of a *finished work* of Christ, a work finished in His death, something done in regard to sin once for all, whether any given soul responds to it or not. As he puts it at the beginning of the Epistle, He made purgation of sins—the thing was done—before He sat down at the right hand of the Majesty in the Heavens. As he puts it later, He has offered one sacrifice for sins for ever, and by the one offering He has brought for ever into the perfect relation to God those who are being sanctified. And though the Epistle does not use the once familiar language about the risen Saviour pleading the merits of His sacrifice, it does undoubtedly represent this sacrifice, offered through eternal spirit, as the basis on which the eternal priesthood of Christ is exercised, and the sinner's access to God assured. Now, a finished work of Christ and an objective atonement are the same thing, and the question once more presents itself: What is it, in Christ's death, which gives it its atoning power? Why is it that, on the ground of this death, God, with whom evil cannot dwell, allows sinners unimpeded, joyful, assured access to Himself, and constitutes them a people of His own?

The one hint of an answer to this question offered by the Epistle itself is that which we find in the words of ix. 14: 'Christ, who through eternal spirit offered Himself without spot to God.' The sinlessness of Jesus entered into the atonement. Only one who knew no sin could take any responsibility in regard to it which would create a new situation for sinners. But more important even than this is the suggestion contained in the words 'through eternal spirit'. This is not the same as through 'indissoluble life' (vii. 16), as though the idea were that the life offered to God on the cross was one which death could not hold, but was rather by death 'liberated' and 'made available' for others. Neither is it the same as 'through His divine nature', as though the idea were that the divine nature or the divine personality through which Christ surrendered His human life to God gave the sacrifice an immeasurable value. These are forms of words rather than forms of thought, and it is difficult to attach to them any intelligible or realizable meaning. If we follow the line of thought suggested by the use of αἰώνιος (eternal) in other passages of the Epistle, we shall say rather that what is meant here is that Christ's offering of Himself without spot to God had an absolute or ideal character. It was something beyond which nothing could be, or could be conceived to be, as a response to God's mind and requirements in relation to sin. It was the final response, a spiritual response, to the divine necessities of the situation. Something of what is included in this may be suggested by the contrast which is here drawn in the Epistle between Christ's offering of Himself through eternal spirit and the sacrifices of the Old Testament. As opposed to these, His sacrifice was rational and voluntary, an intelligent and loving response to the holy and gracious will of God, and to the terrible situation of man. But what we wish to understand is why the holy and gracious will of God, and the terrible situation of man, demanded and were satisfied by this particular response of Christ's death, and not by anything else.

So far as I can see, there is no explanation of this whatever, unless we can assume that the author shared the view of Paul and of primitive Christianity generally, that sin and death were so related to one another, were in some sense, indeed, so completely one, that no one could undertake the responsibility of sin who did not at the same time submit to death.

The connection of ideas which is here suggested is often controverted by appeal to the passage at the beginning of the tenth chapter. There the writer is contrasting the sacrifices of the Old Covenant with that of the New. 'The law,' he says, 'having a shadow of the good things to come, not the very image of the things, could never with the same sacrifices which they offer year by year, continually, make perfect those who draw near. Otherwise would they not have ceased to be offered, owing to the worshippers, having been once purged, having no longer conscience of sins? So far from this being the case, sins are brought to mind in them year by year. It is impossible for blood of bulls and goats to remove them. Accordingly, at His entrance into the world, He says, "Sacrifice and offering Thou didst not desire, but a body didst Thou prepare for me. In whole burnt offerings and offerings for sin Thou hadst no pleasure." Then I said, "Behold I come; in the volume of the Book it is written concerning Me; to do Thy will, O God." Above, in saying "sacrifices and offerings, and whole burnt offerings, and offerings for sin Thou didst not desire nor take pleasure in"—that is, God had no delight in such sacrifices as are offered according to the law—then His Word stands, "Lo, I come to do Thy will." He removes the first to establish the second.'

This passage is often read as if it signified that sacrifice was abolished in favour of obedience, and the inference is drawn that no use can be made of the conception of sacrifice in the interpretation of Christ's death or, as it is sometimes put, that no significance can be assigned to His death which does not belong equally to every part of His life. His obedience is what atones, and His obedience is the same from first to last. But to argue thus is to ignore the very words with which the writer proceeds: *'in which will'*, that is, the will of God which Christ came to do, 'we have been sanctified', that is, constituted a worshipping people of God, *'through the offering of the body of Jesus Christ once for all'*. What is contrasted in this passage is not sacrifice and obedience, but sacrifice of dumb creatures, of bulls and goats and suchlike, with sacrifice into which obedience enters, the sacrifice of a rational and spiritual being, which is not passive in death, but in dying makes the will of God its own. The will of God, with which we are here concerned, is not satisfied by an obedience which comes short of death. For it is not merely the preceptive will of God, His will that men should do right and live according to His holy law, which Christ came to fulfil. It is His gracious will, a will which has as its aim that sinful men should be constituted into a people for Himself, a will which has resolved that their sin should be so dealt with as no longer to keep them at a distance from Him, a will, in short, that sinners should find a standing in His sight. And in that will we are sanctified, not merely by Christ's fulfilment of the law of God as it is binding on man in general, but by His fulfilment of the law as it is binding on sinful men, by His obedient suffering of death as that in which God's mind in relation to sin finds its final expression.

In determining the meaning of obedience and of the will of God in this passage, we touch the quick of the great question about the relations of incarnation and atonement. If we have read it correctly, it confirms what has been already said about the priority of the latter. It is the atonement which explains the incarnation: the incarnation takes place in order that the sin of the world may be put away by the offering of the body of Jesus Christ. The obedience of the incarnate One, like all obedience, has moral value—that is, it has a value for Himself; but its redemptive value, that is, its value for us, belongs to it not simply as obedience, but as obedience to a will of God which requires the Redeemer to take upon Himself in death the responsibility of the sin of the world. That this is done obediently implies that in dying the Son of God acknowledges the justice of God in connecting death and sin, as they are connected for the human conscience; He does right, as it has been put, by the divine law which is expressed in that connection. And in doing so He does perfectly, and therefore finally and once for all, something through which sinful men can enter into fellowship with God. He lays the basis of the new covenant. He does what sinners can look to as a finished work. He makes an objective atonement for sin—exactly what Paul describes as καταλλαγή or reconciliation. There is peace now between God and man. We can draw near to the Holy One.

How it is that Christ's death becomes effective for men is not expressed in the Epistle to the Hebrews as clearly as it is in the Pauline Epistles. The author was not an evangelist so much as a pastor, and it is not the initiation of Christianity but its conservation with which he deals throughout. But in substance it may be said, Christ's work must be appropriated by men identifying themselves with Him. The writer never uses the Pauline expression 'in Christ' to express this identification or its result. He has the vaguer conception of being 'partakers of Christ', μέτοχοι τοῦ Χριστοῦ, which so far answers to it (iii. 14, cf. iii. 1, vi. 4, xii. 8). Christ is not represented as the object of faith so much as the great exemplar of faith. Yet He is the object of the Christian confession, both as Apostle and High Priest (iii. 1). It is to those who obey Him that He is the author of eternal salvation (v. 9). And He is the centre to which the eyes and hearts of Christians are steadily directed. It does not, therefore, exhaust the meaning of the writer to say that He is our Representative, and that He does nothing for us which it is not for us to do over again. It is true that He is our Representative; but He not only acts in our name, and in our interest. In His action He does something for us which we could never have done for ourselves, and which does not need to be done over again. He achieves something which we can look to as a finished work, and in which we can find the basis of a sure confidence toward God. He achieves, in short, 'purgation of sins' (i. 3).

This is the evangelical truth which is covered by the word 'Substitute', and which is not covered by the word 'Representative'. It is the consciousness of this truth that makes the evangelical

Church sensitive and even jealous of a too free and easy use of the ideas that Christ becomes one with us, and we one with Him in all things. There is an immense qualification to be made in this oneness on both sides. Christ does not commit sin, and we do not make atonement. The working in us of the mind of Christ toward sin, which presumably is what is meant by our identification with Him in His death, is not the making of atonement, nor the basis of our reconciliation to God; it is the fruit of the atonement, which is Christ's finished work.

Although faith is not defined in the Epistle directly by relation to Christ, it is nevertheless faith which saves (x. 22, 38 f., xiii. 7), and the well-known description or definition in the eleventh chapter can easily be applied in the Christian religion. Faith is there said to be the assurance of things hoped for, the proof of things not seen (xi. 1). It is to the invisible world what sight is to the visible. It is the means of realizing it, so that its powers and motives enter into the life of men, and enable them after patient endurance and fulfilment of God's will to inherit the promises. What, then, is the unseen world which is realized by Christian faith? It is a world in which Christ holds the central place, and in which, in the virtue of that death in which He made purgation of sins, He appears perpetually in the presence of God on our behalf. It is a world in which everything is dominated by the figure of the great High Priest, at the right hand of the Majesty in the Heavens, clothed in our nature, compassionate to our infirmities, able to save to the uttermost, sending timely succour to those who are in peril, pleading our cause. It is this which faith sees, this to which it clings as the divine reality behind and beyond all that passes, all that tries, daunts, or discourages the soul. It is this in which it finds the *ens realissimum*, the very truth of things, all that we mean when we speak of God. It is holding fast to the eternal realities revealed in Christ, and not some indefinable 'identification' with Him, on which all that is Christian depends. And it is this, more than anything, which, in spite of differences of form, makes the writer akin to Paul. For he too builds everything on Jesus Christ, crucified and exalted.

CHAPTER V

THE JOHANNINE WRITINGS

B Y the Johannine writings we mean the Apocalypse and the fourth Gospel, as well as the three catholic Epistles to which the name of John is traditionally attached. We will consider the Apocalypse first. Its opening words carry us at once to the heart of our subject. John interweaves with the address of his book to the seven churches a sudden doxology: 'Unto Him that loveth us, and loosed us from our sins by His blood; and He made us to be a kingdom, to be priests unto His God and Father; to Him be the glory and the dominion for ever and ever' (i. 5 f.). What is before his mind as he speaks is Christ in His exaltation—the faithful witness, the firstborn of the dead, the prince of the kings of the earth. But he cannot contemplate Him, nor think of the grace and peace which he invokes on the churches from Him, without recurring to the great deed of Christ on which they ultimately depend. Christ's love is permanent and unchanging, and John thinks of it as such (τῷ ἀγαπῶντι ἡμᾶς, to Him that *loveth* us). But the great demonstration of it belongs to the past (καὶ λύσαντι ἡμᾶς ἐκ τῶν ἁμαρτιῶν ἡμῶν ἐν τῷ αἵματι αὐτοῦ). He does not say, 'who liberates us from our sins', as though a progressive purification were in view; but 'who liberated us', pointing to a finished work. It seems to me far the most probable interpretation of ἐν τῷ αἵματι to make ἐν represent the corresponding Hebrew preposition of price. Christ's blood was the cost of our liberation, the ransom price which He paid. This agrees with the word of our Lord Himself in the Gospel about giving His life a ransom for many (Mt. xx. 28), and with other passages in the Apocalypse in which the notion of 'buying' a people for God finds expression (v. 9, xiv. 3 f.). Sin, or rather sins, held men in bondage; and from this degrading servitude Christ purchased their freedom at no less a cost than that of His own life. It is not any undefined goodwill, it is the love revealed in this dear-bought emancipation of the sinful, which inspires the doxology, 'to Him that loveth us'. Redemption, it may be said, springs from love, yet love is a word of which we do not know the meaning until it is interpreted for us by redemption.[1]

The result of the liberty, bought by Christ's blood, is that those who were once held by sin are made a kingdom, even priests, to His God and Father. These words are borrowed from the fundamental promise of the Old Covenant in Ex. xix. 6. 'He made us a kingdom' does not mean 'He made us kings' (so some MSS. and A.V.). It means, 'He constituted us a people over whom God reigns'. The dignity conferred on us is not that of sovereignty, but of citizenship. 'He made us priests' means that in virtue of His action we are constituted a worshipping people of God; on the ground of it we have access to the Father. Both words together imply that we owe our standing in God's sight, and our whole relation to Him so far as it is anything in which we can rejoice, to the action of Christ who died for our redemption. All dignity and all privilege rest on the fact that He set us free from our sins at the cost of His blood. A doxology is not the place at which to seek for the rationale of anything, and we do not find the rationale of these things here. It is the fact only which is brought into view. The vision of Christ calls out the whole contents of the Christian consciousness; the Christian heart is sensible of all it owes to Him, and sensible that it owes it all in some way to His death.

Next in significance to this striking passage come the frequent references in the Apocalypse to the Lamb, and especially to the Lamb as it had been slain. This name occurs twenty-nine times in all. The most important passages are the following:

(1) Rev. v. 6-14. Here the Lamb is represented as sovereign, the object of all praise; as a Lamb which had been sacrificed (ἐσφαγμένον means 'with the throat cut'); as living and victorious (ἐστηκός, standing). It has the character which sacrifice confers, but it is alive. Although it is not dead, it has the virtue of its death in it. It is on the ground of this death, and of the redemption

---

[1] λούσαντι (*washed*) is the reading familiar to us from the Received Text and the Vulgate. It also, as well as λύσαντι, has analogies in the book: cf. vii. 14 and the Text. Rec. at xxii. 14. The sacrament of baptism made the figure of washing an obvious one to Christians, quite apart from such suggestions as are given by Ps. li. 2 Isa. i. 16, 18, and its influence is apparent in 1 Cor. vi. 11, Tit. ii. 14. On the whole, λύσαντι is much the better supported reading.

(or purchase of men for God) effected by it, that all praise is ascribed to the Lamb, and the knowledge and control of all providence put into His hands. 'Worthy art Thou to take the book, and to open the seals thereof: for Thou wast slain, and didst purchase unto God with Thy blood (ἐν τῷ αἵματί σου) men of every tribe, and tongue, and people, and nation, and madest them to be unto our God a kingdom and priests; and they reign upon the earth.' Here we have the ideas of i. 5 repeated, with the further thought that love like that displayed in Christ's death for man's redemption is worthy not only of all praise, but of having all the future committed to its care. It is really a pictorial way of saying that redeeming love is the last reality in the universe, which all praise must exalt, and to which everything else must be subordinate.

(2) The next passage is that about the martyrs in vii. 14. 'One of the elders answered, saying unto me, These which are arrayed in the white robes, who are they, and whence came they? And I say unto him, My lord, thou knowest. And he said to me, These are they which come out of the great tribulation, and they washed their robes and made them white in the blood of the Lamb (ἐν τῷ αἵματι τοῦ ἀρνίου).' Here what is referred to is evidently the power of Christ's death to sanctify men, though how it is exercised we are not told. The people seen in this vision, the endless procession coming out of the great tribulation, were martyrs and confessors. They had taken up their cross and followed Jesus to the end. They had drunk of His cup, and been baptized with His baptism. They had resisted unto blood, striving against sin, and now they were pure even as He was pure. But the inspiration to all this, and the strength for it, was not their own: they owed it to Him. They washed their robes and made them white in the blood of the Lamb; it was the power of His Passion, descending into their hearts, which enabled them to do what they did. Once more, the rationale is wanting. Some may feel that none is needed, that the cross acts immediately in this way on those who are of the truth. At all events, none is given. We can feel only that the cross must have some divine meaning in it when it exercises so overwhelming a constraint.

(3) Rev. xii. 11, the third of the passages which call for special study, has also a relation to martyrdom, or at least to fidelity

in a time of terrible persecution. 'And they overcame him because of the blood of the Lamb, and because of the word of their testimony; and they loved not their life even unto death.' It is implied in this that but for the blood of the Lamb they would not have been able to overcome. The pressure put on them would have been too great, and they would inevitably have succumbed to it.[1] But with a motive behind them like the blood of the Lamb they were invincible. Now nothing can be a motive unless it has a meaning; nothing can be a motive in the sense implied here unless it has a gracious meaning. To say that they overcame because of the blood of the Lamb, is the same as to say that the love of Christ constrained them. With the cross on which He died for them before their eyes, they dared not betray His cause by cowardice, and love their own lives more than He had loved His. They must be His, as He had been theirs. It is taken for granted here that in the blood of the Lamb there had been a great demonstration of love to them. In other words, it is assumed that the death of Christ was capable of being defined in such a way, in relation to their necessities, as to bear this interpretation. It is because it is an incomparable demonstration of love that it is an irresistible motive. And though the relation is not thought out nor defined here, for such a definition would have been utterly out of place, it is not forcing the language in the least to assume that it must have existed in fact for the author.

(4) Rev. xiii. 8 and xxi. 27 are two other passages which might be brought into connection with our subject. In both, reference is made to 'the Lamb's book of life'. In this book the names are written of those who are to inherit life everlasting: those whose names are not found there die the second death. Nothing could express more strongly the writer's conviction that there is no salvation in any other than the Lamb, that in Jesus Christ and Him crucified is the whole hope of a sinful world. It is very common to take the first of the two passages just quoted as though it spoke of 'the Lamb slain from the foundation of the world', and to argue from it that atonement is no after-

---

[1] Compare Moffatt *ad. loc.* in *Expositor's Greek Testament*: 'In opposition to the contemporary Jewish tradition (Ap. Bar. ii. 2, xiv. 12; 4 Esd. vii. 77, etc.), it is not reliance on works but the consciousness of redemption which enables them to bear witness and to bear the consequences of their witness.'

thought, that redemption belongs to the very being of God and the nature of things. But though these are expressions upon which a Christian meaning can be put, they find no support in this passage. The words 'from the foundation of the world' are not to be construed with 'slain', but with 'written', as the parallel passage proves. It is the names of the redeemed that stand from eternity in the Lamb's book of life, not the death or sacrifice of the Lamb which is carried back from Calvary and invested with an eternal, as distinct from its historical, reality. An apostle would probably have felt that the historical reality was compromised by such a conception, or that something was taken away from its absolute significance. But even discounting this, it has no exegetic support.

If we try to put together the various lights which the Apocalypse casts on the death of Jesus, we may say: (i) That death is regarded as a great demonstration of love (i. 5). (ii) It is a death which once for all has achieved something—the aorists λύσαντι (i. 5), ἐσφάγης καὶ ἠγόρασας ἐν τῷ αἵματι (v. 9), prove this. There is a finished work in it. (iii) It is a death which has an abiding power—ἀρνίον ὡς ἐσφαγμένον (v. 6), not σφαγέν.[1] (iv) This abiding power is exercised in this, that it enables men to be faithful to Christ under persecution, to suffer with Him rather than sin, and finally to die rather than sin (xii. 11). Christ Himself was a martyr, and the typical Christian is a martyr too. To be a martyr is to furnish the decisive proof that the abiding power of Christ's blood is being exercised over one's life. (v) Hence the blood of Christ does something both once for all, in breaking the bond by which sin holds us and bringing us into such a relation to God that we are a people of priests, and progressively, in assuring our gradual assimilation to Jesus Christ the faithful witness. In both respects the Christian life is absolutely indebted to it; without it, it could neither begin nor go on. There is the same experience, it may be said, of Christ's death, the same practical appreciation of it, and the same exultant and devout utterance of that appreciation in the language of worship, which we find in Paul; but, as we might expect, when the nature of the com-

[1] Compare Paul's use of the perfect participle ἐσταυρωμένον, 1 Cor. i. 23; 1 Cor. ii. 2; Gal. iii. 1.

position is taken into account, we do not find any such dialectic
treatment of this Christian experience, and of the ideas it involves,
as in the writings of the apostle of the Gentiles.

We may now proceed to the examination of the Gospel. The
general conception of the fourth Gospel is that what we owe
to Christ is life, eternal life. This life, it may further be said, we
owe to Him rather than to anything He does. This is true without any qualification of the prologue (i. 1-18), and it is true of
the Gospel so far as the influence of the prologue can be traced
through it. If we use the word redemption at all, and it occurs
naturally to us as we come from the Apocalypse, we must say
that redemption is conceived in the Gospel as taking place through
revelation. Jesus redeems men, or gives them life, by revealing
to them the truth about God. The revelation is made in His
own person, by His words and deeds, no doubt, but supremely
by what He is. 'This is life eternal, that they should know Thee
the only true God, and Him whom Thou didst send, even Jesus
Christ' (xvii. 3). The work of redemption, to borrow the dogmatic category, is interpreted through the prophetic office of
Christ almost exclusively.

It is on this basis that the ordinary contrasts are drawn between
the theology of Paul and that of the fourth Gospel, and, if we
do not look too closely, they can be drawn in very broad lines.
Or, to change the figure, we may say that they can be put in
epigrammatic and striking forms. Thus it may be said that in
John the great and fundamental idea is revelation. God makes
Himself known to men, and in making Himself known He
redeems them; to see Him in His true nature is to be withdrawn
from the world of sin. In Paul, on the other hand, revelation is
through redemption. It is because God in Jesus Christ takes the
responsibilities of the sinful world upon Himself, so reconciling
the world to Himself, that we know what He is: the relation
of revelation and redemption is reversed. In agreement with this
it has been said that in John the death of Jesus, though it comes
inevitably, comes only because of the flesh. The Word was made
flesh, and therefore must share the fate of all flesh and fulfil the
destiny of man by a perfect death as by a perfect life. In Paul,
on the contrary, it is the death which is the primary thing. Except

for the purpose of dying for man's redemption Christ would never have been here in the flesh at all. It agrees with this further, so it is said, that whereas in Paul (as in the synoptic Gospels), the people in whom Jesus is most interested and who are most interested in Him are the sinners who need redemption and whom He died to redeem, in John the sinners have practically disappeared, and the persons who have an interest in Jesus are the relatively good people who are prepared to appreciate the revelation He has brought. 'He that doeth the truth cometh to the light' (iii. 21). 'Every one that is of the truth heareth My voice' (xviii. 37).

The trick of such contrasts is easily learned, but does not strike one as very valuable. It depends for its plausibility on those generalities in which there is always some delusion hidden. It depends in this case, for example, on taking the somewhat abstract and so-called speculative standpoint of the prologue, and allowing that to dominate the historical parts of the Gospel. But if we turn from the prologue to the Gospel itself, in which Jesus actually figures and in which His words and deeds are before us, we receive a different impression. There is a great deal which resists the speculative solvent supposed to be contained in the Logos theory. There is, in particular, a great deal bearing upon the death of Christ and its significance, which goes to discredit those abstract contrasts which have just been illustrated. When we do take such a closer look at the Gospel, what do we find? We find that the death of Christ comes to the front in a great variety of ways as something which is of peculiar significance for the evangelist.

The first allusion to it comes from the lips of John the Baptist in i. 29: 'Behold, the Lamb of God, which taketh away the sin of the world.' That these words refer to the death of Jesus does not seem to me open to question. Granting that ὁ αἴρων τήν ἁμαρτίαν τοῦ κόσμου is rightly rendered *qui tollit* or *qui aufert peccatum mundi*, who takes *away*, not who takes *on Him*, the sin of the world, we have to take the subject of the sentence into consideration, the Lamb. When sin is taken away by a lamb, it is taken away sacrificially. It is borne off by being in some sense (in the case of an unintelligent sacrifice, only a figurative sense) borne. It is not too much to say that the conception of Christ's death as a sacrifice for sin, found thus, at the very beginning of the Gospel, on the lips of the great witness to Jesus, is meant to convey decisively the evangelist's own conception of Jesus and His work. He is here to put away sin. That sums up His vocation. And He puts it away by a sacrifice in which it has to be borne.

The second allusion to the death of Jesus is in ii. 19: 'Destroy this temple, and in three days I will raise it up.' This, the evangelist records, He spoke concerning the temple of His body.

The third reference is also indisputable, though the terms in which it is expressed may not be free from ambiguity. It is found in iii. 14 where Jesus compares Himself to the brazen serpent. 'Even so must the Son of Man be lifted up.' The expression 'lifted up' occurs in one or two other places, and the same happy or unhappy ambiguity attaches to it in all. Thus in Jn. viii. 28 Jesus says to the Jews: 'When ye have lifted up the Son of Man, then shall ye know that I am He,' etc. In xii. 32 we have: 'And I, if I be lifted up from the earth, will draw all men unto Myself'; and the evangelist adds the note, 'This He said, signifying by what manner of death he should die' (xii. 33). All that the Jews seem to have taken out of the word was the idea of 'removal'; for they contrast the inevitable 'uplifting' of the Son of Man with the 'abiding of the Christ for ever'. It would seem that where in this Gospel the 'uplifting' is spoken of indefinitely, it may be conceived, properly enough, to include the exaltation. But where it is spoken of as the act of the Jews (viii. 28), and compared to the elevation of the brazen serpent on a pole (iii. 14 f.), the allusion to the cross is unmistakable. There is, indeed, an exact parallel to it in Ezra vi. 11, though the word ὑψοῦν is not used: 'Also I have made a decree, that whosoever shall alter this word, let a beam be pulled out from his house, and let him be lifted up and fastened thereon.' That was the death which Jesus died, and to such a death the evangelist understood Him to refer when he used the word which he represents by ὑψοῦν. The word had the advantage—for no doubt it was counted an advantage—of carrying a double meaning, of raising the mind at once to the cross and to the heavenly throne. But nothing is more characteristic of the writer, or of Jesus as He is set before us in this Gospel, than the unification of these two things. They are inseparable parts of the same whole. Hence the peculiar use of the term 'glorify' to express what happens to Christ in His death.[1] There is no conception of a humiliation in death followed and rewarded by an exaltation. On the contrary, Christ is lifted up and ascends through His death. His glory is revealed in that whole experience which death initiates and into which it enters, more than in all His miracles. The mere fact that words like ὑψωθῆναι and δοξασθῆναι are the evangelist's chosen words to describe Christ's death shows how thought had been preoccupied with it, and how, the prologue notwithstanding, the Christian soul felt itself here at the heart of the revelation and of the redeeming power of God.

Our fourth passage is in Jn. vi. Here again the death of Christ seems to be alluded to, this time in close connection with the life which is His supreme gift to men. In it He speaks of His flesh, which He will give for the life of the world, and of eating the flesh and drinking the blood of the Son of Man (verses 51-53). If it were possible, as I do not think it is, to deny that there is any reference in this chapter to the sacrament of the Lord's Supper, it might be possible also to deny that it contained any reference to Christ's death. 'My flesh' and 'My blood' would be in this case only a more concrete and pictorial 'Me'; there would not of necessity be any reference to the death. But when we remember the period at which the Gospel came into use, the sacramental allusion both here and in the third chapter seems to me quite indisputable, and this carries with it the allusion to Christ's death as being in some way or other the life of the world.

In the tenth chapter we again come upon passages in which there is nothing equivocal. 'I am the Good Shepherd: the Good Shepherd layeth down His life for the sheep' (x. 11). This, it might be said, is only an ideal way of putting it; it is what the Good Shepherd would do if the situation emerged which required it. But it is not so recorded by the evangelist. The need has emerged, and the laying down of His life with a view to its resumption is made the sum and substance of the vocation of Jesus. 'Therefore doth the Father love Me, because I lay down My life, that I may take it again. No one taketh it away from

[1] See, for example, xiii. 31, 'Now is the Son of Man glorified.'

Me, but I lay it down of Myself. I have power to lay it down, and I have power to take it again. This commandment received I from My Father' (x. 17 f.). Christ's death is not an incident of His life, it is the aim of it. The laying down of His life is not an accident in His career, but His vocation; in it the divine purpose of His life is revealed.

A peculiar solemnity attaches in the Gospel to a sixth allusion to Christ's death which is found in the unconscious prophecy of Caiaphas. A prophecy is what a man speaks under the impulse of the Holy Spirit, and the evangelist means us to understand that a divine authority attaches for once to the words of this wicked man. 'Being high priest that year, he prophesied that Jesus should die for the nation; and not for the nation only, but that He might also gather together into one the children of God that are scattered abroad' (Jn. xi. 51-52). Some interest of the nation, and this great interest of the family of God, were conditioned by the death of Jesus, however that death may be related to the ends it was to achieve.

In the twelfth chapter there are several significant allusions. There is the corn of wheat which, unless it fall into the ground and die, abides alone, but if it die, bears much fruit (xii. 24), a similitude in which the influence of Jesus is made to depend directly on His death. In close connection with this there is the anticipation of the near and awful future, the shadow of which struck dark and cold upon the Saviour's soul. 'Now is My soul troubled; and what shall I say? Father, save Me from this hour. But for this cause came I unto this hour' (xii. 27). 'This hour' is the great crisis in the life of Jesus, the hour which no one could anticipate (vii. 30, viii. 20), but from which, now that it has come, He will not shrink. It has come, in the sense already explained, as the hour in which the Son of Man is to be *glorified*, the hour in which He is to drink the cup which the Father gives Him to drink, and to crown the work the Father has given Him to do. The way in which He is moved by it, shrinks from it and accepts it, reveals the place it holds in His mind and in that of the evangelist also.

Just as the reference to the Lamb of God at the beginning of the Gospel (i. 29) connected it with Isa. liii, so does the quotation in xii. 38 gives us the same key to its interpretation at the end. 'Though He had done so many signs before them, yet they believed not on Him: that the word of Isaiah the prophet might be fulfilled, which he spake, Lord, who hath believed our report? and to whom hath the arm of the Lord been revealed?' Taken alone, this passage could not be made to bear any special reference to the death of Christ or to its interpretation. But occurring as it does after the triple and unmistakable references of the corn of wheat, the dreaded hour, and the lifting up from the earth (verses 24, 27, 32), it seems to me rather probable than otherwise that it is meant to bring before the reader's mind, by a sufficient hint, the fifty-third chapter of Isaiah as the Old Testament, and therefore the divine solution of the mysteriously disappointing career of Jesus.

If this instance is reckoned doubtful, there can be no doubt about the one in the fifteenth chapter: 'Greater love hath no man than this, that a man lay down his life for his friends' (verse 13). A characteristic thought of John, we are sometimes told, is that of Jesus dying for His friends; Paul, on the other hand, thinks of Him as dying for His enemies (Rom. v. 10). It is an inept remark. Jesus at the moment is speaking to His friends, and about the supreme pledge of love He is going to give them. In other places, John, like Paul, represents Him as giving His flesh 'for the life of *the world*' (vi. 51), and lays stress on the fact that it is God's love for *the world*, in its all-inclusive yet individualizing intensity, which explains His 'lifting up' (iii. 14). The great thing on which they both agree is that the highest revelation of love is made in the death of Jesus.

A singular and striking allusion to His death has been found in our Lord's intercessory prayer: 'For their sakes I sanctify Myself, that they themselves also may be sanctified in truth' (xvii. 19). Tne meaning of this will be considered presently.

Finally there is the story of the Passion itself. That there is a peculiar significance attaching to the death of Jesus is implied (i) by the fulness with which the story is told; (ii) by the references in it to the fulfilment of prophecy, which mean that a divine purpose was being carried out by it (xix. 24; cf. Ps. xxii. 18: xix. 28 f.; cf. Ps. lxix. 21: xix. 36 f.; cf. Ex. xii. 46, Zech. xii. 10);

and (iii) by the peculiarly emphatic attestation given to some mysterious circumstances attendant on it, the sense of which might have remained hidden from us but for the interpretation of them provided in the first Epistle. 'One of the soldiers with a spear pierced His side, and straightway there came out blood and water. And he that hath seen hath borne witness, and his witness is true: and he knoweth that he saith true, that ye also may believe. For these things came to pass, that the Scripture might be fulfilled, A bone of Him shall not be broken. And again another Scripture saith, They shall look on Him whom they pierced' (xix. 34 ff., cf. 1 Jn. v. 6).

This series of passages has not been cited at random, but to dissipate the impression which many people have, and which some writers on New Testament theology propagate, that the death of Christ has no place in the fourth Gospel corresponding to that which it has elsewhere in the New Testament. I think they are sufficient to dissipate such an impression. No doubt there is much in the fourth Gospel which makes it plausible to say, Paul deals with the work of Christ, John with His person; for Paul, Christ only lives to die; for John, He dies because death is the only issue from life; but such contrasts do as much to mislead as to illumine. As soon as we are past the prologue into the scenery of what Jesus actually said, did, thought, feared, and suffered, we see that His death really fills the place it does everywhere in the New Testament, and has the same decisive importance.

But does this prominence of the death of Jesus in the Gospel throw any light upon its meaning? Is it defined by John (or by Jesus as recorded in the fourth Gospel) in any such relations as by Paul? Allowing for the fact that the writer's mind is not of a dialectical turn like that of Paul, but given rather to intuition than to reflection, in other words, to the contemplation of results rather than of processes, of ends rather than of means or conditions, we must answer these questions in the affirmative.

In John, as in Paul, Christ's death is set in relation to the love and saving will of God. 'God so loved the world, that He gave His only begotten Son, that whosoever believeth on Him should not perish, but have eternal life' (iii. 16). Again, in John as in Paul, Christ's death is related to His own love: 'Greater love hath

no man than this, that a man lay down his life for his friends'
(xv. 13). This truth is further emphasized in the allegory of the
Good Shepherd. The perfect freedom with which Christ acts the
shepherd's part, including the final sacrifice which it demands,
is apparently the characteristic of His work to which he attaches
the greatest importance. And it is so because it is through the
freeness with which the surrender of life is made that the love
which is its motive is revealed. 'I lay down My life of Myself.
No one taketh it from Me. I have authority to lay it down, and
I have authority to take it again.' (See x. 14-18.)

This spontaneity on the part of Jesus, when it is put in relation
to the love of the Father in giving the Son, appears as obedience.
The authority or liberty He has to lay down His life and to
take it again is a commandment He has received from the Father.
Equally with Paul or with the writer to the Hebrews, John could
use the term 'obedience' to describe the whole work of Christ.
But as with them, so with him too, it is loving obedience to a
will of love, an attitude at once to God's purpose and to man's
need which makes the passion the sublimest of actions, and
justifies the paradox of the gospel that the cross is a 'lifting up'
or a glorifying of Jesus.

It is possible, however, to go further in defining the death of
Christ in the fourth Gospel. Proceeding as it does from the love
of the Father and the Son, it is nevertheless not conceived as
arbitrary. It is free, but there is a rational necessity for it. The
Son of Man *must* be lifted up if He is to save those who believe.
The corn of wheat *must* fall into the ground and die if it is not
to abide alone. Not much, indeed, is said to explain this. The
various ends secured by Christ's death, the advantage of the flock
for which as the Good Shepherd He lays down His life (x. 11),
the eternal life of those who believe in Him (iii. 14 ff.), the
rallying round Him as a centre of the scattered children of God
so that He becomes the head of a new humanity (xi. 52), these,
no doubt, are all somehow dependent upon it. But just how,
the evangelist is at no pains to tell. We do no violence to his
thought, however, when we put this and that in the Gospel
together in order to discern what he does not say explicitly.

Everything, we have seen, comes from the love of God. The
death of Christ is to be construed in harmony with this, not in

any antagonism to it. But the love of God to the world is never conceived in Scripture abstractly. It is not manifested in some evolutionary process which is necessarily determined *a priori*, as some may have hastily inferred from the prologue to this Gospel. To conceive it so would be to deny its grace. It is conceived, practically, in relation to definite needs of man which it meets. It is manifested not on the analogy of natural forces, which simply are what they are, but on the analogy of the free actions of men, which are determined by specific motives. To deny this is to lose the living and gracious God of revelation, and to take in His place a metaphysical phantom. God so loved the world that He gave His only begotten Son. The giving of the Son includes at least the giving of Him to that death which, as we have seen, pervades the Gospel from beginning to end; indeed, the death is emphasized in the immediate context (iii. 14 ff.). Nor are we left without sufficiently clear hints as to the necessity which determined the gift. In the passage just referred to (iii. 16) we see that apart from it men are lost; they perish, instead of having eternal life. John's mind revolves round these ultimate ideas, death and life, rather than their moral equivalents or presuppositions, sin and righteousness. But we cannot suppose that he did not include in 'death' and 'life' all that we mean by these latter words.

That he did include all this we see when the consequence of refusing the gift of God is presented in the terrible word of Jesus, 'Except ye believe that I am He, *ye shall die in your sins*' (viii. 24); or when the evangelist records the words 'He that believeth on the Son hath eternal life; but he that obeyeth not the Son shall not see life, but *the wrath of God abideth on him*' (iii. 36). The love of God, then, represented in the gift of Christ, has in view, according to the fourth Gospel, the sin of the world, its exposure to the divine wrath, its perishing if left to itself. And the gift in which that love is embodied, if it is to be intelligently apprehended at all, must also have a definite relation to this situation. If it delivers men from perishing under the wrath of God, and from the sin by which that wrath is evoked, then an intelligible relation to sin and to the divine wrath is implicit in the writer's consciousness of it, whether he has given articulate expression to such a relation or not.

It is quite legitimate here to emphasize such passages as i. 29, where, as has been already shown, a sacrificial deliverance from sin is represented as the sum and substance of the gospel, and xx. 23, where the power which the risen Lord confers on His disciples in virtue of all that He has achieved is a power connected with the forgiveness of sins. It may seem to some a less obvious instance, but the striking word of Jesus in xvii. 19 points in the same direction: 'For their sakes I sanctify Myself, that they themselves also may be sanctified in truth.' What men needed was to be sanctified, that is, to be consecrated to God. It was not in their power to consecrate themselves, and surely no reason can be conceived for this but that which lies in their sin. But what they were not able to do for themselves Christ did for them in His own person. He consecrated Himself to God in His death. That the reference is to His death does not seem open to question; the present tense, ἁγιάζω, which suggests something going on at the moment, and the circumstances of our Lord, whose mind as He speaks is full of what is at hand, put out of court the idea that the word is intended to describe His life as a whole. His life was past, and now, in His own person, through death, He is about to establish between God and man a relation which men could never have established for themselves, but into which they can truly enter and into which they will be drawn once it is established by Him. This seems to me the exact equivalent of the Pauline doctrine that Christ dies our death that we may be drawn into the fellowship of His death, and so put right with God. He acts—'I sanctify Myself'; men are acted on—'that they themselves also may be sanctified'. He establishes the reconciliation; they, to use Pauline language, receive it (Rom. v. 11).

In the First Epistle of John we frequently find the connection between the death of Christ and sin explicitly stated, whereas in the Gospel we sometimes have to infer it. Thus 1 Jn. i. 7: 'The blood of Jesus His Son cleanseth us from all sin.' ii. 1 f.: 'These things write I unto you, that ye may not sin. And if any man sin, we have an Advocate with the Father, Jesus Christ the righteous: and He is the propitiation for our sins; and not for ours only, but also for the whole world.' ii. 12: 'I write unto you, my little children, because your sins are forgiven you for His name's sake.' iii. 5: 'Ye know that He was manifested to take away sins.' iv. 10: 'Not that we loved God, but that He loved us, and sent His Son to be the propitiation for our sins.' We see here that the whole person and work of Christ, His whole manifestation in the world, and in some signal way His death, are set in relation to sin.

Here as in the Gospel it is characteristic of the writer that his interest is in the end or result, the actual cleansing of the soul from sin. He thinks of this sanctification not in the sense of 1 Cor. vi. 11, or of Heb. x. 29, but in the sense of modern Protestant theology. It is dependent on the death of Christ. If we walk in the light as God is in the light, the blood of Jesus His Son continuously and progressively cleanses us from all sin: our sanctification is gradually achieved under its influence (i. 7). It is the removal of sin in this sense which is referred to also in iii. 5: 'He was manifested, that He might put sins away.'

It is by no means necessary, for the understanding of the evangelist here, that we should adopt the strange caprice which fascinated Westcott, and distinguish with him in the blood of Christ (i) His death, and (ii) His life; or (i) His blood shed, and (ii) His blood offered; or (i) His life laid down, and (ii) His life liberated and made available for men.[1] No doubt these distinctions were meant to safeguard a real religious interest: they were meant to secure the truth that it is a living Saviour who saves from sin, that He actually does save from sin, and that He does so in the last resort by the communication of His own life. But I venture to say that a more groundless fancy never haunted and troubled the interpretation of any part of Scripture than that which is introduced by this distinction into the Epistle to the Hebrews and the First Epistle of John. The New Testament writers, though they speak often of Christ's death, never think of a dead Christ. Their Christ is One who became dead and is alive for evermore, and in His immortal life the virtue of His death is present. He did something when He died, and that something He continues to make effective for men in His risen life; but there is no meaning in saying that by His death His life, as something other than His death, is 'liberated' and 'made available' for men. On the con-

---

[1] See Westcott, *The Epistles of John*, p. 34 ff.; *Epistle to the Hebrews*, p. 293 ff. For a recent criticism of Westcott's view see *The Meaning of the Word 'Blood' in Scripture*, A. M. Stibbs (Tyndale Press, 1948).

trary, what makes His risen life significant and a saving power for sinners is neither more nor less than this, that His death is in it. It is the life of One who by dying has dealt with the fatal necessities of man's situation, and in doing so has given a supreme demonstration of His love.

This connection of ideas becomes apparent when we notice that John uses a word akin to Paul's ἱλαστήριον in describing the relation of Christ to sin. Jesus Christ the righteous, he says, is the ἱλασμός for our sins (ii. 2); and again, he says, God of His own accord loved us, and sent His Son a propitiation for our sins (iv. 10). It is impossible to suppose that John used this word in any relations other than those in which it is found, or in which the cognate terms are found, in Hebrews or in Paul. The characteristic words of religion cannot be applied in new ways at will.

Now the idea of ἱλασμός or propitiation is not an insulated idea. There cannot, indeed, be any such thing. It is part of a system of ideas, which we have to reconstruct with the means at our disposal. It is related, for one thing, to the idea of sin. It is sin, according to the uniform teaching of the New Testament, which creates the necessity for it, and which is in some sense the object of it. In other words, sin is the problem with which ἱλασμός deals. John agrees with all New Testament writers in regarding sin as a problem. It cannot simply be ignored or suppressed. Something has to be done with it, and the effective something has been done by Christ the ἱλασμός.

Again, the idea of ἱλασμός is related to the ideas of sacrifice and intercession. When John says that Jesus Christ the righteous is the propitiation for our sins, this is implied. He has spoken almost immediately before about the *blood* of Jesus cleansing from all sin; he speaks further on with significant emphasis about His coming in *blood* as well as in water (v. 6). There is no doubt that he conceived Jesus as 'set forth', as Paul has it (Rom. iii. 25), 'in His blood' in this propitiatory character.

Further, the idea of ἱλασμός by being related to sin is related also to some divine law or order which sin has violated, and which is acknowledged in its inviolable rights by the ἱλασμός. This is what is meant when the propitiation is described as Jesus Christ *the righteous*. All that is divine, all the moral order of the world, all that we mean by the law of God, has right done by it in the death of Christ. Sin, in that sense, is neutralized by the propitiation, and if men could enter into it, or if the benefit of it could come to them, sin would no more be a barrier to their fellowship with God. The propitiation would draw them to God, put them right with Him and, as it held their hearts more closely, would more effectually and thoroughly cleanse them from every taint of sin. The power of sanctification is lodged in it as well as the condition of the sinner's primary acceptance with God. The first of these—the power of sanctification—preponderates in the Epistle; but it would be as complete a negation of its teaching, as of that of every New Testament writing, to say that the second —the sinner's acceptance with God—is dependent upon it. The very reverse is the case. The sin of *the whole world* has been atoned for, as the apostle expressly asserts (ii. 2); and it is on the basis of this work finished for all, and assumed to underlie everything, that the progressive purification of the Christian proceeds. It is the virtue of the ἱλασμός, in which all sin has been dealt with for its removal, and dealt with according to the realities of the divine law involved in the case, which eventually effects sanctification.

Perhaps the most striking thing in the first Epistle of John is the manner in which the propitiation of Christ is related to the love of God. The connection of the two things is, as we have seen, universal in the New Testament. No one could teach more emphatically than Paul, for example, that we owe to the love of God the presence of Jesus in the world and His work for men. No one could contrast more emphatically than Paul does what the love of God has done for us in Christ with the utmost which men will do from love for each other. But John rises above all comparisons to an absolute point of view at which propitiation and love become ideas which explain each other, and which have no adequate illustration apart from each other. He defines not only the propitiation by relation to love—'God Himself loved us and sent His Son to be the propitiation for our sins' (iv. 10); he defines love by relation to the propitiation—'in this have we come to know what love is, that He laid down His life for us' (iii. 16). The emphasis in this last sentence is on the expressly contrasted words ἐκεῖνος ὑπὲρ ἡμῶν. It is the contrast of what He is and of what we are, of the sinless Son of God and the sinful sons of men, in which the nerve of the proposition lies. So far from finding any kind of contrast between love and propitiation, the apostle can convey no idea of love to anyone except by pointing to the propitiation—love is what is manifested there; and he can give no account of the propitiation but by saying, 'Behold what manner of love.' For him, to say 'God is love' is exactly the same as to say 'God has in His Son made atonement for the sin of the world.' If the propitiatory death of Jesus is eliminated from the love of God, it might be unfair to say that the love of God is robbed of all meaning, but it is certainly robbed of its apostolic meaning. It has no longer that meaning which goes deeper than sin, sorrow, and death, and which re-creates life in the adoring joy, wonder, and purity of the first Epistle of John.

In speaking of the death of Christ, it would not be just either to the Gospel or to the Epistle of John to ignore the place held in both by the sacraments. That place has been ignored by some and disputed by others. But if we realize the date at which both documents were written, the place which the sacraments had in Christian worship at the time, and the inevitableness with which ordinary Christians must have thought, and as we know did think, of the sacraments when they read, it seems to me indisputable. Baptism and the Lord's Supper, it is no exaggeration to say, were full in the writer's view at many points. He must have thought of baptism when he wrote in the third chapter of the Gospel the words about being born of water and spirit; he must have thought of the Supper as he wrote in the sixth about eating the flesh of the Son of Man and drinking His blood. I cannot doubt that he thought of both when he told in xix. 34 of the blood and water that issued from the pierced side of Jesus, and again in the Epistle (v. 6 f.) urged that Jesus Christ came through water and blood, adding, with unambiguous emphasis, not in the water only, but in the water and in the blood. The water and the blood were always present in the church in the form of the sacraments, and the evangelist uses the sacraments here as witnesses to the historical reality of the life and experiences of Jesus. Christian baptism answers to His baptism. The Christian feast in which faith partakes of His body and blood is a perpetual testimony to His passion.

It is in this death of Christ upon the cross that John is peculiarly interested as he writes the Epistle. There were teachers abroad, of whom Cerinthus is a type, who preached a Christ that had come in the water only, not in the blood. The redeeming love and power of God, they held, had descended on Jesus at His baptism, and been with Him in His ministry of teaching and healing. There is a divine reality in this, therefore, on which we can depend. But they had withdrawn from Him before the Passion: there is therefore no corresponding divine reality there. It is against such a view that the apostle makes the elaborate and emphatic protest of v. 6 f.: 'not in the water only, but in the water and in the blood'. To deny the divine reality and saving significance of the Passion was to rob the most sacred rite of the Christian religion at once of its basis and its import; it was to abolish the Lord's Supper. The apostle appeals to the Lord's Supper against such a view. A Christ who did not come by blood, a Christ whose flesh was not the true meat and His blood the true drink, as the celebration of the Supper and the liturgical language used at it implied, a Christ who did not by His death bring life to men, was not the Christ known to the faith and acknowledged in the worship of the church. Both sacraments, but especially the sacrament of the Supper, are the stronghold of the New Testament doctrine concerning the death of Christ.

But there is another side to this. While the apostle sees in the sacraments a testimony to the historicity of the baptism and death of Christ and to the perpetual presence in the church of the saving power of the Lord's Passion, while he insists upon their historicity as against those who denied that Jesus Christ had come in flesh, and who made the life on earth, and especially the death, phantasmal so far as a revelation of God was concerned, he protests on the other hand against those who would materialize the history. He checks them at every point by introducing and emphasizing the Spirit. Thus in Jn. iii he speaks once of being born of water and spirit, but from that point onward the water is ignored. We hear of the Spirit alone; of His breathing where He will, of being born of the Spirit, of every one who is so born. So also in the sixth chapter, after recording the strongest language about eating the flesh and drinking the blood of the Son of Man, language in which enigmatic defiance to antipathetic minds is carried to the furthest point, he precludes all possibility of religious materialism by the words: 'It is the Spirit which gives life; the flesh is of no use for this; the words that I have spoken to you are spirit and are life' (vi. 63). Words and speech address man on the spiritual side of his nature, and it is on this side that everything included in Christ—'he that eateth *Me*', He says—finds access to us. And finally, in the Epistle, after laying the stress we have seen on the water and the blood, he concludes: 'And it is the Spirit that beareth witness, because the Spirit is the truth. For there are three who bear witness, the Spirit and the water and the blood: and the three agree in one.' In every case the historical is asserted, but care is taken that it shall not be materialized: a primacy is given to the spiritual. On the other hand, there is no such spiritualizing as would leave to the historical merely a position of vanishing or relative importance. There is no sublimation of Christianity into 'ethical' or 'spiritual prin-ciples', or into 'eternal facts', which absolve us from all obligation to a Saviour who came in blood. Except through the historical, there is no Christianity at all, but neither is there any Christianity till the historical has been spiritually comprehended.

This is closely connected with our subject. Christianity is as real as the blood of Christ. It is as real as the agony in the garden and the death on the cross. It is not less real than this, nor more real; it has no reality whatever which is separable from these historical things. Yet it is not in their mere externality, as events in past time, that they establish Christianity or save men from their sins. It is as their spiritual meaning is recognized, and makes a spiritual appeal to men, and awakes a spiritual response. When that awful experience of Jesus is revealed as a propitiation for sins, an assumption of our responsibilities by One who does right by the eternal law which we have wronged, and does it for us at this tremendous cost, then the soul of man is reached by the divine love, and through penitence and faith drawn away from evil, and born again of God. Then the blood of Jesus, God's Son, cleanses from all sin. Then the Son of Man is glorified in His death, and God is glorified in Him.

A friendly critic of this book pointed out what he regarded as a serious omission in it—the want of any reference to the death of Christ as a victory over Satan. This is a point of view which is principally found in the fourth Gospel. Thus it is with His death and its consequences in view that Jesus says, 'Now is the judgment of this world: now shall the prince of this world be cast out. And I, if I be lifted up from the earth, will draw all men unto Myself' (Jn. xii. 31 f.). As His hour comes nearer He says again, 'I will no more speak much with you, for the prince of the world cometh: and he hath nothing in Me' (Jn. xiv. 30). And finally, in the description of the work and power of the Spirit, who is to take His place in the hearts of the disciples after His departure, the same conception recurs. 'He, when He is come, will convict the world . . . of judgment, because the prince of this world hath been judged' (Jn. xvi. 11). A mind which does not naturally personalize the principle of evil—turning the principle into a prince—has the same embarrassment in dealing with these passages as with the Pauline ones previously mentioned. Possibly we get out too easily with our abstract nouns. The evil in the world may be represented as a principle, or an atmosphere, or an abstraction of some kind, by a spectator who is not engaged in conflict with it. But for One whose life is spent in conflict, for One who resists unto blood in the strife against it and finds it impossible not to do so, evil may assume a more malignant, and therefore a more personal aspect. It is not an unconscious but a wilful and wicked force. It is not a *vis inertiæ* in the moral world, but an awful enemy of God. It reveals the intensity of the conflict, the stress of the battle which Jesus fought, that the power which He vanquished is represented thus. There is no suggestion in the fourth Gospel that the Prince of this World had any rights in it, even relative and temporary rights, such as might be supposed to belong to the angels who gave the law, and who were superseded in their authority by Christ. The Prince of this World has no rights at all, and that is what Jesus demonstrates by His death. He has nothing in Christ. He is judged; he is cast out. Through the death on the cross the kingdom of this world is taken from him, and becomes the kingdom of God and of His Christ.

CHAPTER VI

THE DEATH OF CHRIST IN PREACHING
AND THEOLOGY

IF the series of studies which we have now completed has
reproduced with any adequacy or accuracy the mind of the
New Testament writers, certain conclusions of importance
may fairly be deduced from it. One is that there really is such
a thing as the New Testament. There is, as we were disposed
to assume, a real and substantial unity of thought in the books
which we call by that name. They were not written with a view
to incorporation in a canon. To repeat the paradox referred to
in the introduction, New Testament theology is the theology of
the Church at a time when as yet it had no New Testament. But
the New Testament books have a unity, nevertheless, neither
external nor imposed, nor due to the accident of their being
approximately contemporary, but inward, essential, and spiritual.
This qualifies them to be canonical.

Another conclusion to which we are led is that the death of
Christ is the central thing in the New Testament and in the
Christian religion as the New Testament understands it. And
when we say the death of Christ, we include, of course, the
significance which the New Testament ascribes to it. Apart from
that significance the death of Christ has no more right to a place
in religion than the death of the penitent or the impenitent thief.
The cross and the word of the cross, the cross and the rationale
of it in relation to the love of God and the sin of man, are for
religion one thing. This being so, it is apparent that both for
the propagation and for the scientific construction of the Christian
religion the death of Christ is of supreme importance. Not that
I should draw too abstract a distinction. The propagation of
Christianity and its interpretation by intelligence—in other words,
preaching and theology—should never be divorced. At the vital
point they coincide. The simplest truth of the gospel and the
profoundest truth of theology must be put in the same words

—'He bore our sins.' If our gospel does not inspire thought, and if our theology does not inspire preaching, there is no Christianity in either. Yet vitally related as they are, there is a sufficiently clear distinction between them, and in considering some consequences for preaching and theology of New Testament teaching on Christ's death, it will be convenient to take preaching first.

It is an immediate inference, then, from all that we have seen in the New Testament, that where there is no atonement there is no gospel. To preach the love of God out of relation to the death of Christ, or to preach the love of God in the death of Christ but without being able to relate it to sin, or to preach the forgiveness of sins as the free gift of God's love while the death of Christ has no special significance assigned to it, is not, if the New Testament is the rule and standard of Christianity, to preach the gospel at all. Many ministers have suffered from the charge of not preaching the gospel, and have resented it as an injustice. In any given case it may quite well have been so. There are those who are unable to separate form from substance in thinking, and who are only too ready to believe that if the familiar form in which the truth has been expressed is varied, the substance is being injured or dissipated. But it is not a hard or unjust thing to say that in some cases the charge may not be groundless. It may be made not merely by the unintelligent, who fail to distinguish form from substance, but by the simple Christian spirit which has the anointing from the Holy One, and knows instinctively whether that by which it lives is present in the message it hears or not. There is such a thing as preaching in which the death of Christ has no place corresponding to that which it has in the New Testament. There is preaching in which the New Testament interpretation of Christ's death is ignored, or carped at, or exploded. We do not need to argue that no man can preach the gospel until he has absorbed into his mind and heart the whole significance of Christ's death as the New Testament reveals it. In that case, who could preach at all? But it is not unjust to say that no man will so preach as to leave the impression that he has the Word of God behind him if he is inwardly at war with the idea of atonement, constantly engaged in minimizing it or maintaining an attitude of reserve, or even of self-defence, in relation to it. We may take it or leave it, but it is idle to attempt to propagate the Christian religion on the basis and with the authority of the New Testament, unless we have welcomed it with our whole heart.

It is proper to remember in this connection that very often it is the simplest expressions, and those most open to abstract criticism, in which the profoundest truth is most tellingly expressed and most really apprehended. When this is the case, if we are compelled to criticize, we should be careful that we do not discredit the essential truth as well as the inadequate form. It is easy, for instance, to criticize the insufficiency of any commercial figure, like that of 'debt', to exhibit the personal and spiritual relations subsisting between man and God. Yet Christ used this figure habitually, and the whole impression which it makes upon the conscience is sound. The words of the revival hymn, 'Jesus paid it all, All to Him I owe,' have the root of the matter in them. However inadequate they may be as an interpretation of Christ's work and of Christian experience as a whole, they are infinitely more true than the most balanced, considerate, or subtle statement which denies them. Hence, whatever the motive which prompts criticism of such forms, we should be sensitive to the meaning they bear. Even if we think they are morally inadequate, and leave the new life unprovided for, we should remember that in the New Testament the new life is the immediate response to the very truth which such forms convey. The new life springs out of the sense of debt to Christ. The regenerating power of forgiveness depends upon its cost: it is the knowledge that we have been bought *with a price* which makes us cease to be our own, and live for Him who so dearly bought us. And we should remember also that it is not always intellectual sensitiveness, nor care for the moral interests involved, which sets the mind to criticize statements of the atonement. There *is* such a thing as pride, the last form of which is unwillingness to become debtor even to Christ for forgiveness of sins. And it is conceivable that in any given case it may be this which makes the words of the hymn stick in the throat. In any case, I do not hesitate to say that the sense of debt to Christ is the most profound and pervasive of all emotions in the New Testament, and that only a gospel which evokes this, as the gospel of atonement does, is true to the primitive and normal Christian type.

Not only must atonement by the death of Christ be preached if we would preach the New Testament gospel, but the characteristics of the atonement must be clearly reflected in the preaching if justice is to be done to the gospel. As the finished work of Christ the atonement is complete, and the perfection which belongs to it belongs also to the new relation to God into which we enter when the atonement is appropriated by faith. There is *no* condemnation to them that are in Christ Jesus. Their relation to God is not determined now in the very least by sin or law; it is determined by Christ the propitiation and by faith. The position of the believer is not that of one trembling at the judgment seat, or of one for whom everything remains somehow in a condition of suspense. It is that of one who has the assurance of a divine love which has gone deeper than all his sins, and has taken on itself the responsibility of them, and the responsibility of delivering him from them. A relation to God in which sin has nothing to say, but which is summed up in Christ and His perfect atonement for sin—in John Wesley's words, *full salvation now*—is the burden of the gospel. If it is not easy to believe this or to preach it, it is because, as the heavens are higher than the earth, so are God's thoughts higher than our thoughts, and His ways than our ways. In the New Testament itself there is always something startling, something almost incredible, which breaks again and again on the soul with a sense of wonder, in the experience of reconciliation through the death of Christ. But it is this great gospel which is the gospel to win souls—this message of a sin-bearing, sin-expiating love, which pleads for acceptance, which takes the whole responsibility of the sinner unconditionally, with no preliminaries, if only he abandon himself to it. Only the preaching of full salvation now, as Wesley tells us—and who knew better from experience than he?—has any promise in it of revival.

Further, preaching which would do justice to the atonement must hold out in the gospel an assurance corresponding to the certainty of Christ's death and to the sin-bearing love demonstrated in it. Nothing is more characteristic of churches than their attitude to assurance, and the place they give it in their preaching and in their systems of doctrine. Speaking broadly, we may say that in the Roman Catholic church it is regarded as essentially akin to presumption; in the Protestant churches it is a privilege or a duty. But in the New Testament religion it is simply a fact. This explains the joy which, side by side with the sense of infinite obligation, is the characteristic note of apostolic Christianity. The great invincible certainty of the reconciling love of God, which even when we were enemies made peace for us, underlies all things, embraces all things, makes all things work together for good to those who love God, makes us more than conquerors in all things. Take away the certainty of it, and the New Testament temper expires. Joy in this certainty is not presumption; on the contrary, it is joy in the Lord, and such joy is the Christian's strength. It is the impulse and the hope of sanctification. To deprecate it and the assurance from which it springs is no true evangelical humility, but a failure to believe in the infinite goodness of God who in Christ removes our sins from us as far as the east is from the west and plants our life in His eternal reconciling love. The New Testament spirit is not meant for our despair, but for our inspiration. That assurance of sin-bearing love, that sanctifying strength and gladness, are typical of genuine Christian life.

We can understand and appreciate the motive which, in both the Roman Catholic and the Protestant churches, has fostered in relation to assurance a temper which is not that of the New Testament, and which does not answer to the completeness and certainty of Christ's finished work. The motive is in both cases a desire to safeguard moral interests and to put a check upon self-deception. The Roman Church safeguards moral interests by making justification and the new life identical. Men are justified as, and only in proportion as, they are actually and morally renewed. The objection to this method is that the security is too good. An absolute justification is needed to give the sinner a start. He must have the certainty of 'no condemnation', of being, without reserve or drawback, right with God through God's gracious act in Christ, before he can begin to live the new life. As Chalmers put it with magnificent simplicity, 'What could I do if God did not justify *the ungodly*?' It is not by denying outright the gospel from the very beginning that we are to guard against the possible abuse of it.

In the Protestant churches, on the other hand, the attempt to check presumption and to safeguard moral interests was usually made by laying stress on the proper kind of faith. The German Pietists, in opposition to a dead orthodoxy in which faith had come to mean no more than the formal recognition of sound doctrine, spoke with emphasis of penitent faith, living faith, true faith, obedient faith, and so on. The fact that they are foreign to the New Testament is somewhat against qualifications like these. What they come to in practice is this. 'Before the mercy of God in Christ the propitiation can be available for you, O sinful man, you must have a sufficient depth of penitence, a sufficiently earnest desire for reconciliation and holiness, a sufficient moral sincerity. Otherwise grace would only minister to sin.' But such qualifications infringe upon the graciousness of the gospel and overlook its absolute freeness. They are inconsistent with the New Testament where the atonement is explained as originating in the love of God and in terms of the necessity, not the merits of men. Christ did not die for those who were sufficiently penitent. He is the propitiation for the whole world, and He bore the sins of all that all might believe and receive through Him repentance and remission. To try to take some preliminary security for the sinner's future morality before you make the gospel available for him is not only to strike at the root of assurance, it is to pay a very poor tribute to the power of the gospel. The truth is that morality is best guaranteed by Christ and not by any precautions we can take before Christ gets a chance or by any virtue that is in faith except as it unites the soul to Him. Now the Christ who is the object of faith is the Christ whose death is the atonement, and the faith which takes hold of Christ as He is held out in the gospel conducts, if we may use such a figure, the virtue of the atonement into the heart. The mercy of God which we welcome in it and welcome as the first and last of spiritual realities with invincible assurance is a mercy which has God's judgment upon sin deep in its heart. And such a mercy, absolutely free as it is and able to evoke in sinful men a joy unspeakable and full of glory, can never foster either immorality or presumption. But when its certainty, completeness, and freeness are so qualified or disguised that assurance becomes suspect and joy is quenched, the Christian religion has ceased to be.[1]

There is one other characteristic of the atonement which ought to be reflected in gospel preaching as determined by it, and which may for want of a better word be described as its finality. Christ died for sins once for all, and the man who believes in Christ and in His death has his relation to God once for all determined not by sin but by the atonement. The sin for which a Christian has daily to seek forgiveness is not sin which annuls his acceptance with God and casts him back into the position of one who has never had the assurance of the pardoning mercy of God in Christ. On the contrary, that assurance ought to be the permanent element in his life. The forgiveness of sins has to be received again and again as sin emerges into act. But when the soul closes with Christ the propitiation, the assurance of God's love is laid at the foundation of its being once for all. It is not to isolated acts it refers, but to the personality; not to sins, but to the sinner; not to the past only, in which wrong has been done, but to time and eternity.

There will inevitably be in the Christian life experiences of sinning and of being forgiven, of falling and of being restored. But the grace which forgives and restores is not some new thing, nor is it conditioned in some new way. It is not dependent upon penitence, or works, or merit of ours. It is the same absolutely free grace which meets us at the cross. From first to last, it is the blood of Jesus, God's Son, which cleanses from sin. The daily pardon, the daily cleansing, are but the daily virtue of that one all-embracing act of mercy in which, while we were yet sinners, we were reconciled to God by the death of His Son.

---

[1] I venture to quote two sentences in illustration of this paragraph. Dr. Dale (*Life*, p. 666), who read Pusey's life 'with a deep impression of the nobleness and massiveness of his nature, and feeling more than ever that the power of God was with him', had nevertheless to add: 'The absence of joy in his religious life was only the inevitable effect of his conception of God's method of saving men; in parting with the Lutheran truth concerning justification (it might equally well be said with the New Testament truth of Christ's finished work) he parted with the springs of gladness.' It is in the same line that Dr. Fairbairn has said of Pusey, that the sense of sin was 'more a matter for himself to bear than for grace to remove' (*Philosophy of the Christian Religion*, p. 333). The other sentence is from Chalmers, a great nature who had an original experience of the New Testament religion and often found original utterance for it: 'Regaled myself with the solidity of the objective part of religion, and long to enter a field of enlargement in preaching on the essential truths of the gospel' (*Life*, by Hanna, vol. ii, p. 417).

To say that there is no gospel without atonement, and that the characteristics of the atonement must be impressed upon Christian preaching and reflected in the completeness, assurance, and joy of the Christian life which is the response to it, does not mean that the preacher is always to be expressly and formally engaged with the death of Christ, nor does it determine in what way that death in its redeeming significance is to be presented to men. It is impossible to forget the example of our Lord, though we are bound to remember that what was natural and inevitable before the Passion and the Resurrection may not be either wise or natural now. But looking to the Gospels, we cannot fail to see that our Lord allowed His disciples every opportunity to become acquainted with Him, and to grow into confidence in Him, before He began to teach them about His death. He allowed them to catch the impression of His Personality before He initiated them into the mystery of His Passion. As for outsiders, He seems not to have spoken to them on the subject at all. Yet it would be a mistake, as we have seen, to suppose that the death of Jesus was not present in His mind and in His life even where nothing was said of it. The more we study the Gospels, and the more thoroughly we appreciate such incidents as the Baptism, the Temptation, and the Transfiguration, with the heavenly voices attendant on them, not to mention the occasions on which His death rises even in early days to the surface of our Lord's mind, the more we shall be convinced that the sense and the power of it pervade everything we know of Him. He lived in the same spirit in which He died, and in a true sense we are in contact with the Passion and the atonement whenever we are in contact with the soul of Jesus. To preach the Gospels, therefore, it may be said, is to preach the gospel. On the other hand we must remember, and allow the remembrance its full weight as a directory for teaching and preaching, that a time came when Jesus set Himself deliberately, systematically, and with unwearied reiteration to bring home to His disciples the meaning of His death.

Everything conspires to make us see how deeply it moved Him, and how deeply He was concerned to have it apprehended by the disciples for what it was. The very names by which He names it, 'My baptism', 'My cup', the profound virtue He ascribes to it as a ransom, and as the basis of a new covenant between God and man, the striking ordinances of baptism and the Supper which He associated with it, and which in spite of intelligible yet misconceived protests will guard its meaning while the world stands; all these separately, and still more in combination, warn us that whatever method may be prescribed in any given case by pedagogic considerations, it must not be one which leaves it optional to us to give the death of Christ a place in our gospel or not, as we please. It is as certain as anything can be that He meant us to be His debtors and to feel that we are so. He meant to represent Himself as the mediator between God and sinners, and to evoke in sinners an infinite sense of obligation to Himself as they realized that they had peace with God.

It always comes to this in the long run. Men may come into contact with Christ at different places. They may approach Him from all quarters of the compass, under various impulses, yielding to a charm and constraint in Him as manifold as the beatitudes or as gracious as the words and deeds of the gospel. But if they are in dead earnest as He is, they will come sooner or later to the strait gate. And the ultimate form the strait gate assumes— for it is a gate that goes on straitening till the demand for death is made as the price of life—is that to which Jesus leads His disciples in His last lessons. 'Are you willing to humble yourselves so as to owe to Me, and to My death for you, the forgiveness of sins and the life which is life indeed?' There is a straight line from every point in the circumference of a circle to the centre, and when we get to the quick of almost anything in the relations of men to Jesus, it leads with wonderful directness to this decisive point.

A striking passage from Kierkegaard's diary may help to reconcile in our minds what seem to be conflicting assertions: the one, that there is no preaching of the gospel unless the atonement is preached; the other, which, as we have seen, has a superficial support in the life and practice of Jesus, that the atonement is the last thing in Christ to which the mind can be opened or reconciled. In general, Kierkegaard says,[1] the relation between God

[1] *The Journals of Soren Kierkegaard* (English translation, O.U.P., 1938), section 1282.

and man is represented thus: Christ leads us to God; man requires a mediator in order to have access to the Father. But this, he argues, is not how the New Testament puts it. Nor can this by any possibility be the true way of putting it if, as he further argues, our relation to God is to become continually higher and more real; for it can become such only through a continual experience on our part of being more deeply humbled in God's presence. But there is no sense of being deeply humbled in the first stages of our religion. We begin, in short, with the Father, quite easily and naturally, and without any mediator. This and nothing else is the childlike way of beginning. For the child nothing is too high; he says *Du* to the Kaiser just as he does to his nurse, and finds it perfectly intelligible and proper that God should be his Father. It would have no meaning to him if he heard a voice which said, 'No man cometh unto the Father but by Me.' But as soon as man has attained to a certain degree of maturity, God's greatness or sublimity, moral as well as metaphysical, becomes so overwhelming to him that it is no longer natural or easy to call Him Father. There is something presumptuous in it, or something quite unreal.

Now this sense of the relation between himself and God, which grows upon man as his moral consciousness matures, is true, and there is something which answers to it in the mind of God Himself. Hence at this stage God points us to His Son, the Mediator. 'It is written in the prophets,' says Jesus, 'And they shall all be taught of God. Every one that hath heard from the Father, and hath learned, cometh unto Me' (Jn. vi. 45). This is the remedy for the presumption and unreality just referred to. It is as though God said: You must not assert or claim sonship in your own right; you must not take Fatherhood for granted; but through the Mediator I can be your Father. This, however, is not all. The Mediator also, like the Father at first, is apt to be taken for granted with the assurance of youth, if not of childhood. For the Mediator is at first conceived as example. It is in imitation of Him, in likeness to Him (to use the phrase which is most popular in our own day and is charged to the full with this unreflecting youthful assurance), it is in self-identification with Him that we must realize the Fatherhood of God.

There is an amiable youthfulness, says Kierkegaard, the token of which is that it finds nothing too high for it. It seems to it quite natural and becoming that it should have such an infinitely lofty example as Jesus, the Son of God. Among its amiable illusions is to be counted a pious conviction that it is within its power to attain to this example. It takes for granted that the example and he who is striving to follow it are so much of one kind that nothing can really come between them. But once more, as the moral consciousness matures, a change comes. The example towers to such a height before man's eyes, the sinless Son of God is so remote and inaccessible in His sinlessness and Sonship, that man can no longer think of imitating Him, or of trying to do so, in the independent style of good comradeship. He cannot take it for granted that he can make himself what Christ is, that he can 'identify' himself with Christ offhand simply because he wants to do so.

In view of this we shall not be surprised to find that it is another and a more dependent relation, with a deeper sense of obligation in it, which our Lord requires from His followers. The example has another side, of which amiable and aspiring youth is at first ignorant: Jesus Christ is also the Reconciler. Experience reveals, Kierkegaard argues, to one who is trying to imitate Jesus, or to identify himself with Him, that he needs reconciliation first. He must become debtor to Jesus for this one thing needful before he can have a sound start in the filial life. He must owe it to Christ as Reconciler, and owe it from the very beginning, if he is ever to stand in the relation of a son to the Father. He may think at first that he can identify himself with the Son of God at any point over the whole area of his life, but he discovers experimentally that this is not so. He finds out in a way surer than any logical demonstration that Christ is in the last resort as inaccessible to him as the God to whom he would draw near by imitating Christ, and that the only hope he has of getting to God in this way depends upon Christ making Himself one with him in that responsibility for sin which separates him from the Father. His one point of contact with Christ, when his whole situation is taken seriously, is Christ's character as a propitiation for sin; and sooner or later he is driven in upon that.

The type of experience here described may be common enough in Christian lands, but what, it may be asked, is its relation to such a practice as Paul describes in 1 Cor. xv. 3: 'I delivered unto you *first of all* that which also I received, how that Christ died for our sins according to the Scriptures'? Is this consistent with what has just been said, or with what we have seen of our Lord's method of teaching? Is there a rule in it for all evangelistic preaching?

Paul's expression, ἐν πρώτοις, is not quite so pointed as 'first of all'. It is certainly to be taken, however, in a temporal sense. Among the first things the apostle transmitted to the Corinthians were the fundamental facts of the Christian religion, the death and resurrection of Jesus in the significance which belonged to them 'according to the Scriptures', that is, in the light of the earlier revelation. And among these first things the death of Christ in its relation to sin had a foremost place.

It is, I think, a fair inference from this that in preaching the gospel the main appeal is to be made to the conscience, and that it cannot be made too soon, too urgently, too desperately, or too hopefully. It is because the atonement is at once the revelation of sin and the redemption from sin, that it must inspire everything in preaching which is to bring home to the conscience either conviction of sin or the hope and assurance of deliverance from it. 'Eternity', Halyburton said, 'is wrapt up in every truth of religion'; the atonement, it is not too much to say, is wrapt up in every truth of the Christian religion, and should be sensible through every word of the Christian preacher. In this sense at least it must be delivered ἐν πρώτοις. We may begin as wisely as we please with those who have a prejudice against it, or whose conscience is asleep, or who have much to learn both about Christ and about themselves before they will consent to look at such a gospel, to say nothing of abandoning themselves to it; but if we do not begin with something which is essentially related to the atonement, presupposing it or presupposed by it or involved in it, something which leads inevitably, though it may be by an indirect and unsuspected route, to the Lamb of God that taketh away the sin of the world, we have not begun to preach the gospel at all.

This may seem a hard saying to those who have wearily listened to the repetition of orthodox formulae on this subject, and have realized that even under the new covenant there are conditions

which compel us to say, 'the letter killeth'. But it is not because
the formulae are orthodox that they weary; it is because they
are formal. The vital interest of the great realities which they
enshrine has slipped away through lack of faith and left the
preacher with nothing to deliver but words. A fresh realization
of the truth which they embody would bring new words or put
new life into the old; and in any case the fact remains that there
is nothing which is so urgently and immediately wanted by
sinful men, nothing which strikes so deep into the heart, answers
so completely to its need and binds it so irrevocably and with
such a sense of obligation to God, as the atoning death of Jesus.
Implicit or explicit, it is the Alpha and Omega of Christian
preaching.

Most preachers in any sympathy with this line of thought
have deplored the present-day decay of the sense of sin.[1] Now,
the atonement is addressed to the sense of sin. It presupposes the
bad conscience. Where there is no such thing, it is like a lever
without a fulcrum. Great as its power might be, it is actually
powerless, and often provokes resentment. The phenomenon is
a curious one, and though it cannot be permanent, it calls for
explanation. A partial explanation may be that the atonement
itself was once preached too much as though it had relation only
to the past and had no assurance or guarantee in it for man's
future. It contained the forgiveness of sins, but not the new life.
Where this was the case we can understand that it ceased to be
interesting to those whose hearts were set on holiness. We can
understand how Bushnell could speak of the forgiveness of sins
as 'only a kind of formality, or verbal discharge, that carries
practically no discharge at all'. But it is not easy to understand
how this could be brought into any kind of relation to the New
Testament. There, as we have seen, the forgiveness of sins, and
the atonement which is its ground, are no formality. They are
the supreme miracle of revelation, the hardest, most incredible,
most wonderful work of the God who alone does wondrous
things. The whole promise and potency of the new life are to
be found in them alone. The atonement, or God's justification
of the ungodly, which takes effect with the acceptance of the
atonement, regenerates, and there is no regeneration besides.

[1] For a typical illustration, see Dale's *Christian Doctrine*, pp. 251 ff.

But while a defective appreciation of the New Testament may have done something to discredit the atonement, and to make men think of forgiveness, and of the sense of sin which demands it, as alike 'formalities' in contrast with actual sanctification, the deadening of conscience is probably to be traced to other causes. It is due in great part to the dominance in the mind for the last forty or fifty years of the categories of natural science, and especially of a naturalistic theory of evolution. All things have been 'naturalized', if we may so speak; the spiritual being no longer retains, in the common consciousness, his irreducible individuality; he has lapsed to some extent into the vast continuity of the universe. Even to speak of the individual is to use language which is largely unreal, and with individuality individual responsibility has lost credit. It is the race which lives, and it is the qualities and defects of the race which are exhibited in what we call the virtues and vices of men. When we look at the lives of others, the last thing we now think of is the responsibility which attaches to each of them for being what he is. And it is apt to be the last thing also which we think of when we look at ourselves. Heredity and environment, these are the dominant realities in our minds. So inevitable, so importunate is their pressure, that what was once known as freedom passes out of view. We are afraid to speak as the Bible speaks about personal responsibility—we are afraid to say the tremendous things it says about sin and sinful men—both because we would not be unjust to others, and because we wish to be considerate to ourselves.

For the same reason we are afraid to give that decisive importance to the atoning death of Christ which it carries in the New Testament. But of one thing we may be certain: sooner or later there will be a reaction against this mental condition. When our sense of the unity of the race in itself, and of its unity with the 'nature' which is the theatre of its history, has done its work, when the social conscience has been quickened, when the feeling of corporate responsibility has attained adequate intensity so that the duties of society to the individual shall be no longer overlooked, the responsibility of the individual will come back in new strength. The naturalistic view of the world cannot permanently suppress the moral one. Even while it has seemed to threaten it, it has been preparing for its revival in a more profound and adequate form. The sense of personal responsibility, when it does come back, will be less confined, more far reaching and mysterious. It will be more than ever such a sense of responsibility as will make the doctrine of a divine atonement for sin necessary, credible, and welcome.

Meanwhile, surely, the preaching of the atonement has something to do with producing the very state of mind on which its reception depends. It is the highest truth of revelation: and the highest truth is like the highest poetry; it has to generate the intellectual and moral atmosphere in which alone it can be appreciated and taken to the heart. To say that there is no sense of sin, or that the sense of sin is defective, is only to say in other words that there is no repentance, or no adequate repentance, no returning of the mind upon itself deeply enough, humbly enough, tenderly and hopefully enough, to have any healing or restoring effect.

But how is this spiritual condition to be altered? What is the cure for it? There are those who cannot be convinced that any cure is necessary. In spite of all Christian confession to the contrary, they cling to the idea that such a returning of the mind upon itself as would constitute repentance unto life and be the proper condition of pardon and acceptance with God is an experience which the sinful soul can produce out of its own resources and clothed in which it can come hopefully to meet God. But true repentance, that is, repentance which is not self-centred, but which realizes that sin is something in which God has an interest as well as we, repentance which is not merely a remorseful or apathetic or despairing regret, but a hopeful, healing, sanctifying sorrow, such repentance is born of the knowledge of God, and of what God has done for us in our sins. It is not a preliminary to the atonement, nor a substitute for it, nor a way in which we can be reconciled to God without being indebted to it. It is its fruit. It is born at the cross where we see sin put away, not by our own regret, however sincere and profound, but by the love of God in the passion of His dear Son. Hence, if we give the atonement anything less than the central place in our preaching, we lose the only chance of seeing it, and of seeing in its true intensity the sense of individual responsibility which is part and parcel of it. No one is really saved from sin until he

has in relation to it that mind which Christ had when He bore
our sins in His own body on the tree. And no motive is potent
enough to generate that mind in sinful men but the love with
which Christ loved us when He so gave Himself for us. It is
true to say that the atonement presupposes conscience and appeals
to it, but it is truer still to say that of all powers in the world it
is the supreme power for creating and deepening conscience. One
remembers again and again the story of the first Moravian
missionaries to Greenland, who, after twenty years of fruitless
toil in indirect approaches to the savage mind, found it suddenly
responsive to the appeal of the cross.

Paul made no mistake when he delivered to the Corinthians
ἐν πρώτοις the message of the atonement. No one can tell how
near conscience is to the surface, or how quickly in any man it
may respond to the appeal. We might have thought that in
Corinth much preliminary sapping and mining would have been
requisite before the appeal could be made with any prospect of
success. But Paul judged otherwise, and preached from the very
outset the great hope of the gospel, by which conscience is at
once evoked and redeemed. We might think that in a Christian
country conscience would be nearer the surface, more susceptible,
more conscious of its needs, more quickly responsive to the
appeal of the atonement; and if we do not always find it so, it
is only, as Paul himself puts it, because all men have not faith.
We cannot get behind this melancholy fact, and give the rationale
of what is in itself irrational. Yet all experience shows that the
gospel wins by its magnitude, and that the true method for the
evangelist is to put the great things in the forefront. If this is
not the way to the conscience, this sublime demonstration of the
love of God in Christ, in which our responsibility as sinful men
is taken by Him in all its dreadful reality and made His own,
what is? In what, if not in this, can we find the means of appealing
to all men, and to that which is deepest in all?

One other characteristic ought to distinguish evangelical
preaching if it is to be determined by the atonement. It ought
to have a deep impression of the absoluteness of the issues in
faith and unbelief, or let us say in the acceptance or rejection of
the reconciliation. In one way, it may be said, this is always the
note of religion. It is a form of the absolute consciousness, and

deals not with a sliding scale but with the blank, unqualified antithesis of life or death, weal or woe, salvation or perdition, heaven or hell. This is true; yet of no religion is it more emphatically true than of that which is exhibited in the New Testament. We are concerned with a life and death matter when we come face to face with Christ and with what He has done for us.

It is quite possible to preach with earnestness, and even with persuasiveness, from another standpoint. It is quite possible to have a very sincere admiration for goodness, and a very sincere desire to be better men than we are and to see others better; it is quite possible even to see the charm and beauty of Christ's goodness and to commend it in the most winning way to men, and yet to lack in preaching the very note which is characteristic both of Christ and of the apostles. Christ knew that He was to give His life a ransom; the apostles knew that He had done it, and had made peace through the blood of His cross. Thus their preaching, though it is never overbearing or unjust, though it never tries to intimidate men, or, as one may sometimes have been tempted to think in a mission service, to bully them into faith, is as urgent and passionate as the sense of the atoning death can make it. To receive the reconciliation, or not to receive it —to be a Christian, or not to be a Christian—is not a matter of comparative indifference. It is not a question of being a somewhat better man, or a man, perhaps, not quite so good; it is a question of life or death.

It is difficult to speak of this as it ought to be spoken of, and to urge it in any given situation may easily expose the preacher to the charge of intolerance, uncharitableness, or moral blindness. But difficult as it may be to preach the gospel in the spirit of the gospel, with a sense at the same time of the infinite love which is in it, and the infinite responsibility which it puts upon us, it is not a difficulty which the preacher's vocation will allow him to evade. He may easily be represented as saying that he is making the acceptance of his own theology the condition of acceptance with God, and arrogating to himself the right to judge others. But while he repudiates such charges as inconsistent with his whole relation both to God and man, he will not abandon his conviction that the apostolic sense of the infinite consequences determined by man's relation to the gospel is justified, and that it is justified because it is in harmony with all that the New Testament teaches about the finished work of Christ. God has spoken His last word in His Son. He has done all that He can do for men. Revelation and redemption are complete, and the finality on which the Epistle to the Hebrews lays such emphasis as characteristic of everything belonging to the new covenant ought to have an echo in every proclamation of it. If therefore we are conscious that this note is wanting in our preaching, that it fails in urgency and entreaty, that it is expository merely, or attractive, or hortatory, that it is interpretative or illuminative, or has the character of good advice, very good advice indeed, when we come to think of it, it is probably time to ask what place in it is held by the atonement.

The proclamation of the finished work of Christ is not good advice; it is good news, good news that means immeasurable joy for those who welcome it, irreparable loss for those who reject it and infinite and urgent responsibility for all. The man who has this to preach has a gospel about which he ought to be in dead earnest. Just because there is nothing which concentrates in the same way the judgment and the mercy of God, there is nothing which has the same power to evoke seriousness and passion in the preacher.

Leaving out of account its importance to the sinner, the supreme interest of the doctrine of the atonement is, of course, its interest for the evangelist. Without a firm grasp of it he can do nothing whatever in his vocation. But what is central in religion must be central also in all reflection upon it, and the theologian no less than the evangelist must give this great truth its proper place in his mind. I have no intention of outlining a system of theology in which the atonement made in the death of Christ should be the determinative principle. But short of this, it is possible to indicate its bearing and significance in regard to some vital questions.

For example, if we have been correct in our appreciation of its place in the New Testament, it is not too much to say that as the focus of revelation it is the key to all that precedes. The nature of the unity which belongs to Scripture has always been a perplexing question—so perplexing, indeed, that the very existence of any unity at all has been denied; yet there is an answer to it. Scripture converges upon the doctrine of the atonement; it has the unity of a consentient testimony to a love of God which bears the sin of the world. How this is done we do not see clearly till we come to Christ, or till He comes to us. But once we get this insight from Him, we get it for revelation as a whole. To Him bear all the Scriptures witness; and it is as a testimony to Him, the Bearer of sin, the Redeemer who gave His life a ransom for us, that we acknowledge them. This is the burden of the Bible, the one fundamental omnipresent truth to which the Holy Spirit bears witness by and with the word in our hearts. This, at bottom, is what we mean when we say that Scripture is inspired.

It is worth while to insist on this in view of the widespread confusion which prevails in regard to inspiration. We are all aware of the apparent readiness, on the part of some, to give it up as an insignificant or irrelevant idea, if not an utterly discredited one, and the haphazard attempts, on the part of others, to save it piecemeal, after abandoning it as a whole. The truth is that the unity of the Bible and its inspiration are correlative terms. If we can discover a real unity in it, as I believe we can and do when we see that it converges upon and culminates in a divine love bearing the sin of the world, then that unity and its inspiration are one and the same thing. And it is not only inspired as a whole, it is the only book in the world which is inspired. It is the only book in the world to which God sets His seal in our hearts when we read in search of an answer to the question, How shall a sinful man be righteous with God? And when we approach Scripture with this problem, we find not only sympathy, but a solution; and with the solution is identified all that we mean by inspiration. All the suggestions of the Bible with reference to this problem converge upon the cross. The cross dominates everything. It interprets everything. It puts all things in their true relations to each other.

We shall never know what inspiration really is until Scripture has resolved itself for us into a unity. That unity, I venture to say, will be its testimony to a love in God which we do not earn, which we can never repay, but which comes to meet us with mercy, dealing, nevertheless, in all earnest with our sins, and at infinite cost of doing right by God's holy law in regard to them. This love becomes incarnate in the Lamb of God bearing the sin of the world, and putting it away by the sacrifice of Himself. It is in its testimony to this that the unity of Scripture and its inspiration consists, and whoever believes in this believes in inspiration in the only sense which can be rationally attached to the word.

The doctrine of the atonement, in the central place which Scripture secures for it, has decisive importance in another way. It is the proper evangelical foundation for a doctrine of the person of Christ. To put it in the shortest possible form, Christ is the person who can do this work for us. This is the deepest and most decisive thing we can know about Him, and in answering the questions which it prompts we are starting from a basis in experience. There is a sense in which Christ confronts us as the reconciler. He is doing the will of God on our behalf, and we can only look on. We see in Him the judgment and the mercy of God in relation to our sins. His presence and work on earth are a divine gift, a divine visitation. He is the gift of God to men, not the offering of men to God, and God gives Himself to us in and with Him. We owe to Him all that we call divine life.

On the other hand, this divine visitation is made, and this divine life is imparted, through a life and work which are truly human. The presence and work of Jesus in the world, even the work of bearing sin, does not prompt us to define human and divine by contrast with each other: there is no suggestion of incongruity between them. Nevertheless, they are both there, and the fact that they are both there justifies us in raising the question as to Jesus' relation to God on the one hand, and to men on the other. We become sensible, as we contemplate this divine visitation, this achievement of a work so necessary to man yet so transcending his powers, that Jesus is not, as far as the human race is concerned, just one man more to whom our relation may be as fortuitous as to any other. Rather does the whole phenomenon justify us in putting such a question as Dale's: 'What must Christ's relation to men be in order to make it possible that He should die for them?' This question leads to an essentially evangelical argument. Christ must have had a unique and central relation to the human race and to every member of it. Whether this is the best way to express the conclusion need not here be considered, but that this is the final way to approach the problem is not open to doubt.

In this connection I venture to emphasize again a point referred to at the close of the first chapter. The doctrine of the atonement secures for Christ His place in the gospel, and makes it inevitable that we should have a Christology or a doctrine of His person. Reduced to the simplest religious expression, the doctrine of the atonement signifies that we owe to Christ and to His finished work our whole being as Christians. We are His debtors, and it is a real debt, a debt infinite, never to be forgotten, never to be discharged. The extraordinary statement of Harnack—as extraordinary, perhaps, in its ambiguity as in its daring—that in the gospel as Jesus preached it the Son has no place but only the Father, owes whatever plausibility it has, under the most favourable construction, to the assumption that in the gospel as Jesus preached it there is no such thing as an atoning work of Jesus. Jesus *did* nothing in particular by which men become His debtors; He only showed in His own life what the state of the case was between God and men, quite apart from anything He did or had to do. He was 'the personal realization and the power of the gospel, and is ever again experienced as such'.

One might be tempted to criticize this from Kierkegaard's point of view, and to urge that it betrays no adequate appreciation of the gulf between Christ and sinful men, and of the dreadful difficulty of bridging it. It is sufficient to say, however, that it departs so widely not only from the consciousness of primitive Christianity as it is reflected in the Epistles, but from the mind of Christ as we have seen cause to interpret it through the gospels, that it is impossible to assent to it. Christ not only *was* something in the world, He *did* something. He did something that made an infinite difference, and that puts us under an infinite obligation. He bore our sins. That secures His place in the gospel and in the adoration of the church. That is the impulse and the justification of all Christologies.

Harnack's statement, quoted above, is meant to give a religious justification for lightening the ship of the church by casting

Christological controversy overboard. But the atonement always says to us again, 'Consider how great this Man was!' As long as it holds its place in the preaching of the gospel, and asserts itself in the church, as it does in the New Testament, as the supreme inspiration to praise, so long will Christians find in the person of their Lord a subject of high and reverent thought. It is a common idea that Socinianism, or Unitarianism, is specially connected with the denial of the incarnation. It began historically with the denial of the atonement. It is with the denial of the atonement that it always begins anew, and it cannot be too clearly pointed out that to begin here is to end, sooner or later, with putting Christ out of the Christian religion altogether.

It is the more necessary to insist on this point of view because there is in some quarters a strong tendency to put the atonement out of its place, and to concentrate attention on the incarnation as something which can be appreciated in entire independence of it. The motives for this are various. Sometimes they may not unfairly be described as speculative. Those whose interest is in the cosmic process, or in articulating all that is known as Christian into the framework of the universe, devote their attention to the person of Christ, and seek in it the natural consummation, so to speak, of all that has gone before. Without that person the universe would be without a crown or a head. It is so constituted that only He gives it unity and completeness. But those who think in these terms tend to overlook the fact that its unity had been broken before He came to earth, and that He completed it by a work of reversal and not of direct evolution, a work which, however truly it may be said to have carried out the original idea of God, is yet in the strictest sense supernatural, a redemption, not a natural consummation.

With others, again, the motive may be said to be ethical. To put the atonement at the foundation of Christianity seems to them to narrow it morally in the most disastrous way. It is as though they fear losing the breadth and variety of interest and motive which appeal to the conscience from the life of Christ in the pages of the evangelists. But there is a misconception here. Those who make the atonement fundamental do not turn their backs on the Gospels. They are convinced, however, that the *whole* power of the motives which appeal to us from the life of

Jesus is not felt until we see it condensed, concentrated, and transcended in the love in which He bore our sins in His own body on the tree.

Others displace the atonement for what may be called a dogmatic reason. It is a fixed point with them that so great a thing as the incarnation could not be in any proper sense contingent. The presence of the Son of God in the world cannot be an 'afterthought' or an 'accident'; the whole intent of it cannot be given in such an expression as 'remedial'. The universe must have been constituted from the first with a view to it, and it would have taken place all the same even though there had been no sin and no need for redemption. When it did take place, indeed, it could not be exactly as had been intended. Under the conditions of the fall, the incarnation entailed a career which meant atonement. It was incarnation into a sinful race, and the atonement was made when the Son of God accepted the conditions which sin had determined, and fulfilled man's destiny under them.

Perhaps the truth might be put within the four corners of such a formula, but the tendency in those who adopt this point of view is to minimize all that is said in the New Testament about the death of Christ in relation to sin. The specific assertions and definitions of the apostolic writings are evaded. They are interpreted emotionally but not logically, as if the men who say the strong things on this subject in the New Testament had said them without thinking, or would have been afraid of their own thoughts. The most distinguished representative of this tendency in our own country was Bishop Westcott. Not that what has just been said is applicable in its entirety to him; but the assumption that the incarnation is something which we can estimate apart from the atonement, something which has a significance and a function of its own, independent of man's redemption from sin, underlies much of his writing, and tends to keep him from doing full justice to apostolic ideas on this subject.

There are three broad grounds on which the evangelist and the theologian alike ought to discount any interpretation of the atonement as a mere incident, or consequence, or modification of the incarnation, the incarnation being regarded as something in itself natural and intelligible on grounds which have no relation to sin. In the first place it shifts the centre of gravity in the New

Testament. The incarnation may be the thought round which everything gravitates in the Nicene Creed, and in the theology of the ancient Catholic Church which found in that creed its first dogmatic expression. But that only shows how far from doing justice to New Testament conceptions was the first ecclesiastical apprehension of Christianity. Even in the Gospel and the Epistles of John, as has been shown above, the incarnation cannot be said, without serious qualification, to have the character here claimed for it, and it cannot be asserted with the faintest plausibility for the synoptic Gospels or the Epistles of Paul. The New Testament knows nothing of an incarnation which can be defined apart from its relation to atonement; it is to put away sin, and to destroy the works of the devil, that even in the evangelist of the incarnation the Son of God is made manifest. It is not in His being here, but in His being here as a propitiation for the sins of the world, that the love of God is revealed. Not Bethlehem, but Calvary, is the focus of revelation, and any construction of Christianity which ignores or denies this distorts Christianity by putting it out of focus.

A second ground for resisting the tendency to put the incarnation into the place which properly belongs to the atonement is that it is concerned under these conditions with metaphysical, rather than with moral problems. Now Scripture has no interest in metaphysics except as metaphysical questions are approached through and raised by moral ones. The atonement comes to us in the moral world and deals with us there. It is concerned with conscience and the law of God, with sin and grace, with alienation and peace, with death to sin and life to holiness; it has its being and its efficacy in a world where we can find our footing, and be assured that we are dealing with realities. The incarnation, when it is not defined by relation to these realities, when it is not conceived, in other words, as the means to the atonement but as part of a speculative theory of the world quite independent of man's actual moral necessities, can never attain to a reality as vivid and profound. It can never become thoroughly credible just because it is not essentially related to anything in human or Christian experience sufficiently great to justify it. Approached in this way it does not answer moral questions, especially those which bring the sinful man to despair. At best it answers metaphysical questions about the relation of the human to the divine, about the proper way to define these words in relation to each other, whether it be by contrast or by mutual affinity, about the divine as being the truth of the human and the human as being the reality of the divine, and so forth. It does not contain a gospel for lost souls, but a philosophy for speculative minds.

Now the New Testament is a gospel for lost souls, or it is nothing; and whatever philosophy it may lead to or justify, we cannot see that philosophy itself in the light in which it demands to be seen, unless we keep the gospel in its New Testament place. If we start in the abstract speculative way there is no getting out of it, or getting any specifically Christian good out of it either. It is only when the person of Christ is conceived as necessarily related to a work in which we have a life and death moral interest, that it has religious import, and can be a real subject for us. There is in truth only one religious problem in the world—the existence of sin. Similarly there is only one religious solution of it—the Atonement, in which the love of God bears the sin, taking it, in all its terrible reality for us, upon itself. And nothing can be central or fundamental either in Christian preaching or in Christian thinking which is not in direct and immediate relation to this problem and its solution.

The third ground on which we should deprecate the obtrusion of the incarnation at the cost of the atonement is that in point of fact it tends to sentimentality. Whether this is an inevitable result or not need not be inquired. It is dangerous, however, to bring into religion anything which is not vitally related to morals, and incarnation not determined by atonement is open to this charge. The Christmas celebrations in many churches supply all the proof that is needed: they are an appeal to anything and everything in man except that to which the gospel is designed to appeal. The New Testament is just as little sentimental as it is metaphysical: it is ethical, not metaphysical; passionate, not sentimental. And its passionate and ethical characters are condensed and guaranteed in that atoning work of Christ which is in every sense of the word its vital centre.

If it is a right conception of the atonement which enables us to attain to a right conception of the person of Christ, similarly we may say it is through a right conception of the atonement that we come to a right conception of the nature or character of God. In the atonement revelation is complete, and we must have it fully in view in all affirmations we make about God as the ultimate truth and reality. The more imperfect our conceptions of God, the more certainly they tend to produce scepticism and unbelief; and nothing presents greater difficulties to faith than the idea of a God who either gives no heed to the sin and misery of man, or saves sinners, as it were, from a distance, without entering into the responsibility and tragedy of their life and making it His own. To put the same thing in other words, nothing presents greater difficulties to faith than a conception of God falling short of that which the New Testament expresses in the words, 'God is love.'

Now this conception is not self-interpreting or self-accrediting, as is often supposed. There is no proposition which is more in need both of explanation and of proof. We may say 'God is love', and know just as little what love means as what God means. Love is like every word of moral or spiritual import; it has no fixed meaning, and in this respect differs from words denoting physical objects or attributes. It stands, so to speak, upon a sliding scale, and it stands higher or lower in the position where the experience of those who use it enables them to place it.

John, when he placed it where he did, was enabled to do so only by the experience in which Christ was revealed to him as the propitiation for sins. It is with this in his mind that he says, '*Hereby* perceive we love.' The word love, especially in such a proposition as 'God is love', has to have its proper meaning before it can be said to have any meaning at all. It is used in a thousand senses which in such a proposition would be only absurd or profane. Now the person who first uttered that sublime sentence felt his words to be pregnant with meaning as he contemplated Christ sent by God a propitiation for the whole world. A God who could do that, a God who could bear the sin of the world in order to restore to man the possibility of righteousness and eternal life, such a God is love. Such love, too, is the ultimate truth about God. But apart from this the apostle would not have said that God is love, nor is it quite real or specifically Christian for anyone else to say so. There is no adequate way of

telling what he means. Until it is demonstrated as it is in the
atonement, love remains an indeterminate sentimental expression,
with no clear moral value, and with infinite possibilities of moral
misunderstanding. But when it has a specific meaning through
the contemplation of the atonement, the danger of mere senti-
mentalism and other moral dangers are provided against, for love
in the atonement is inseparable from law. The universal moral
elements in the relations of God and man are unreservedly
acknowledged, and it is in the cost at which justice is done to
them in the work of redemption that the love of God is revealed
and assured. We then see its reality and its scale. We see what
it is willing to do, or rather what it has done. We see something
of the breadth and length and depth and height which pass knowledge. We believe and know the love which God has in our case,
and can say God is love.

From the vantage ground of this assurance we look out henceforth on all the perplexities of the world and of our own life
in it. We are certain that it is in God to take the burden and
responsibility of it upon Himself. We are certain that it is in the
divine nature not to be indifferent to the tragedy of human life,
not to help it from afar off, not to treat as unreal in it the very
thing which makes it real to us—the eternal difference of right
and wrong—but to bear its sin, and to establish the law in the
very act and method of justifying the ungodly. It is a subordinate
remark in this connection, but not for that reason an insignificant
one, that this final revelation of love in God is at the same time
the final revelation of sin. For sin, too, needs to be revealed,
and there is a theological doctrine of it as well as an experience
antecedent to all doctrines. Love is that which is willing to take
the responsibility of sin upon it for the sinner's sake, and which
does so; and sin, in the last resort—sin as that which cuts man
finally off from God—is that which is proof against the appeal
of such love.

There is another great realm of Christian thinking to which
the atonement is of fundamental importance—the department of
Christian ethics, the scientific interpretation of the new life. It has
undoubtedly been a fault in much systematic theology that in
dealing with the work which Christ finished in His death it has

shown no relation, or no adequate and satisfactory relation, between that death and the Christian life which is born of faith in it. There must be such a relation, or there would be no such thing in the world as Christian life or the Christian religion. The only difficulty, indeed, in formulating it is that the connection is so close and immediate that it might be supposed to be impossible to hold apart, even in imagination, the two things which we wish to define by relation to each other. But it may be put as follows.

The death of Christ, interpreted as the New Testament interprets it, constitutes a great appeal to sinful men. It appeals for faith. To yield to its appeal, to abandon oneself in faith to the love of God which is manifested in it, is to enter into life. It is the only way in which a sinful man can enter into life at all. The new life is constituted in the soul by the response of faith to the appeal of Christ's death, or by Christ's death evoking the response of faith. It does not matter which way we put it. We may say that we have received the atonement, and that the atonement regenerates; or that we have been justified by faith, and that justification regenerates; or that we have received an assurance of God's love which is deeper than our sin, and extends to all our life past, present, and to come, and that such an assurance, which is the gift of the Spirit shed abroad in our hearts, regenerates: it is all one. It is the same experience which is described, and truly described, in every case. But both the power and the law of the new life, the initiation of which can be so variously expressed, are to be found in the atoning death of Christ, by which faith is evoked, and there only. The atonement, therefore, is the presupposition of Christian ethics just as it is the inspiring and controlling force in Christian life. Nothing can beget in the soul that life of which we speak except the appeal of the cross, and what the appeal of the cross does beget is a life which, in its moral quality, corresponds to the death of Christ itself. It is a life, as it has been put already, which has that death in it, and which lives only upon this condition. It is a life to which sin is all that sin was to Christ, to which law, and holiness, and God are all that law and holiness and God were to Christ as He hung upon the tree. It is a life which is complete and self-sufficing, because it is sustained at every moment by the inspiration of the atonement.

This is why Paul is not afraid to trust the new life to its own resources, and why he objects equally to supplementing it by legal regulations afterwards, or by what are supposed to be ethical securities beforehand. It does not need them, and is bound to repel them as dishonouring to Christ. To demand moral guarantees from a sinner before you give him the benefit of the atonement, or to impose legal restrictions on him after he has yielded to its appeal, and received it through faith, is to make the atonement itself of no effect. Paul, taught by his own experience, scorned such devices. The Son of God, made sin for men, so held his eyes and heart, entered into his being with such annihilative, such creative power, that all he was and all he meant by life were due to Him alone. He does not look anywhere but to the cross for the ideals and motives of the Christian: they are all there. And the more one dwells in the New Testament, and tries to find the point of view from which to reduce it to unity, the more one is convinced that the atonement is the key to Christianity as a whole. 'The Son of Man came to give His life a ransom for many.' 'Christ died for the ungodly.' 'He bore our sins in His own body on the tree.' 'He is the propitiation for the whole world.' 'I beheld, and lo, a Lamb as it had been slain.' It is in words like these that we discover the open secret of the new creation.

CHAPTER VII

THE ATONEMENT AND THE MODERN MIND

WE have seen that our conception of the relations subsisting between God and man, of the manner in which these relations are affected by sin, and particularly of the Scripture doctrine of the connection between sin and death, must determine, to a great extent, our attitude to the atonement. The atonement, as the New Testament presents it, assumes the connection of sin and death. Apart from some sense and recognition of such connection, the mediation of forgiveness through the death of Christ can appear only an arbitrary, irrational, unacceptable idea. But leaving the atonement meanwhile out of sight, and looking only at the situation created by sin, the question inevitably arises, What can be done with it? Is it possible to remedy or to reverse it? It is an abnormal and unnatural situation; can it be annulled, and the relations of God and man put upon an ideal footing? Can God forgive sin and restore the soul? Can we claim that He shall? And if it is possible for Him to do so, can we tell how or on what conditions it is possible?

When the human mind is left to itself, there are only two answers which it can give to these questions. Perhaps they are not specially characteristic of the modern mind, but the modern mind in various moods has given passionate expression to both of them. The first says roundly that forgiveness is impossible. Sin is, and it abides. The sinner can never escape from the past. His future is mortgaged to it, and it cannot be redeemed. He can never get back the years which the locust has eaten. His leprous flesh can never come again like the flesh of a little child. Whatsoever a man soweth, that shall he also reap, and reap for ever and ever. It is not eternal punishment which is incredible; nothing else has credibility. Let there be no illusion about this: forgiveness is a violation, a reversal, of law, and no such thing is conceivable in a world in which law reigns.

The answer to this is that sin and its consequences are here conceived as though they belonged to a purely physical world, whereas, if the world were only physical, there could be no such thing as sin. As soon as we realize that sin belongs to a world in which freedom is real, a world in which reality means the personal relations subsisting between man and God, and the experiences realized in these relations, the question assumes a different aspect. It is not one of logic or of physical law, but of personality, of character, of freedom. There is at least a possibility that the sinner's relation to his sin and God's relation to the sinner should change, and that out of these changed relations a regenerative power should spring, making the sinner, after all, a new creature. The question, of course, is not decided in this sense, but it is not foreclosed.

At the opposite extreme from those who pronounce forgiveness impossible stand those who give the second answer to the great question, and calmly assure us that forgiveness may be taken for granted. They emphasize what the others overlooked—the personal character of the relations of God and man. God is a loving Father; man is His weak and unhappy child; and of course God forgives. As Heine put it, *c'est son métier*, it is what He is for. But the conscience which is really burdened by sin does not easily find satisfaction in this cheap pardon. There is something in conscience which will not allow it to believe that God can simply condone sin. To take forgiveness for granted when you realize what you are doing seems to a live conscience impious and profane. In reality, the tendency to take forgiveness for granted is the tendency of those who, while they properly emphasize the personal character of the relations of God and man, overlook their universal character—that is, exclude from them that element of law without which personal relations cease to be ethical. But a forgiveness which ignores this stands in no relation to the needs of the soul or the character of God.

What the Christian religion holds to be the truth about forgiveness—a truth embodied in the atonement—is something quite distinct from both the propositions which have just been considered. The New Testament does not teach with the naturalistic or the legal mind that forgiveness is impossible; neither does it teach with the sentimental or lawless mind that it may be taken for granted. It teaches that forgiveness is mediated to sinners through Christ, and specifically through His death. Its message, in other words, is that it is possible for God to forgive, but possible for Him only through a supreme revelation of His love, made at infinite cost, and doing justice to the uttermost to those inviolable relations in which alone, as I have already said, man can participate in eternal life, the life of God Himself. There is an inexorable divine reaction against sin, finally expressing itself in death. But forgiveness is possible on these terms, and it becomes actual as sinful men open their hearts in penitence and faith to this marvellous revelation, and abandon their sinful life unreservedly to the love of God in Christ who died for them.

From this point of view it seems to me possible to present in a convincing and persuasive light some of the truths involved in the atonement to which the modern mind is supposed to be specially averse.

Thus it becomes credible—we say so not *a priori*, but after experience—that there is a *divine necessity* for it. In other words, there is no forgiveness possible to God without it; if He forgives at all, it must be in this way and in no other. To say so beforehand would be inconceivably presumptuous, but it is quite another thing to say so after the event. What it really means is that in the very act of forgiving sin, or, to use the daring word of Paul, in the very act of justifying the ungodly, God must act in consistency with His whole character. He must demonstrate Himself to be what He is in relation to sin, a God with whom evil cannot dwell, a God who maintains inviolate the moral constitution of the world, taking sin as all that it is in the very process through which He mediates His forgiveness to men.

The divine necessity is not just to forgive, but to forgive in a way which shows that God is irreconcilable to evil, and can never treat it as other or less than it is. It is the recognition of this, or the failure to recognize it, which ultimately divides interpreters of Christianity into evangelical and non-evangelical, those who are true to the New Testament and those who cannot digest it.

No doubt the forms in which this truth is expressed are not always adequate to the idea they are meant to convey, and if we are acquainted with them only at second hand they will probably appear even less adequate than they are. When Athanasius, for example, speaks of God's *truth* in this connection, and then reduces God's truth to the idea that God must keep His word, the word which made death the penalty of sin, we may feel that the form only too easily loses contact with the substance. Yet Athanasius is dealing with the essential fact of the case, that in all His dealings with sin for man's deliverance from it God must be true to Himself, and to the moral order in which men live. Furthermore, He has been thus true to Himself in sending His Son to live our life and to die our death for our salvation.

Or again, when Anselm in the *Cur Deus Homo* speaks of the satisfaction which is rendered to God for the infringement of His honour by sin, a satisfaction apart from which there can be no forgiveness, we may feel again, and even more strongly, that the form of the thought is inadequate to the substance. But what Anselm means is that sin makes a real difference to God, and that even in forgiving God treats that difference *as* real, and cannot do otherwise. He cannot ignore it, or regard it as other or less than it is. If He did so, He would not be more gracious than He is in the atonement; He would cease to be God. It is Anselm's profound grasp of this truth which, in spite of all its inadequacy in form, and of all the criticism to which its inadequacy has exposed it, makes the *Cur Deus Homo* the truest and greatest book on the atonement that has ever been written.

It is the same truth of a divine necessity for the atonement which is emphasized by Paul in Rom. iii, where he speaks of Christ's death as a demonstration of God's righteousness. Christ's death, we may paraphrase his meaning, is an act in which (so far as it is ordered in God's providence) God does justice to Himself. He who is moved with compassion for sinners does justice to His character as a gracious God. If He did not act in a way which displayed His compassion for sinners, He would *not* do justice to Himself; there would be no ἔνδειξις of His δικαιοσύνη: it would be in abeyance. He would do Himself an injustice, or be untrue to Himself.

It is with this in view that we can appreciate the arguments of writers like Diestel and Ritschl, that God's righteousness is synonymous with His grace. Such arguments are true to this extent, that God's righteousness includes His grace. He could not demonstrate it, He could not be true to Himself, if His grace remained hidden. We must not, however, conceive of this as if

it constituted on our side a claim upon grace or upon forgiveness:
such a claim would be a contradiction in terms. All that God
does in Christ He does in free love, moved with compassion for
the misery and doom of men.

But though God's righteousness as demonstrated in Christ's
death—in other words, His action in consistency with His
character—includes, and, if we choose to interpret the term
properly, even necessitates, the revelation of His grace, it is not
this only, nor, I believe, is it this primarily, which Paul has here
in mind. God, no doubt, would not do justice to Himself if He
did not show His compassion for sinners. But, on the other hand
—and here is what the apostle is emphasizing—He would not
do justice to Himself if He displayed His compassion for sinners
in a way which made light of sin, which ignored its tragic reality,
or took it for less than it is. In this case He would again be doing
Himself injustice. There would be no demonstration that He
was true to Himself as the author and guardian of the moral
constitution under which men live. As Anselm put it, He would
have ceased to be God. The apostle combines the two sides. In
Christ set forth as a propitiation in His blood—in other words,
in the atonement in which the sinless Son of God enters into the
bitter realization of all that sin means for man, yet loves man
under and through it all with an everlasting love—there is an
ἔνδειξις of God's righteousness, a demonstration of His self-consistency. In virtue of this we can see how He is at the same time
Himself just and the justifier of him who believes on Jesus, a
God who is irreconcilable to sin, yet devises means that His
banished be not expelled from Him. We may say reverently that
this was the only way in which God could forgive. The phrase
'He cannot deny Himself' means both that He cannot deny His
grace to the sinful, and that He cannot deny the moral order in
which alone He can live in fellowship with men. And we see
the inviolableness of both asserted in the death of Jesus. Nothing
else in the world demonstrates how real is God's love to the
sinful, and how real the sin of the world is to God. And the love
which comes to us through such an expression, bearing sin in all
its reality, yet loving us through and beyond it, is the only love
which at once forgives and regenerates the soul.

It becomes credible also that there is a *human necessity* for the atonement. In other words, the conditions of being forgiven could no more be fulfilled by man, apart from it, than forgiveness could be bestowed by God.

There are different tendencies in the modern mind with regard to this point. On the one hand, there are those who frankly admit the truth here asserted. Yes, they say, the atonement is necessary for us. If we are to be saved from our sins, if our hearts are to be touched and won by the love of God, if we are to be emancipated from distrust and reconciled to the Father whose love we have injured, there must be a demonstration of that love so wonderful and overpowering that all pride, alienation and fear shall be overcome by it. And this is what we have in the death of Christ. It is a demonstration of love powerful enough to evoke penitence and faith in man, and it is through penitence and faith alone that man is separated from his sins and reconciled to God. A demonstration of love, too, must be given in act. It is not enough to be told that God loves: the reality of love lies in a region other than that of words. In Christ on His cross the very thing itself is present, wonderful, beyond all hope of telling. Without its irresistible appeal our hearts could never have been melted to penitence, and won for God. On the other hand, there are those who reject the atonement on the very ground that for pardon and reconciliation nothing is required but repentance, the assumption being that repentance is something which man can and must produce out of his own resources.

On these divergent tendencies in the modern mind the following may be said.

First, the idea that man can repent as he ought, and whenever he will, without coming under any obligation to God for his repentance, but rather, it might almost be imagined, putting God under obligation by it, is one to which experience lends no support. Repentance is an adequate sense not of our folly, nor of our misery, but of our *sin*. As the New Testament puts it, it is repentance *toward God*. It is the consciousness of what our sin is to Him, of the wrong it does to His holiness, of the wound which it inflicts on His love. Now it is not in the power of the sinner to produce such a consciousness at will. The more deeply he has sinned, the more, so to speak, repentance is needed, the less is it in his power. It is the very nature of sin to darken the mind and harden the heart, to take away the knowledge of God alike in His holiness and in His love. Hence it is only through a revelation of God, and especially of what God is in relation to sin, that repentance can be evoked in the soul. Of all terms in the vocabulary of religion, repentance is probably the one which is most frequently misused. It is habitually applied to experiences which are not even remotely akin to true penitence. The self-centred regret which a man feels when his sin has found him out, the wish, compounded of pride, shame, and anger at his own inconceivable folly, that he had not done it, these are spoken of as repentance. But they are not repentance at all. They have no relation to God. They constitute no fitness for a new relation to Him. They are no opening of the heart in the direction of His reconciling love. It is the simple truth that that sorrow of heart, that healing and sanctifying pain in which sin is really put away, is not ours in independence of God. It is a saving grace which is begotten in the soul under that impression of sin which it owes to the revelation of God in Christ. A man can no more repent than he can do anything else without a motive, and the motive which makes repentance toward God possible does not enter into any man's world till he sees God as God makes Himself known in the death of Christ. All true penitents are children of the cross. Their penitence is not their own creation: it is the reaction towards God produced in their souls by this demonstration of what sin is to Him, and of what His love does to reach and win the sinful.

In the second place there are those who admit the death of Christ to be necessary *for us*, necessary, in the way I have just described, to evoke penitence and trust in God, but who on this very ground deny it to be *divinely* necessary. It had to be, because the hard hearts of men could not be touched by anything less moving: but that is all. This, I feel sure, is another instance of those false abstractions to which reference has already been made. There is no incompatibility between a *divine* necessity and a necessity *for us*. It may very well be the case that nothing less than the death of Christ could win the trust of sinful men for God, and at the same time that nothing else than the death of

Christ could fully reveal the character of God in relation at once
to sinners and to sin. For my own part I am persuaded, not only
that there is no incompatibility between the two things, but that
they are essentially related, and that only the acknowledgment
of the divine necessity in Christ's death enables us to conceive
in any rational way the power which it exercises over sinners in
inducing repentance and faith. It would not evoke a reaction
Godward unless God were really present in it, that is, unless it
were a real revelation of His being and will. But in a real revelation of God's being and will there can be nothing arbitrary,
nothing which is determined only from without, nothing, in
other words, that is not divinely necessary. The demonstration of
what God is, which is made in the death of Christ, is no doubt
a demonstration singularly suited to call forth penitence and faith
in man, but the necessity of it does not lie simply in the desire
to call forth penitence and faith. It lies in the divine nature itself.
God could not do justice to Himself, in relation to man and sin,
in any way less awful than this. And it is the fact that He does
not shrink even from this, that in the person of His Son He
enters, if we may say so, into the whole responsibility of the
situation created by sin, which constitutes the death of Jesus a
demonstration of divine love, compelling penitence and faith.
Nothing less would have been sufficient to touch sinful hearts
to their depths; in that sense the atonement is humanly necessary.
But neither would anything else be a sufficient revelation of
what God is in relation to sin and to sinful men; in that sense it
is divinely necessary. And the divine necessity is the fundamental
one. The power exercised over us by the revelation of God at
the cross is dependent on the fact that the revelation is true—in
other words, that it exhibits the real relation of God to sinners
and to sin. It is not by calculating what will win us, but by acting
in consistency with Himself, that God irresistibly appeals to men.
We dare not say that He must be gracious, as though grace
could cease to be free. But we may say that He must be Himself,
and that it is because He is what we see Him to be in the death
of Christ, understood as the New Testament understands it, that
sinners are moved to repentance and to trust in Him. What the
eternal being of God made necessary to Him in the presence of
sin is the very thing which is necessary also to win the hearts of

sinners. Nothing but what is divinely necessary could have met the necessities of sinful men.

When we admit this twofold necessity for the atonement, we can tell ourselves more clearly how we are to conceive Christ in it, in relation to God on the one hand and to man on the other. The atonement is God's work. It is God who makes the atonement in Christ. It is God who mediates His forgiveness of sins to us in this way. This is one aspect of the matter, and probably the one about which there is least dispute among Christians. But there is another aspect of it. The Mediator between God and man is Himself Man, Christ Jesus. What is the relation of the Man Christ Jesus to those for whom the atonement is made? What is the proper term to designate, in this atoning work, what He is in relation to them? The doctrine of atonement most generally current in the Reformed churches answered frankly that in His atoning work Christ is our Substitute. He comes in our nature, and He comes into our place. He enters into all the responsibilities that sin has created for us, and He does justice to them in His death. He does not deny any of them. He does not take sin as anything less or else than it is to God. In perfect sinlessness He consents even to die, to submit to that awful experience in which the final reaction of God's holiness against sin is expressed. Death was not *His* due: it was something alien to One who did nothing amiss. But it was our due, and because it was ours He made it His. It was thus that He made atonement. *He* bore *our* sins. He took to Himself all that they meant, all in which they had involved the world. He died for them, and in so doing acknowledged the sanctity of that order in which sin and death are indissolubly united. In other words, He did what the human race could not do for itself, yet what had to be done if sinners were to be saved: for how could men be saved if there were not made in humanity an acknowledgment of all that sin is to God, and of the justice of all that is entailed by sin under God's constitution of the world? Such an acknowledgment, as we have just seen, is divinely necessary, and necessary, too, for man, if sin is to be forgiven.

This was the basis of fact on which the substitutionary character of Christ's sufferings and death in the atonement was asserted. It may be admitted at once that when the term Substitute is interpreted without reference to this basis of fact it lends itself very easily to misconstruction. It falls in with, if it does not suggest, the idea of a transference of merit and demerit, the sin of the world being carried over to Christ's account, and the merit of Christ to the world's account, as if the reconciliation of God and man, or the forgiveness of sins and the regeneration of souls, could be explained without the use of higher categories than are employed in book-keeping. It is surely not necessary at this time of day to disclaim an interpretation of personal relations which makes use only of sub-personal categories. Merit and demerit cannot be mechanically transferred like sums in an account. The credit, so to speak, of one person in the moral sphere cannot become that of another, apart from moral conditions. It is the same truth, in other words, if we say that the figure of paying a debt is not in every respect adequate to describe what Christ does in making the atonement. The figure, I believe, covers the truth; if it did not, we should not have the kind of language which frequently occurs in Scripture. But it is misread into falsehood and immorality whenever it is pressed as if it were exactly equivalent to the truth.

But granting these drawbacks which attach to the word, is there not something in the work of Christ, as mediating the forgiveness of sins, which no other word can express? No matter on what subsequent conditions its virtue for us depends, what Christ did had to be done, or we should never have had forgiveness; we should never have known God, and His nature and will in relation to sin; we should never have had the motive which alone could beget real repentance; we should never have had the spirit which welcomes pardon and is capable of receiving it. We could not procure these things for ourselves, we could not produce them out of our own resources. But He, by entering into our nature and lot, by taking on Him our responsibilities and by dying our death, has so revealed God to us as to put them within our reach. We owe them to Him. In particular, and in the last resort, we owe them to the fact that He bore our sins in His own body on the tree. If we are not to say that the atonement, as a work carried through in the sufferings and death of Christ, sufferings and death determined by our sin, is vicarious or substitutionary, what are we to call it?

The only answer which has been given to this question, by those who continue to speak of atonement at all, is that we must conceive Christ not as the Substitute but as the Representative of sinners. I venture to think that, with some advantages, the drawbacks of this word are quite as serious as those which attach to Substitute. It makes it less easy, indeed, to think of the work of Christ as a finished work which benefits the sinner *ipso facto*, and apart from any relation between him and the Saviour. But of what sort is the relation which it does suggest? A representative, in all ordinary circumstances, is provided or appointed by those whom he represents, and it is practically impossible to divest the term of the associations which this involves, misleading as they are in the present instance.

The case for Representative as opposed to Substitute was put forward with great earnestness by a critic of the views which I have stated earlier in this book. He was far from saying that a writer who finds a substitutionary doctrine throughout the New Testament is altogether wrong. He was willing to admit that if we look at the matter from what may be called an external point of view, no doubt we may speak of the death of Christ as in a certain sense substitutionary. But no one, he held, can do justice to Paul who fails to recognize that the death of Christ was a racial act; and 'if we place ourselves at Paul's point of view, we shall see that to the eye of God the death of Christ presents itself less as an act which Christ does for the race than as an act which the race does in Christ'. In plain English, Paul teaches less that Christ died for the ungodly, than that the ungodly in Christ died for themselves.

This brings out the logic of what Representative means when Representative is opposed to Substitute. The Representative is ours; we are in Him; and we are supposed to get over all the moral difficulties raised by the idea of substitution just because He is ours, and because we are one with Him. But the fundamental fact of the situation is that, to begin with, Christ is *not* ours, and we are *not* one with Him. In the apostle's view, and in point of fact, we are 'without Christ' *(χωρὶς Χριστοῦ)*. It is not we who have put Him there. It is not to us that His presence and His work in the world are due. If we had produced Him and put Him forward, we might call Him our Representative in

the sense suggested by the sentences just quoted. We might say
it is not so much He who dies for us, as we who die in Him. But
a Representative not produced by us, but given to us, not chosen
by us, but the elect of God, is not a Representative at all in
the first instance, but a Substitute. He stands in our stead, facing
all our responsibilities for us as God would have them faced. And
it is what He does for us, and not the effect which this produces
in us, still less the fantastic abstraction of a 'racial act', which is
the atonement in the sense of the New Testament. To speak of
Christ as our Representative, in the sense that His death is to
God less an act which He does for the race than an act which
the race does in Him, is in principle to deny the grace of the
gospel, and to rob it of its motive power.

To do justice to the truth here, both on its religious and its
ethical side, it is necessary to put in their proper relation to one
another the aspects of reality which the terms Substitute and
Representative respectively suggest. The first is fundamental.
Christ is God's gift to humanity. He stands in the midst of us,
the pledge of God's love, accepting our responsibilities as God
would have them accepted, offering to God, under the pressure
of the world's sin and all its consequences, that perfect recognition
of God's holiness in so visiting sin which men should have offered
but could not; and in so doing He makes atonement for us. In
so doing, also, He is our Substitute, not yet our Representative.
But the atonement thus made is not a spectacle, it is a motive.
It is not a transaction in business, or in book-keeping, which is
complete in itself. In view of the relations of God and man it
belongs to its very nature to be a moral appeal. It is a divine
challenge to men designed to win their hearts. And when men
are won, when that which Christ in His love has done for them
comes home to their souls, when they are constrained by His
infinite grace to the self-surrender of faith, then we may say He
becomes their Representative. They begin to feel that what He
has done for them must not remain outside of them, but be
reproduced somehow in their own life. The mind of Christ in
relation to God and sin, as He bore their sins in His own body
on the tree, must become their mind. This and nothing else is
the Christian salvation.

The power to work this change in them is found in the death

of Christ itself. The more its meaning is realized as something there, in the world, outside of us, the more completely does it take effect within us. In proportion as we see and feel that out of pure love to us He stands in our place, our Substitute, bearing our burden, in that same proportion are we drawn into the relation to Him that makes Him our Representative. But we must be careful here not to lose ourselves in soaring words. The New Testament has much to say about union with Christ, but, as we have already noticed, it has no such expression as mystical union. The only union it knows is a moral one, a union due to the moral power of Christ's death, operating morally as a constraining motive on the human will and begetting in believers the mind of Christ in relation to sin.

This moral union, however, remains the problem and the task, as well as the reality and the truth, of the Christian life. Even when we think of Christ as our Representative and have the courage to say we died with Him, we have still to *reckon* ourselves to be dead to sin and to *put to death* our members which are upon the earth. And to go past this and speak of a mystical union with Christ in which we are lifted above the region of reflection and motive, of gratitude and moral responsibility, into some kind of metaphysical identity with the Lord, does not promote intelligibility, to say the least. If the atonement were not, to begin with, outside of us, if it were not in that sense objective, a finished work in which God in Christ makes a final revelation of Himself in relation to sinners and sin, if, in other words, Christ could not be conceived in it as our Substitute, given by God to do in our place what we could not do for ourselves, there would be no way of recognizing or preaching or receiving it as a motive. On the other hand, if it did not operate as a motive, if it did not appeal to sinful men in such a way as to draw them into a moral fellowship with Christ, if, in other words, Christ did not under it become representative of us, our surety to God that we should yet be even as He in relation to God and to sin, we could say only that it had all been vain. Union with Christ, in short, is not a presupposition of Christ's work, which enables us to escape all the moral problems raised by the idea of a substitutionary atonement, it is its fruit. To see that it is its fruit is to have the final answer to the objection that substitution is immoral. If substitution, in the sense in which we must assert it of Christ, is the greatest moral force in the world, if the truth which it covers, when it enters into the mind of man, enters with divine power to assimilate him to the Saviour, uniting him to the Lord in a death to sin and a life to God, obviously to call it immoral is an abuse of language. The love which can literally go out of itself and make the burden of others its own is the radical principle of all the genuine and victorious morality in the world. And to say that love cannot do any such thing, that the whole formula of morality is 'every man shall bear his own burden', is to deny the plainest facts of the moral life.

Yet this is a point at which difficulty is felt by many in trying to grasp the atonement. On the one hand, there seem to be analogies to it, and points of attachment for it, in experience. No sin that has become real to conscience is ever outlived and overcome without expiation. There are consequences involved in it that go far beyond our perception at the moment, but they work themselves out inexorably, and our sin ceases to be a burden on conscience, and a fetter on will, only as we 'accept the punishment of our iniquity', and become conscious of the holy love of God behind it. But the consequences of sin are never limited to the sinner. They spread beyond him in the organism of humanity, and when they strike visibly upon the innocent, the sense of guilt is deepened. We see that we have done we know not what, something deeply and mysteriously bad beyond all our reckoning, something that only a power and goodness transcending our own avail to check. It is one of the startling truths of the moral life that such consequences of sin, striking visibly upon the innocent, have in certain circumstances a peculiar power to redeem the sinful. When they are accepted, as they sometimes are accepted, without repining or complaint, when they are borne, as they sometimes are borne, freely and lovingly by the innocent, because to the innocent the guilty are dear, then something is appealed to in the guilty which is deeper than guilt, something may be touched which is deeper than sin. A new hope and faith may be born in them to take hold of love so wonderful and, by attaching themselves to it, to transcend the evil past. The suffering of such love they are dimly aware, or rather the power of such love persisting through all the suffering brought on it by sin, opens the gate of righteousness to the sinful in spite of all that has been. Sin is outweighed by it; it is annulled exhausted, transcended in it.

The great atonement of Christ is somehow in line with this, and we do not need to shrink from the analogy. As one writer has well said, 'If there were no witness in the world's deeper literature'—if there were no witness, that is, in the universal experience of man—'to the fact of an atonement, the atonement would be useless, since the formula expressing it would be unintelligible.' It is the analogy of such experiences which makes the atonement credible; yet it must always in some way transcend them. There is something in it which is ultimately incomparable.

When we speak of others as 'innocent', the term is used in only a relative sense; there is no human conscience pure to God. When we speak of the sin of others falling in its consequences on the innocent, we speak of something in which the innocent are purely passive; if there is moral response on their part, the situation is not due to moral initiative of theirs. But with Christ it is different. He knew *no* sin, and He entered *freely*, deliberately, and as the very work of His calling, into all that sin meant for God and brought on man. Something that I experience in a particular relation, in which another has borne my sin and loved me through it, may help to open my eyes to the meaning of Christ's love. But what I see when they are opened is the propitiation for the whole world. There is no guilt of the human race, there is no consequence in which sin has involved it, to which the holiness and love made manifest in Christ are unequal. He reveals to all sinful men the whole relation of God to them and to their sins—a holiness which is inexorable to sin, and cannot take it as other than it is in all its consequences, and a love which through all these consequences and under the weight of them all, will not let the sinful go. It is in this revelation of the character of God and of His relation to the sin of the world that the forgiveness of sins is revealed. It is not intimated in the air. It is preached, as Paul says, 'in this Man'. It is mediated to the world through Him and specifically through His death, because it is through Him, and specifically through His death, that we get the knowledge of God's character which evokes penitence and faith and brings the assurance of His pardon to the heart.

From this point of view we may see how to answer the question that is sometimes asked about the relation of Christ's life to His death, or about the relation of both to the atonement. If we say that what we have in the atonement is an assurance of God's character, does it not follow at once that Christ's teaching and His life contribute to it as directly as His death? Is it not a signal illustration of the false abstractions which we have so often had cause to censure, when the death of Christ is taken as if it had an existence or a significance apart from His life, or could be identified with the atonement in a way in which His life could not?

I do not think this is so clear. Of course it is Christ Himself who is the atonement or propitiation—He Himself, as John puts it, and not anything, not even His death, into which He does not enter. But it is He Himself, as making to us the revelation of God in relation to sin and to sinners. And apart from death, as that in which the conscience of the race sees the final reaction of God against evil, this revelation is not fully made. If Christ had done less than die for us, therefore, if He had separated Himself from us, or declined to be one with us, in the solemn experience in which the darkness of sin is sounded and all its bitterness tasted, there would have been no atonement. It is impossible to say this of any particular incident in His life, and to this extent at least the unique emphasis laid on His death in the New Testament is justified.

But I should go further than this, and say that even Christ's life, taken as it stands in the Gospels, enters into the atonement, and has reconciling power only because it is pervaded from beginning to end by the consciousness of His death. There is nothing artificial or unnatural in this. There are plenty of people who never have death out of their minds an hour at a time. They are not cowards, nor mad, nor even sombre: they may have purposes and hopes and gaieties as well as others. But they see life steadily and see it whole; and of all their thoughts the one which has most determining and omnipresent power is the thought of the inevitable end. There is death in all their life. It was not, certainly, as the inevitable end, the inevitable 'debt of nature', that death was present to the mind of Christ. But if we can trust the Evangelists at all, from the hour of His baptism it was present to His mind as something involved in His vocation; and it was a presence so tremendous that it absorbed everything into itself. 'I have a baptism to be baptized with, and how am I straitened till it be accomplished.'

Instead of saying, therefore, that Christ's life as well as His death contributed to the atonement, that His active obedience, to use the theological formula, as well as His passive obedience was essential to His propitiation, we should rather say that His life is part of His death, a deliberate and conscious descent, ever deeper and deeper, into the dark valley where at the last hour the last reality of sin was to be met and borne. And if the objection is made that after all this means only that death is the most vital point of life, its intensest focus, I should not wish to make any reply. Our Lord's passion *is* His sublimest action—an action so potent that all His other actions are absorbed in it, and we know everything when we know that He *died* for our sins.

The desire to bring the life of Christ as well as His death into the atonement has probably part of its motive in the feeling that when the death is separated from the life it loses moral character, and is reduced to a merely physical incident, which cannot carry such vast significance as the atonement. Such a feeling certainly exists, and finds expression in many forms. How often, for example, do we hear it said that it is not the death which atones, but the spirit in which the Saviour died, not His sufferings which expiate sin, but the innocence, the meekness, the love to man and obedience to God in which they were borne. The atonement, in short, was a moral achievement, to which physical suffering and death are essentially irrelevant. This is our old enemy, the false abstraction, once more, and that in the most aggressive form. The contrast of physical and moral is made absolute at the very point at which it ceases to exist. As against such absolute distinctions we must hold that if Christ had not really died for us, there would have been no atonement at all; and on the other hand that what are called His physical sufferings and death have no existence simply as physical, but are essential elements in the moral achievement of the passion. It leads to no truth to say that it is not His death, but the spirit in which He died, that atones for sin: the spirit in which He died has its being in His death, and in nothing else in the world.

It seems to me that what is really wanted here, both by those who seek to co-ordinate Christ's life with His death in the atonement and by those who distinguish between His death and the spirit in which He died, is some means of keeping hold of the person of Christ in His work. This, I believe, cannot effectively be done apart from the New Testament belief in the Resurrection. There is no doubt that in speaking of the death of Christ as that through which the forgiveness of sins is mediated to us we are liable to think of it as if it were only an event in the past. We take the representation of it in the Gospels and say, 'Such and such is the impression which this event produces upon me. I feel in it how God is opposed to sin, and how I ought to be opposed to it. I feel in it how God's love appeals to me to share His mind about sin. And, as I yield to this appeal, I am at once set free from sin and assured of pardon. This is the only ethical forgiveness. To know this experimentally is to know the gospel.' No one can have any interest in disputing another's obligation to Christ, but it may fairly be questioned whether this kind of obligation to Christ amounts to Christianity in the New Testament sense. There is no living Christ here, no coming of the living Christ to the soul in the power of the atonement to bring it to God. But this is what the New Testament shows us. It is *He* who is the propitiation for our sins, He who died for them and rose again. The New Testament preaches a Christ who was dead and is alive, not a Christ who was alive and is dead. It is a mistake to suppose that the New Testament conception of the gospel, involving as it does the spiritual presence and action of Christ in the power of the atonement, is a matter of indifference to us, and that in all our thinking and preaching we must remain within purely historical limits if by purely historical limits is meant that our creed must end with the words 'crucified, dead, and buried'. To preach the atonement means not only to preach One who bore our sins in death, but One who by rising again from the dead demonstrated the final defeat of sin, and One who comes in the power of His risen life—which means, in the power of the atonement accepted by God—to make all who commit themselves to Him in faith partakers in His victory. It is not His death, as an incident in the remote past, however significant it may be; it is the Lord Himself, appealing to us in the virtue of His death, who assures us of pardon and restores our souls.

One of the most singular phenomena in the attitude of many modern minds to the atonement is the disposition to plead against the atonement what the New Testament represents as its fruits. It is as though it had done its work so thoroughly that people could not believe that it ever needed to be done at all. The idea of fellowship with Christ, for example, is constantly urged against the idea that Christ died for us, and by His death made all mankind His debtors in a way in which we cannot make debtors of each other. The New Testament itself is pressed into the service. It is pointed out that our Lord called His disciples to drink of His cup and to be baptized with His baptism, where the baptism and the cup are figures of His passion, and it is argued that there cannot be anything unique in His experience or service, anything which He does for men which it is beyond the power of His disciples to do also. Or again, reference is made to Paul's words to the Colossians: 'Now I rejoice in my sufferings for your sake, and fill up on my part that which is lacking of the afflictions of Christ in my flesh for His body's sake, which is the Church' (Col. i. 24); and it is argued that Paul here represents himself as doing exactly what Christ did, or even as supplementing a work which Christ admittedly left imperfect. The same idea is traced where the Christian is represented as called into the fellowship of the Son of God, or more specifically as called to know the fellowship of His sufferings by becoming conformed to His death. It is seen pervading the New Testament in the conception of the Christian as a man *in Christ*. And to descend from the apostolic age to our own, it has been put by an American theologian into the epigrammatic form that Christ redeems us by making us redeemers. What, it may be asked, is the truth in all this? and how is it related to what we have already seen cause to assert about the uniqueness of Christ's work in making atonement for sin, or mediating the divine forgiveness to man?

I do not think it is impossible or even difficult to reconcile the two. It is done, indeed, whenever we see that the life to which we are summoned, in the fellowship of Christ, is a life which we owe altogether to Him, and which He does not in the least owe to us. The question really raised is this: Has Jesus Christ a place of His own in the Christian religion? Is it true that there is one Mediator between God and man, Himself Man, this Man, Christ Jesus?

In spite of the paradoxical assertion of Harnack to the contrary, it is not possible to deny with any plausibility that this was the mind of Christ Himself, and that it has been the mind of all who call Him Lord. He knew and taught, what they have learned by experience as well as by His word, that all men must owe to Him their knowledge of the Father, their place in the Kingdom of God, and their part in all its blessings. He could not have taught this of any but Himself, nor is it the experience of the Church that such blessings come through any other. Accordingly, when Christ calls on men to drink His cup and to be baptized with His baptism, while He may quite well mean, and does mean, that His life and death are to be the inspiration of theirs, and while He may quite well encourage them to believe that sacrifice on their part, as on His, will contribute to bless the world, He need not mean, and we may be sure He does not mean, that their blood is, like His, the blood of the covenant, or that their sinful lives, even when purged and quickened by His Spirit, could be, like His sinless life, described as the world's ransom.

The same considerations apply to the passages quoted from Paul, and especially to the words in Col. i. 24. The very purpose of the Epistle to the Colossians is to assert the exclusive and perfect mediatorship of Christ, alike in creation and redemption. All that we call being, and all that we call reconciliation, has to be defined by relation to Him, and not by relation to any other persons or powers, visible or invisible. However gladly Paul might reflect that in his enthusiasm for suffering he was continuing Christ's work, and exhausting some of the afflictions— they were Christ's own afflictions—which had yet to be endured ere the Church could be made perfect, it is nothing short of grotesque to suppose that in this connection he conceived of himself as doing what Christ did, atoning for sin, and reconciling the world to God. All this was done already, perfectly done, done for the whole world. And it was on the basis of it, and under the inspiration of it, that the apostle sustained his enthusiasm for a life of toil and pain in the service of men.

Always, where we have Christian experience to deal with, it is the Christ through whom the divine forgiveness comes to us at the cross, the Christ of the substitutionary atonement, who bore all our burden alone and did a work to which we can for ever recur, but to which we did not and do not and never can contribute at all, who constrains us to find our Representative with God in Himself, and to become ourselves His representatives to men. It is as we truly represent Him that we can expect our testimony to Him to find acceptance. But that testimony far transcends everything that our service enables men to measure. What is anything that a sinful man, saved by grace, can do for his Lord or for his kind, compared with what the sinless Lord has done for the sinful race? It is true that He calls us to drink of His cup, to learn the fellowship of His sufferings, even to be conformed to His death. But under all the intimate relationship the eternal difference remains which makes Him *Lord*. He knew no sin, and we could make no atonement. It is the goal of our life to be found in Him. But I cannot understand the man who thinks it more profound to identify himself with Christ and share in the work of redeeming the world, than to abandon himself to Christ and share in the world's experience of being redeemed. And I am very sure that in the New Testament the last is first and fundamental.

INDEX OF SCRIPTURE PASSAGES

No attempt has been made to include in this index every Scripture reference given in the text. The list has been limited to those passages to which it has been necessary to give fairly detailed consideration.